ABOUT THE AUTHORS

Wayne Martino has been a high-school English teacher and now lectures in Education at Murdoch University. He has written books for teachers on masculinity, including *Gender and Texts* (AATE 1998), *From the Margins* (Fremantle Arts Centre Press 1997) and *What About the Boys?* (Open University Press 2001).

Maria Pallotta-Chiarolli is well-known for her work on equity issues in schools and youth sexual health, and is senior lecturer in the School of Health Sciences at Deakin University. Maria is also editor of *Girls' Talk: Young Women Speak their Hearts and Minds* (Finch 1998) and author of *Someone You Know* (Wakefield 1991), about a friend living with AIDS, and *Tapestry* (Random 1999), the story of four generations of Italian women.

Together they are writing *So What's a Boy?* (Open University Press 2002).

D1088543

Maria wishes to dedicate this book to the most important young man in her life, her nephew Steven, with wishes for a life full of love and fulfilment.

Wayne wishes to dedicate this book to his parents, Roma and Armando Martino, for their love and support.

This book is also for the incredible and inspirational guys who have contributed to this project. May your lives always be lived with strength and love.

BOYS' STUFF

BOYS TALKING ABOUT WHAT MATTERS

WAYNE MARTINO & MARIA PALLOTTA-CHIAROLLI

ALLEN&UNWIN

First published in 2001

Copyright © Edited by Wayne Martino and Maria Pallotta-Chiarolli 2001
Copyright in individual pieces remains with the authors

All rights reserved. No part of this book may be reproduced or
transmitted in any form or by any means, electronic or mechanical,
including photocopying, recording or by any information storage and
retrieval system, without prior permission in writing from the publisher.
The Australian Copyright Act 1968 (the Act) allows a maximum of one
chapter or 10 per cent of this book, whichever is the greater, to be
photocopied by any educational institution for its educational purposes
provided that the educational institution (or body that administers it)
has given a remuneration notice to Copyright Agency Limited (CAL)
under the Act.

This project has been assited by the Commonwealth
Government through the Australia Council, its arts funding
and advisory body.

Allen & Unwin
83 Alexander Street
Crows Nest NSW 2065
Australia
Phone: (61 2) 8425 0100
Fax: (61 2) 9906 2218
Email: info@allenandunwin.com
Web: www.allenandunwin.com

National Library of Australia
Cataloguing-in-Publication entry:

Boys' stuff: boys talking about what matters.
   ISBN 1 86508 555 3.

   1. Teenage boys—Australia—Attitudes. 2. Sex differences.
   I. Pallotta-Chiarolli, Maria. II. Martino, Wayne.

305.235

Designed and typeset by Antart
Printed by Griffin Press, Adelaide
10 9 8 7 6 5 4 3 2 1

CONTENTS

WHAT'S THIS STUFF ABOUT?

So you've opened this book and you're probably thinking what's this all about? Well it's about boys, their lives, their relationships and other stuff that matters to them. But this time it's not some expert saying what to think, feel and do. It's actually guys doing the talking about what's really going on for them.

Sure, we're in this book too. We wanted to find out about the stuff that was happening for guys out there in Australia and we pop up every now and again with some of our own thoughts about what the guys are saying.

We decided to create a book like this because we wanted to give guys the opportunity to tell it as it is for them. It's raw and it's honest and that means it's really going to make you stop and think about your life, your feelings and where

you stand. But it's also going to get you thinking about what's really going on in other guys' heads and hearts.

Over the past couple of years we've been out there talking to all sorts of boys from all sorts of places around Australia, from Port Hedland in Western Australia to Townsville in Queensland to Rosedale in Victoria. Some guys we interviewed, some guys sent us stuff like artwork, poetry, essays and stories. Along with that came their experiences and opinions.

So have a read. Can you relate to these guys? Have you been through some of the same stuff? Is there anything that you'd want to add to a book like this to share with others? Write to us at **boysstuff01@hotmail.com** and let us know what you think.

CHAPTER ONE

BEING A GUY

So what's it like growing up as a guy? This is what several boys have to say about the adventures and the pressures. What would you say?

PUBERTY POEM

The hormone holocaust has begun . . .
And I've got the 'hots' for Gillian
   Anderson,
Parts of me are growing—I never
   knew they would
Some of it's terrible, some of it's
   good,
Blackheads are developing on my
   nose and chin
I play CDs
And make a din!
My parents (the olds)
Often do nag
To get me to take out the rubbish bag
Sometimes they forget I'm past being a kid,
And I do things differently to what they
   did!
I'm sometimes scared, mixed up and just
   plain shitty . . .
   And that's the end of my puberty ditty!

DAVID'S DOMAIN — KEEP OUT!

Daggy sports curtains, skull lamp, bag of chips under the bed for emergencies. Smelly stinky feral shoes, 34 basketball and babe posters covering one wall—a 3m cardboard cut-out of Allan Border. CDs ready to rock. MY SPACE MY PLACE.

Drop dead gorgeous

Argumentative

Value for money

Is always fighting with sister

Dangerous

DAVID FREIR 13

A STRONG HEART

I'M INDIGENOUS and I've learnt that you've got to have a strong heart when you're growing up because if you have a strong heart you know right from wrong. If you have a weak heart you just sort of take  whatever your friends are doing . . . usually what I do when people call me names or something, I make them real shamed and then they know not to do that again because boys don't like to be shamed . . . So I like to teach people, it changes the community and stuff like that. So if you're teaching people as you react it helps heaps. Because Nigel and I used to just hang around mainly head-butting—it just used to be us two and then everyone who didn't smoke drugs and drink—they started hanging around us because we didn't do that and they thought we were cool. We talk to people, and we ask people about their weekends, what they're doing, and they say, 'Oh, we just started smoking drugs', we usually ask why, 'Why do you do it? It's not good for you.' We make them feel like nothing so that they know not to do it again. I think that's a good thing to do.

BEADE 16

BEADE 16

ALL ABOUT ME

I FEEL THAT THE last two or three years have brought the most change to my life, such as the changing of my physical appearance, hormones and gaining a lot of different aspects of maturity. I guess that I have changed in the aspect of physical appearance by really only getting bigger, growing. With hormones I basically disliked the other sex until I was about ten then I realised that some of these people I am actually attracted to. In the way of maturity I feel I have changed my attitude towards everything and also started to look at being as responsible as possible.

TIM MARSTERS 12

G IS FOR GROW IN THE MIND AND BODY.

R IS FOR REACH, REACH FOR THE TOP.

O IS FOR OPENING. THE WORLD IS OPENING UP FOR YOU.

W IS FOR WORRY. YOU START TO WORRY ABOUT WHAT PEOPLE THINK OF YOU.

I IS FOR INTEREST. YOU GAIN AN INTEREST WHEN YOU'RE GROWING UP.

N IS FOR NOBODY, SOMEONE YOU DON'T WANT TO BE.

G IS FOR GAIN. YOU GAIN THINGS AS YOU GET OLDER.

U IS FOR UNDERSTAND. YOU UNDERSTAND THINGS BETTER WHEN YOU GROW.

P IS FOR PERSONALITY, THAT IS WHAT YOU GAIN.

BRENDAN LINDSAY 13

Rules for being a boy

Being a boy means there are rules you're expected to follow. Many boys feel that they have to act and think in certain ways to be accepted, to be popular, to be something called 'normal'. These rules are taught to boys from a very young age. The following boys let us in on what they think the rules are and how they've impacted upon their lives. But you'll also see that many guys are questioning the rules for boys and are choosing to break them. They feel that these Stereotype Straitjackets are restricting their choices in life. As you read about what these guys have to say, think about:

> **WHO MAKES THE RULES FOR BOYS?**

> **HOW AND WHERE DO BOYS LEARN THESE RULES?**

> **WHY DO BOYS WHO BREAK THE RULES OFTEN GET PUNISHED?**

> **WHO DOES THE PUNISHING?**

> **WHY?**

ONE OF THE other major issues is to be cool and macho in a world where those who play sport and are strong are supreme, and those skinny 'four-eyed nerds' are the 'underworld rats'.

CHRISTIAN 16

AS ABORIGINAL BOYS we got a lot of pressure on us because we have to be role models for younger students. We can't really misbehave that much around the younger students or they'll start copying us. We have to be on our best behaviour most of the time.

SEAN 17

I FOUND IN BOTH South Africa where I'm from and in Australia that boys are faced with the dilemma that they have to live up to their friends' expectations and not their own, i.e. they have to be macho and brutal all the time when in actual fact they aren't, but if they don't act like that they are considered a faggot or gay!!!

TIM 16

YOU'LL KNOW YOU'RE a man once you've got a steady girlfriend and you've finished school and you've had children and you've got married. They're all things that make you a man. Basically the only thing that I reckon is the difference between being a man and a woman is your private parts and that's it. If you're born with one you're a man, if you're born without one you're not. Like that's basically it. But lots of people think if you've lost your virginity that makes you a man. If you're big and tough you're a man. If you own a car you're a man, if you can drive a car you're a man.

KEVIN 16

BASICALLY THE ONLY thing you need to have to be a boy is a penis, and that can be surgically removed or added at any point in time. The rest is completely irrelevant. I think that as a society we are too caught up in this big debate about what makes us all different when really there is very little that separates us all.

XANDER 19

BEING GOOD WITH your hands mechanically and being stronger than females. Always having to be strong in a relationship. Girls can cry a lot over a death and you're there for them. They've always got a shoulder to lean on. The car comes first for guys, but some guys are always on about girls, girls, girls.

JARROD 16

I'M ABORIGINAL and my dad always says to me, if you're young don't act as a man, because when it comes to being a man you're going to be tired to be a man.

MARK 15

BEING A MAN MEANS YOU LOVE YOUR SPORT, YOU FIX YOUR CAR AND YOU DIG CHICKS AND YOU DRINK BEER.

BEING A MAN means you love your sport, you fix your car and you dig chicks and you drink beer. At the end of primary school I decided that I wanted to take up dancing, which initially was this big taboo. It was like 'No, you are not a poofter, you do not dance'. I was very adamant and eventually I was allowed to dance. So the first time my father actually came to see me it was all pride and big eyes and, 'Oh, this is really good'.

XANDER 19

A LOT OF BOYS talk about what girl they were with on the weekend. But some boys just don't do it. I don't do it because I know that a girl wouldn't like it if she heard me talking like that, so I don't do it.

BEADE 16

BOYS HAVE TO FACE not looking like a fairy, not being too dumb, not being too smart, every pressure available, fitting in the right groups. No matter how hard you try and how much effort you put in you always end up back at the bottom—to fit in is the hardest thing of all.

GRANT 16

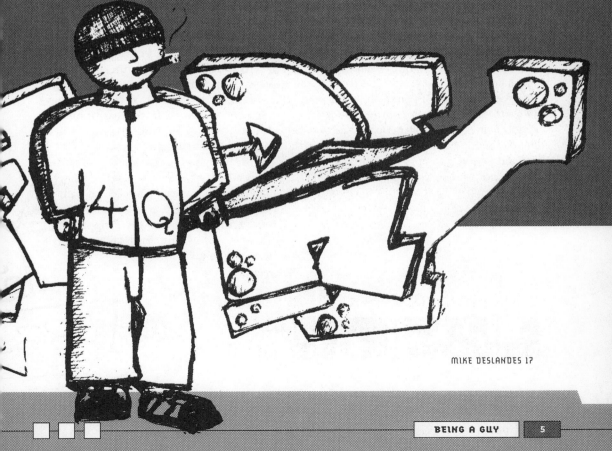

MIKE DESLANDES 17

YOU'RE SUPPOSED TO GO to the footy, you're supposed to drink a six-pack every week and you're supposed to watch action movies over and over again. I don't like football, I don't like cricket and I can cook. All that probably makes me, in society's view, not all that flash. There's a real male stereotype out there for football watchers and beer-swilling hillbillies, but I think you can't really put a definition onto manhood. I think being a man is whatever you want it to be. I think disability has a lot to do with how I challenge male stereotypes because I've had to deal with a lot of things. The only thing I miss out from what the footballer guys are getting is probably the popularity.

You've got to be popular, and you've got to wear $300 sunglasses, which I think is stupid, but you've got to wear certain types of clothes and you've got to hang out with certain types of people and you've got to go to certain types of parties and you've got to learn to ride a skateboard and you've got to do dope and you've got to drink a lot and you've got to spew up in class, you've got to sleep in class or just not do any work.

ANDREW 16

MALES ARE SUPPOSED to be big, tough, never cry, a person who drinks all the time, doesn't really care about their reputation. That's false because not everyone is like that. You got males who are quiet or outgoing but don't like to drink. Some guys won't cry and try being tough and then they'll probably go around the corner and cry. They keep that image but when no one's looking they admit that it hurts.

When guys are by themselves, they are totally different than when they're in a group. In a group they show off, 'I'm a big tough guy, look at me', so when they've got other friends around you can't associate with them. It's real pressure—I've got to be big and tough, I'm the male, I've got to do weights, I've got to have muscles, I can't shave my legs, I can't dye my hair. It puts pressure on us definitely. Like pressure on females—they've got to stay home and cook and clean, but males have to go out and work. If we wear women's clothes we get hassled for that. But what's the difference if a male wears a girl's T-shirt? They're not that much different, but it all comes down to what you look like. If you have long curly blond hair, people think, 'Oh, you're a female'. I've got four earrings, I want to get a nipple ring and an eyebrow ring. I get called a female because I've got earrings.

GLENN 16

BEING IN A WHEELCHAIR at school, I felt totally inadequate as a male. I admired and felt so envious of these dudes whose bodies were developing. When you go to a friend's house or party, you'd hear adults say to other guys, 'Oh, look at you, you're growing, you're getting tall and strong', and on and on and on, and I felt really inadequate. On a more positive note, I think I know that all this stuff is constructed. I know now that it's the system. I think that if I ever again met those guys who were all muscly and had those fantastic bodies and I asked them, 'What are you up to?', half of them [would] have just gotten married and divorced and are doing jobs they don't like. It's really not that bad for me now.

TONY 24

I'M A TORRES STRAIT Islander and what I think would be a man is maybe not having the thing between your legs, but having a stand, knowing what to do when situations go wrong, to stand up and say, 'Yes, I know what to do, I can do it'. Sort of be the big mother bird and take other little birds underneath your wing and show them what to do, show them how to fly, stuff like that.

JASON 18

AN ISSUE THAT BOYS have to deal with a lot is how strong they are. Often boys will just start pushing each other for no reason and if you show that you are hurt by what they have done then they will keep on doing it to you until you do something back to them. Also if a boy looks weak but is actually strong but people don't know he is strong, then they will call him lanky, weak, faggot and other abusive names.

JEREMY 15

You're supposed to go to the footy, you're supposed to drink a six-pack every week and you're supposed to watch action movies over and over again.

THE FIRST TIME

WHEN WAS THE FIRST TIME YOU FIGURED OUT:

YOU HAD TO STIR GIRLS WHEN YOU WERE WITH OTHER GUYS?

IT WASN'T OKAY TO BE GAY?

YOU COMPARED YOUR BODY TO OTHER BOYS' BODIES?

WHAT BEING A 'NORMAL BOY' WAS SUPPOSED TO MEAN?

WHAT A PENIS WAS MEANT TO LOOK LIKE, WHAT SIZE IT WAS MEANT TO BE?

IT WAS NO LONGER OKAY TO HUG ANOTHER GUY AND YOU BEGAN TO PUNCH YOUR FRIENDS INSTEAD?

YOU HAD TO PRETEND TO BE TOUGH WHEN YOU WERE REALLY SCARED?

WHAT 'SISSY STUFF' WAS?

YOU WEREN'T SUPPOSED TO CRY EVEN IF YOU REALLY FELT LIKE IT?

YOU COULD AVOID BEING HASSLED BY BOYS BY HASSLING BOYS?

More rules for boys

YOU'VE GOT TO BE macho. I don't mind because you get to do some pretty cool stuff like ride bikes. But you just do what they say—like when they say fight you do it. They say, 'Go, come on, don't be a chicken', and stuff like that. Guys see you and they go, 'Oh, you chicken', and 'You big girl'.

NATHAN 15

GUYS WHO WATCH so many Arnold Schwarzenegger movies or Van Damme movies might actually start acting like that, but strength is in your brain and your heart. A person on the 'Guinness Book of Records' who jumps off a building or whatever, that's not guts, that's being crazy.

ABDU 16

DRIVING WAS DEFINITELY risky among guys, especially amongst the petrol heads. It was definitely a big issue to do the biggest burn-outs or have the loudest car or the fastest car, and there was definitely a lot of challenges to a drag race flying around.

CHRISTIAN 22

WE JUST JOKE AROUND and put each other down in front of girls sometimes. Put each other down, make each other look stupid. Just in front of the girls to show off.

AARON 15

YOU HAVE TO BE TOUGH, you have to swear, be rude to girls, you have to have a deep voice because if you don't you'll get hassled. They used to hassle me because of my higher voice, calling me gay. It's just that everyone's voice matured before mine.

JACOB 15

EVEN ABORIGINAL BOYS don't really like the idea of boys liking other boys . . . They start calling them names. But I see it as if they want to be gay or something, they can be. I can't stop them! I'm not going to hit them for it.

BEADE 16

WHEN YOU SEE A WOMAN upset, she'll cry about it. You see a guy who gets upset, he'll throw punches.

PAUL 16

PEOPLE EXPECT YOU to be tougher. I stay away from a lot of that. If someone did try to get into a fight with me, I wouldn't be afraid to protect myself. But as far as I'm concerned it's a waste of time.

JOSH 15

OFTEN PEOPLE THINK boys are meant to be muscular and very into sport. They're meant to love bugs and monsters and all that kind of stuff. But that's just what the stereotype is. It doesn't apply to me. I hate bugs and stuff. I like sport except I've never wanted to play football.

EDDIE 11

YOU'RE LOOKED DOWN UPON if you're mentally disabled, or not 'macho', or don't take an active interest in girls. If not, you're considered gay! I'm a pacifist. I hate violence and I try my best never to put down anybody. I always try to say something encouraging, I guess that's my nature. As a Chinese Australian I know that boys have to deal with the issues of 'fitting in'. They have to try to be rough and tough and swear. I always get so much crap because I don't do that kind of stuff.

I've also been described as 'very naive and ignorant in the sex department'. Boys have to be wanting to be interested in pornographic girls. I find that stuff very filthy, and I thank my parents so much for protecting me from this kind of stuff. People have been contemplating whether I was gay. I personally hate humanity and how they act. School life is full of spiteful people and if I could get a private tutor to get me through high school, I would. I dislike people at this school. Family life is much better. People say their siblings and parents are hated the most and they like their friends. I am the opposite.

MICHAEL 14

BEING SPORTY, being strong, to a certain extent being rude, alcohol drinkers. I don't really model myself on all that because I'm not sporty and I'm not all that strong so I don't really pay much attention to all that.

JOHN 16

I THINK IT'S HARD for boys to express themselves because they think, 'Oh, he's a girl, getting all mushie'. But I think that boys should express themselves more to get things off their chest, because maybe something has happened and they could end up killing themselves, suicide and stuff like that.

JASON 18

SOME PEOPLE EXPECT all men to be tough and some think that men should be the income earners, that men never cry, that men shouldn't show emotions. It's quite ridiculous because we're all human, male or female. I act as an individual. I don't care what other people think. I was hassled a lot in primary school and now I just think, 'Well, stuff the rest of the world. I'll just get on with what I'm doing and do it well. I don't care what other people think.'

JASON 14

BOYS, THEY ACT DIFFERENT. Like they don't put on make-up, only girls do that! And they don't wear a dress and high heels. Boys don't wear that.

CARL 13

I CAN DO MOST OF the schoolwork but I just don't show it because if I showed that I was good at it I would get paid out. If I ask lots of questions or if I answer a lot of questions, I might get paid out more. So you just sort of sit back and don't really act like you're real smart. Yesterday we were looking at a poem and if I put my hand up and talked about what I thought the poem was about, people might think I was a bit weird or something, because it's almost like it's cool to be stupider than be smarter. You just don't act like you're real smart.

MAX 16

IF YOU WERE GAY you would be treated like shit, you would be treated way differently even by Aboriginal boys. You'd be treated like an outcast except if you were in a girls' group. [A gay guy] wouldn't mix with the boys because they're all macho and he's not macho. Girls are in a different category—they're not sexist or anything, they're more not into sport and that's sort of how he'd fit under that category better than with boys. He'd get along with girls well, better. So that's probably why he'd hang around the girls and not mix with any boys. And boys would think he's different to us because he doesn't walk around like us and doesn't fight like us. So he'd be an outcast to every boy.

NIGEL 17

ILLUSTRATIONS: MICHAEL BOKODY 13

I DO ASSOCIATE MOST forms of prejudice with traditional masculinity especially homophobia. Having lesbian parents meant that I grew up in an atmosphere that was relatively unprejudiced. So I always felt that that set me apart from more traditional guys straight away. And then being bisexual was another issue which gave me a whole different perspective on masculinity. I used to do things at school like wear nail polish or eyeliner and other guys would comment on it and make an issue of it. I still don't dress traditionally at all today. I don't even really like talking about the way I dress because I think it's so superficial. I think about the way men and women are treated because it has always been something that my parents talk about. Gender relations is something I've always taken into consideration, to a greater extent as I got older.

ROWAN 19

MEN IN THE PHILIPPINES are closer to each other than men in Australia. In the Philippines they could hold hands and there's no malice about doing that, it's just friendly actions. Whilst in Australia touching hands is just a no no. You have to walk in a certain way, like in a businesslike manner. It's more about conformity here. You have to be with your friends all the time and you all have to act in the same way. You have to be a wild person, an adventurous person. You have to have a girlfriend.

JONARD 18

Does money make the man?

His clothes have holes and I've been to his house and they have expired dates on the cereal. Other boys tease him, 'Oh you're a povvo, you can't even afford proper pants, you can't get a bike'. Girls don't really tease people about how poor they are but the boys just try to make themselves look more important.

MARK 12

What difference does having lots of money or little money, 'povvo' pants or Calvin Kleins, make to you as a guy? Does where you live, what school you go to, how much money you have, what you wear, matter for the kind of guy you want to be? In the following Simon and Cory let us in on their experiences in a 'posh' school.

A Punk Out of Place

I HATE SCHOOL. I hate the narrow-minded middle-class people. I always get screwed around by them. They suck up to teachers. I'm not the typical upper-class snob! I try not to be judgmental but my school fucks me around. Most of my mates are from the social 'extremes' of Perth. I stay at this school so I can earn money when I leave to do the things I want to do, like music. I want to be more free flowing and not tied down. When it comes down to it, I'm a bit of a punk out of place, but I don't boot in heads and I don't parade myself. The school tries to fit me in but they just grind me against the grain more. I hate the way they go on at this school. It's a middle-class school but you still get idiots who try to scum money off you that you don't have. They also nick your CD walkman that you got fair and square after working for a year. Theft is screwing our school. It's like a product of putting people who aren't quite so well off in a fucked up upper-class system. They presume everyone can afford to lose a bit. This is so stuffed. I want to go somewhere else.

CORY 16

RICH BOYS

WE HAVE VERY, very rich parents at my school, parents who are earning millions of dollars in a year, and their sons have whatever they want. And then you've got people like myself with parents who don't own a house and they struggle and make a lot of concessions to send their sons to a private school. You notice the differences in the clothes people wear.

I can't have a good social life because my parents don't have the money. I might get asked to a party or movie and I'll say I can't or something like that. It's not that I don't want to. People might say, 'Oh, you're being anti-social', but it's because I don't have the money but I won't say it. And you're not going to invite anybody around so they can bag your house because it's not as big as theirs or you're living in a poor suburb.

It's not that people get teased because they don't have enough money, it's just that it does make it hard for some kids to be accepted if there's a huge difference in wealth between certain groups. A lot of the guys who go out every Friday night and Saturday night stay out all night and get a taxi home. They might spend $60 or more

THE JUMPER I HAVE ON TOOK ME THREE MONTHS OF ARGUING WITH MY PARENTS TO GET.

AND YOU'RE NOT GOING TO INVITE ANYBODY AROUND SO THEY CAN BAG YOUR HOUSE BECAUSE IT'S NOT AS BIG AS THEIRS OR YOU'RE LIVING IN A POOR SUBURB.

each night by the time they've had dinner and paid for the taxi home or drinks or whatever. Whereas someone like me, it takes me three weeks to con $20 out of my parents.

I can remember once being round at this friend's place and they have a really nice house and a tennis court, and they got a spa and a swimming pool, and he's got all these nice clothes like Calvin Klein, and you do feel a bit uncomfortable. They don't make you feel uncomfortable deliberately but they might make comments about your T-shirt or something like that. The jumper I have on took me three months of arguing with my parents to get.

But I don't get angry with my parents at all because they've given up so much to send me to a private school when really they can't afford it, and I know that. A lot of the kids who are better off don't realise that there is a huge difference between how much some of the people are earning.

SIMON MOSS 16

Disability=gay? Dancing=gay?

Andrew's got a disability. Aaron's a dancer. They may seem different from each other but they have something in common—they both get called 'gay'! Seems like having a disability and being a dancer don't measure up to those rules for being a 'real man'! And of course, making sure no one thinks you're gay is a major job. It means that some guys are spending each moment of their lives freaking out if they're not fitting into the Stereotype Straitjacket!

Let's hear from Andrew and Aaron about how they do their masculinity and live their lives unstraitjacketed!

THEY THINK I'M DIFFERENT

I GET CALLED NAMES. The traditional one is 'spastic', but I also get called 'gay' and 'faggot'. It's a macho male thing to hate homosexuals. I get called gay because I've got cerebral palsy and my right hand and wrist hangs limp, which is an easy target for that sort of comment. I'm called 'soft' because I don't play football, I don't do drugs, I don't drink 24 hours a day. It's a social status thing. If you haven't got bleached blond hair and [aren't] playing football for the local team and drinking and sticking needles in your arm, then you're not worth anything. They think I'm different because I've got cerebral palsy and they think I'm different because I don't play sport and they think I'm different because I'm not drinking and I'm not doing drugs.

The more people stand up for me, that's fantastic, but if they're being patronising about it, that's very annoying.

It would be stupid of me to say I haven't got a disability. I know I'm disabled and it really doesn't bother me much anymore. Yes, some people treat me like an invalid. For example, since I was born my grandparents have treated me like an invalid. Like I go to their place and my dinner will be cut up, even the potatoes will be cut up into little squares, and I say to them, 'Look, I don't need everything cut up for me'. Some teachers have come up and said, 'Oh, can you do this exercise?' and I've said, 'I can read, I can write, I can do this exercise'.

Being disabled has probably made me more aware of, more sensitive to, people's feelings. If someone's homosexual, that doesn't bother me in the slightest. If someone's black, it doesn't bother me either but I know people who would line them up and shoot them all.
ANDREW 16

THEY THINK IT'S A GIRLS' THING

I'VE BEEN DOING LINE dancing for six years. A lot of guys keep paying me out but when they see me do it they think, 'Oh, that's pretty good. Good on you.' But they also say, 'Oh, you're a queer, you're a poof, you're a wanker', and it really gets you down. They don't know what it's like to do stuff like that because they mainly just sit around their home all day and do nothing. It's because they don't really know what I'm like. They think it's a girls' thing, and if a girl does skateboarding or something like that, they pay her out too. They think guys are going to get extinct or something. They think there's nothing going to be left for us guys to do because all the girls do all the boys' stuff like roller blading and liking cars.

I also like sewing and usually get called a girl for sewing. Sewing is a subject which I really like doing because you can make stuff you want. Like the pair of boxer shorts I made. And it's such fun sitting on the machine and making something. Some of the boys think it's okay because if they need anything done they go to me, 'Could you fix this for us?'. And I go 'Why don't you just join the sewing class?'. The girls think it's good for us to do stuff they do. I think, 'Oh well, if they think it's okay, it's okay.' My mum taught me to always say yes, never say no, and one day you'll surprise them all.

I also think boys need to learn about their bodies. A friend's mum told him that wet dreams are men's periods. He walked

up to his mates and he's going, 'Oh, man!', and they go, 'What's the matter with you?', and he goes 'I got men's periods', and all his mates turned around and started laughing at him. I tried to talk to him on the phone and he said, 'I don't know what to do, man, my mum says they're men's periods', and I told him, 'No, they are nothing like that'.

I have a goatee and moustache. Other guys go 'Shave it off', or the girls look at it and go 'Ugh'. I like to look older than what I am. I started shaving when I was twelve and my voice broke when I was ten. A lot of guys are scared of getting old, waking up in the morning when you're 40 years old and you have grey hairs and you have to work to pay off the loan.

AARON 14

Undoing masculinity

The rules say you're supposed to 'do' either masculinity or femininity, but what if you like doing both? What if you like playing with the gender rules? What if you like living up to some of the rules and trashing the rest?

Did you know that in some cultures people believe there are more than two genders? For example, in some Native American communities a third gender existed called the 'berdache'. It was acceptable for people of this gender to mix different aspects of traditional male and female roles.

But the two-gender rule says that being male means you're standing on a cliff on one side of a gully while being female is what happens on the cliff on the other side. And of course, all the males on one cliff are meant to be the same and all the females on the other are meant to be the same. And if you dare to leap to the other side, it's emotional danger and social death!

But if you get real, look around and check out some history, it's like this:

In the following, Stephen's having fun with gender, making up his own labels and just living his own life.

I'M A TOMGIRL

PEOPLE PICK ON ME sometimes because I'm different to other boys. I call myself 'a tomgirl' because I sometimes dress up like a girl. I'm always playing with mum's make-up, I do things that girls do. I used to be into Barbie dolls too. I never wear make-up and certain clothes at school because that would be really embarrassing and I'd get picked on a lot, although we had this concert at school and I thought I'd dress up as a girl, and at every costume party we've had at school, I've always dressed up as a girl. When I'm wearing girls' clothes I always walk around wiggling my butt and walking sort of curvy. When I walk as a boy I just walk up and down, straight. I prefer bobbing up and down in the middle of both.

I got the word 'tomgirl' from kids, because girls who dress and act like boys get called 'tomboys' and I've heard teachers saying it, and guys who dress like girls are called 'tomgirls'. I'm neither a boy or girl, there are different mixes. I'm in the middle, right in the middle. I'm both, I dress up as a girl sometimes and a boy sometimes. My parents don't mind my dressing up. My mum doesn't mind but she reckons it's a bit weird. Boys are supposed to have muscles, be strong and have good bodies. Girls have to be wearing all the girls' clothes like skirts and make-up. I'm better off, I suppose. I can do a bit of both.

STEPHEN 13

DOING MASCULINITY

1 WHAT'S IT BEEN LIKE 'GROWING UP MALE'?

2 WHO'S BEEN TELLING YOU HOW TO DO MASCULINITY— HOW TO LOOK, HOW TO THINK, WHAT TO DO?

3 DO YOU FOLLOW THE RULES ABOUT BEING A BOY? DO YOU BREAK THEM? WHEN WAS THE FIRST TIME YOU REALISED THERE WERE RULES FOR BOYS?

4 DO YOU THINK THERE ARE RULES FOR GIRLS ON HOW TO 'DO FEMININITY'? HOW DO SOME GIRLS BREAK THESE RULES? WHAT HAPPENS TO GIRLS WHO BREAK THE 'FEMININITY RULES'?

5 HAS THE FOLLOWING EVER BEEN SAID TO YOU? WHEN? BY WHOM? HOW DID YOU REACT?

'WE'RE GOING TO MAKE A MAN OUT OF YOU.'

'ARE YOU MAN ENOUGH TO DO IT?'

'REAL MEN DON'T . . .'

'BOYS WILL BE BOYS.'

So where does masculinity come from?

 Did you know that some people say that being a guy is ruled by testosterone, and that boys have got one kind of brain and girls have got another. But as the guys you've been hearing from tell us, it's not that simple.

At different points in history and in different parts of the world, biology has been used to explain and reinforce the 'fact' that men and women should have different social roles and that men are 'naturally' more powerful, and even more intelligent.

Did you know that in nineteenth-century British, European and American society biology was used to explain the 'scientific fact' that women were less intelligent? This was then used to keep women out of school and universities, which just made the 'scientific fact' seem more justified.

Yet in some cultures, like that of the Yoruba people of south-western Nigeria in Africa, there was no concept of two genders doing different things. And in other cultures like that of the Wayana Indians in the Amazon rainforest, men raised children and women gathered food.

You often hear people say, 'It's just boys being boys', when guys are pushing, shoving, mucking around and scragging on the oval. Someone will say, 'That's just what boys do, they've just got too much testosterone', or 'It's the hormones!'. But does this really explain why some boys act and think in the ways that they do? Is this really how all boys act? Why do some guys think they have to act in this way? Where do you think guys are getting these 'mixed' messages from?

Let's see how Tom and Ben sort through what it means to be a guy.

ON HEAT

WHEN I SOMETIMES think about being a guy I relate it back to how I think we evolved from animals and how men have testosterone. When you look at the animal kingdom, the male is the one who's 'on heat'. I guess you could say that's all he has on his mind. Reproduction couldn't occur otherwise. It's the male who just goes around and I think that side comes out in the human species because guys are just, 'Any time!', because the testosterone's there! But with the females, they're more emotionally attached. Guys will look at sexual experiences as something that's just there to be used for enjoyment, whereas the females look at it from the emotional and the relationship side. I think about that because females are human like us—that's not the way guys should be. I like to think that I'm not like that and that I like to show my emotions. I guess you could say I've been in touch with my feminine side, since the stereotype is that girls are more in touch with their emotions. I like to think of myself like that.

TOM 16

MASCULINITY ISN'T REAL!

MASCULINITY—JUST THE word makes me mad! Masculinity is nothing but a concept—it isn't real, it doesn't really exist. Men are supposed to aspire to it but are all incapable of doing so. How can males be expected not to hurt or break with all the crap and injustice that goes on in our world? It's impossible. Masculinity is a cruel concept dreamed up by some ancient sadistic psychopath as a way of oppressing men and making them feel inadequate. It is something that must be challenged! You can punch someone's head in or have your head punched in but you can never cry or try to talk it out. You're expected to swear and be rude, to drink and get involved with drugs and all that crap. There's a whole big contradiction in society at the moment. Men are now expected to have strength of character, conscience and sensitivity while still having the above 'macho' qualities. If you can't do that then you're not a 'man'. How can you be expected to maintain a balance of such extremes? You can't!

BEN GERRARD 17

JAMES WALL'S GRANDFATHER, WILLIAM WESTON, AGED 17, IN THE BRITISH CAVALRY IN WORLD WAR ONE

Trashing masculinity

The following guys have some challenging things to say about masculinity—one of them calls men 'pigs'. Men don't call other men pigs do they? They don't usually think about masculinity as a disease either! These boys break all the rules!!! They trash dominant views of what makes a man a man. Podge, for example, figures that, in the end, masculinity is all about power and proving that you are hard and not weak. It's just a mask, a front to hide 'our weak and scrawny selves'. Have a read, have a think, and figure out where you stand.

MASCULINITY IS A DISEASE

EXPRESSING AND DISPLAYING your emotions doesn't really fit with being masculine. Masculinity is basically a form of power and displaying emotions isn't masculine and therefore isn't powerful. So because guys want to fit this powerful masculine image, they have to reject anyone who doesn't and they try and seek out who has this masculine powerful image and who doesn't. Like people with complexes or disabilities, they get weaseled out and targeted. I guess because they're always targeted, people who display their emotions or have disabilities, grow up being very quiet, reclusive almost and they don't fit the image of being powerful, manipulative. Guys make people become like this. They do it through the intimidation. They force people into becoming recluses.

Masculinity is a disease and I've had an injection which has made me immune to it. I just shrug it off, it doesn't affect me really. It does sometimes, I think, with people I care about. If something doesn't fit the masculine image, I'd like to think that my friends are okay with it, that they don't reject it. Some guys who fit the masculine image, all they want to talk about is sex, women, 'poofs'—they put everything down, they attack things, they don't talk about their emotions and how they feel. I've had conversations with a lot of them and it's like talking to the same person because they all fit into this image of putting guys down who don't fit the masculine image. You try and bring something up, something you feel about, 'Well that's gay, that's stupid, that's dumb', they just reject it, because it's not masculine. As soon as you start talking about a certain girl who may be targeted, they start going on about their experiences with her and what they've done. They start almost bragging to prove themselves as this masculine guy who's done this and that, 'Oh, yeah, I drink, I smoke, I do drugs', but I don't drink or do drugs or smoke.
TOM 16

'ALL MEN ARE PIGS'

or 'What is man and why and how do we avoid letting it loose?'

MAN'S DEFINING FEATURE, the genitals, give a fine symbol of what a man is. The erect penis is strong, powerful, demanding; it is masculinity embodied—for what an emasculating experience it is for a man to be impotent . . . Impotence is a failure of manhood, the inability to use the one thing that makes a man a man. Erectionless, a man is powerless. But with an erection, he is ambitious, powerful and conceited ('Gonna be a big-time operator . . . I'm gonna have my name in lights . . . I'm gonna have lots of friends').

But an erection's companions, the testicles, are odd, more than slightly comical, fragile, and exposed and vulnerable in their scrotum—yet they are the seat of a man's maleness (the ephemeral essence of man-ness), as the erect penis is the seat of his masculinity. So pathetic to look at, but with a power awe-inspiring and awful to contemplate.

A woman thinks with her heart, a man thinks with his balls. A great deal of mankind's advances are due to this pair of megalomaniacal, conceited organs. But when the area is not aroused, and the penis ceases to be so vigorous, domineering and altogether male, it shrinks and grows timid and joins the testicles in insignificant boyish cuteness. Unobtrusive, unarresting, so innocent-looking that one almost forgets what it is capable of. In this mode, the genitals are serene, peaceful . . . man at his least male.

Rape is man at his most male: thoughtless; uncompassionate; unfeeling; unempathising; arrogant; violent; hard (in all respects); and ruled by, and thinking with, his groin. All these define maleness and rape is the most male behaviour. The domain of MAN—POWERFUL but small; nameless and not the person you know, not any person, but a MAN—anonymous, departed from self and identity in animal evolutionary regression (or someone with a retarded animal self).

Beastly regression—maleness is animal; it has not evolved with the human race as femaleness has. This is most evident with emotions and sensitivity. Men get angry where women are compassionate. A man cannot feel as deeply as a woman because of the emotionally retarded maleness crowding his self; he cannot be sensitive because men don't cry. SNAGs do, but SNAGs are guys, not men, and even that sensitivity and emotional quality rarely match a woman's; and it is still looked upon as weakness, a threat to one's masculinity and manhood. No one ever saw a man with a hard throbbing cock in tears, save of pain.

A hard throbbing cock is like a little soldier at attention, his heart beating with excitement and anticipation at serving his country—MAN. And war, like rape, is also dominantly a male activity, is also telling of males. Arrogant, detached generals relishing the power over men's lives and deaths, and the proud, brave, somewhat naive men with noble intentions and hideous lack of foresight who see the horror and find out how small they are in the fray.

As the nurse in *Lady Chatterley's Lover* says: 'All men are babies, when you come to the bottom of them. Why I've handled some of the toughest customers as ever went down Tevershall pit. But let anything ail them so that you have to do for them, and they're babies, just big babies.' Because, like pufferfish, peacocks or our own cocks, men are not as big, pretty or tough as they make out to be. Maleness is really just a front, a frill around our necks that used to be permanently erect, but is now only occasionally inflated, and our weak and scrawny inner selves become increasingly obvious. And we are getting weaker and scrawnier as the emasculating effect of civilisation takes its toll on our primeval maleness.

One can hardly argue that men today are as manly as those who have gone before us. An equal comparison could never be made between gruff, strong, marauding Vikings hacking monks and villagers to death and the snivelling little accountants we are now. We no longer need to be so masculine and physically powerful to succeed in the world. Indeed, in many respects, a maleful man encounters more problems in today's society than a complacent guy. For one, a MAN is never complacent about his status in the world around him, he is always striving for power, recognition, admiration. But here we have the mischievous entity of adversity, without which none of this can be obtained. And all-conquering, hairy chested Genghis discovers that in the modern age, quite to his chagrin, there exist *things over which he has no control.* A wall of adversity is fine, once overcome, for propelling a man's ego, but when it gets to the point where there is nothing he can do about it, the bull-headed MAN will either repeatedly ram his head against it or quietly gnaw his leg off in the corner. (All this while the accountant is sitting peacefully at his desk in his dimly lit office, a vacant look on his face.) Frustration is not a MAN's best friend.

He needs to be able to exercise every MAN's right to be an all-powerful ruler. And every king needs a kingdom, so a MAN's home is his castle—a serene (to him at least) location where his every word is gospel and everyone is his loyal and devoted subject. His home is a retreat from the vast, perplexing, stupefying world, a place where he can have his slippers put on for him, lie back in a reclining chair, read the newspaper and puff on his pipe—all in silence and awe from his family. Here a MAN's ego has the space to inflate to its natural size and recover from the battering it has received in the outside world, with the sycophantic respect from those around him that it needs and therefore deserves.

But no! Now we discover, to our amazement, that *women* have rights too! and even *children*! And suddenly a MAN's world has gone all topsy-turvy, because now he is not the only one in it. *Others* too are deserving of respect, and so the admiration cannot go to him exclusively. Not only does the outside world become all the more a daunting challenge to enter, but MAN has lost his sanctuary from it; he is not the unquestionable ruler of his domain, but he has to do housework, cook meals, even change nappies! All this only occasionally, of course, because even though, to his dismay, he is no longer the sole breadwinner, he is still thankfully the major one, so nothing can make him give up everything. But this is small compensation for what he has lost—what since the dawn of time has sustained his maleness: a

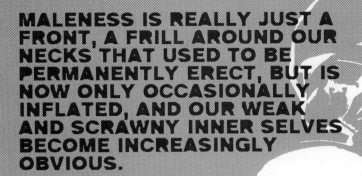

MALENESS IS REALLY JUST A FRONT, A FRILL AROUND OUR NECKS THAT USED TO BE PERMANENTLY ERECT, BUT IS NOW ONLY OCCASIONALLY INFLATED, AND OUR WEAK AND SCRAWNY INNER SELVES BECOME INCREASINGLY OBVIOUS.

sense of importance and omnipotence.

With this loss we are losing our masculinity, fast becoming males without maleness. The chemical, artificial maleness of Viagra may well be a clever way of synthetically counteracting the castrating result of stress, adversity and emotion on the male mind (the genitalia) but it is a vehicle and excuse for its physical escalation. 'LOST BOYS: Why boys are searching for an identity', sounds the hopelessly fundamentalist Christian *Philadelphia Trumpet* magazine on its front cover, accompanied by the reproachful image of a blue-eyed little boy. They are searching for an identity because the identity once bestowed by default upon all men—that of demi-god—is no longer possible. Now men are being forced into a search that was once reserved only for rejects, a search for what a man may be if not a MAN. To dispose of all natural maleness, or to be wiped out. But is this decline of MAN lamentable? One may feel sorry for the individual male being crushed by the burden of emotions and sensitivity he has not evolved to cope with. But the fall of the male empire, which, with its rape, war and

tactlessness, has terrorised women and the world since there have been sexes, would not be lamented by anyone but a male.

The complete eradication of the male half of the species, a wistful fantasy close to many a woman's heart, would solve a great many problems. There would be the possibility of a truly compassionate society, no more war, premature ejaculation, or men who are not equipped to deal with life in the civilisation they have created. Women at last could have their turn at dominating and fucking up the earth. In a best case scenario, taking men out of the world could have the effect of taking the gusto out of the human race—the exploratory drive, the BIG-TIME OPERATOR syndrome that has us reaching up to the stars and down to the uranium, conquering disease and subjugating people—all in the male quest to *make his mark*, all too often a boot mark on the face of our planet. Oh, what the lack of MAN could do.

But I will stand up and be the first to say that it wouldn't solve all our problems, because men are not the only imperfect creatures.

PODGE 17

SO WHAT DO YOU THINK BEING A GUY IS ALL ABOUT?
DO YOU AGREE WITH THESE GUYS?

	AGREE	DISAGREE	DON'T KNOW
1. MASCULINITY IS A KIND OF STRAITJACKET THAT PREVENTS GUYS FROM EXPRESSING WHAT THEY REALLY FEEL.	☐	☐	☐
2. MASCULINITY IS BEST UNDERSTOOD AS POWER THAT IS USED TO INTIMIDATE OTHERS.	☐	☐	☐
3. AS A GUY YOU HAVE TO PROVE THAT YOU'RE NOT GAY OR WEAK.	☐	☐	☐
4. THESE WRITERS DO NOT PRESENT A BALANCED VIEW OF MASCULINITY OR WHAT IT MEANS TO BE A GUY.	☐	☐	☐
5. THE ERECT PENIS IS A SYMBOL OF POWER AND THE SEAT OF A MAN'S MASCULINITY.	☐	☐	☐
6. WOMEN THINK WITH THEIR HEARTS AND MEN THINK WITH THEIR BALLS.	☐	☐	☐
7. MEN ARE EMOTIONALLY RETARDED.	☐	☐	☐
8. MEN SHOULD NO LONGER FEEL THE NEED TO BE 'MACHO' AND PHYSICALLY POWERFUL.	☐	☐	☐
9. MEN FEEL THEY ARE LOSING THEIR MASCULINITY AND ARE SUFFERING AN IDENTITY CRISIS.	☐	☐	☐
10. THE LOSS OF MASCULINITY AND THE FALL OF THE 'MALE EMPIRE' WOULD BE A GOOD THING!	☐	☐	☐
11. WITHOUT MEN THE WORLD WOULD BE A BETTER PLACE.	☐	☐	☐
12. MEN ARE RESPONSIBLE FOR DOMINATING AND DESTROYING THE PLANET.	☐	☐	☐
13. YOU CAN BE A MAN WITHOUT DOING DOMINANT MASCULINITY.	☐	☐	☐
14. WOMEN WOULDN'T NECESSARILY SOLVE THE WORLD'S PROBLEMS.	☐	☐	☐
15. SOME WOMEN KNOW HOW TO DO DOMINANT MASCULINITY TOO!	☐	☐	☐

CHAPTER TWO
BOYS &
THEIR BODIES

As guys and girls are growing up, their bodies change—but you already know that! How, though, do guys understand and relate to their bodies? And what's it like growing up in a boy's body? Read what these guys have to say.

WHAT'S GOING ON?
Puberty

WHAT'S THAT?
When your body begins to change.

WHAT'S IT LIKE?
Different.

BRENDAN HALLIDAY 13

YOU START TO GROW pubic hair at the age of ten or eleven. Also your voice gets deeper if you are a boy. I can't wait to shave my face and wear nice aftershave. Growing up is hard because you are getting older and changing into a man.

TONY 13

I can't wait to shave my face and wear nice aftershave.

FRANKIE FANTASIA 17
(PHOTO COURTESY THE LOOK STUDIO)

BRENDAN HALLIDAY 13

I HAVE FOUND A part of growing up is that your muscles get really sore because they are growing stronger and bigger. Sometimes you get migraines and sometimes this results in throwing up. Your voice cracks and that means it gets deeper, and sometimes when you talk it goes high and squeaky. I don't like it when it goes squeaky because sometimes people laugh at you and keep reminding you that it happened and it is really annoying.

TRENT 13

THE PROBLEM IS THE NEEDLES. I HAVE TO GIVE THEM TO MYSELF. YOU JUST STICK THEM INTO THE LEG. IT HURTS THOUGH.

I WAS IN HOSPITAL because I had a kidney transplant. They were just pretty much gone. Mum gave me a kidney, good match. I've had that for ages now, about seven years. I'm on growth hormones now because I'm a little bit short, it's a bit obvious. But I've grown four centimetres in a month, last month, so it's good. The problem is the needles. I have to give them to myself. You just stick them into the leg. It hurts though.

I can't do much. I want to start doing weights and stuff but I find it hard because all my stomach muscles have been cut. I've got scars across my body. I'm just cut up. My dad says I have to take it slowly, not straight away, with just little weights first, then work up. I do it for my golf, it helps a lot. My arms and my legs are all okay. It's just building up my stomach muscles. It's hard because sometimes if I pull a muscle it just hurts for weeks. I have to be careful. I play cricket and if I get hit in a certain place, I can lose my kidney because it's just under the skin here, it's not under the ribs. So I've got to be careful playing sports.

LANCE 15

So growing up for guys and girls is a time of physical change but it's not always easy, and guys like Lance are faced with particular challenges.

As Trent points out, sometimes your body can become a target. You can get teased if you have a voice others decide is 'funny' or if you're not slim, and your life can be miserable. The toilets at school and the change rooms can become scary places because that's when guys can easily judge other guys' bodies. There are many different kinds of bodies—all shapes and sizes—and unfortunately, rather than accepting these differences, it seems certain kinds of bodies are more acceptable and desirable than others.

How important to you is it to have a gym-toned body or to be slim? Just how important *is* body image to guys? Check out what the following guys who were involved in a study conducted by Dr Murray Drummond from the University of South Australia have to say. These guys' ages range from thirteen to fifteen years old. Which do you think are healthy attitudes toward their bodies? Which do you think are unhealthy or 'obsessive' attitudes, or attitudes formed by peer and other social pressure?

I'D RATHER BE SKINNY!

I WOULD LIKE TO be a little skinnier. Not anorexic or anything. But you know, everywhere. Like some people can't find any fat anywhere, but I can when I pinch myself.

IUAN

I CHANGED THE WAY I ate because I wanted to look better. I wanted to feel better and healthier. I don't like eating the unhealthy foods because of what they have in them and how they look and feel. I guess I don't want to get fat.

GEORGE

WE DEFINITELY GET THE messages from the media. I think there are a lot of people in the magazines who look good and other people see that and want to be like it. I mean it's not just girls either. It's happening to guys too.

LEONG

I HAVE STARTED TO DO more exercise to lose weight and I have cut down on foods a little bit too. I am more conscious of my weight now because of the society we live in.

LAWRY

OCCASIONALLY PEOPLE WILL SAY some bad stuff. I think if you're skinny, people pick on you less.

SHANTON

GYM-TONED BODIES

I DON'T FEEL THAT good about my body and I don't like the way it looks. I would like to improve it. I would like to improve the fitness and I would like to have a big body, you know, muscly. Because I have always been into muscles and that sort of thing. I have always followed wrestling and I saw the wrestlers with big bodies. I look at them in awe.

RORY

I WOULD LIKE TO be a bit muscular. I have thought it would be nice to be a bit stronger. But I can't be bothered going to a gym.

GENNARO

I DO A LOT OF exercise. I do push-ups to make my chest bigger and sit-ups to make the stomach flat. It's important to have a six-pack.

NEVILLE

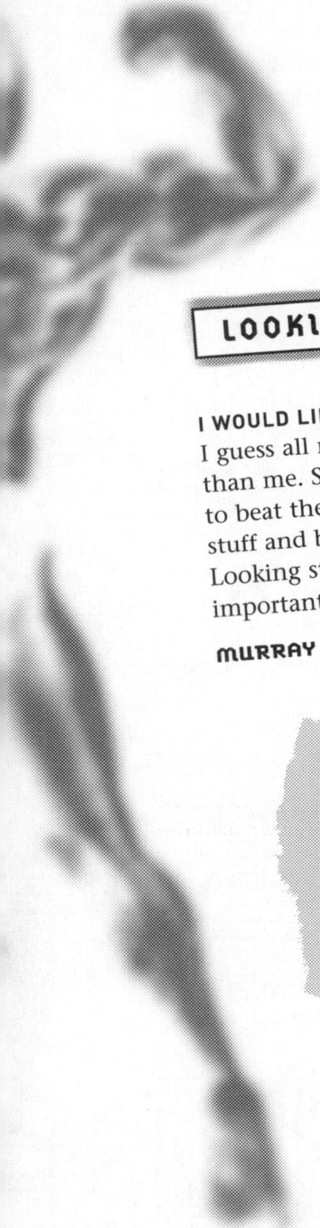

LOOKING STRONGER

I WOULD PREFER TO have both strength and muscularity. I think if you are strong you should try and look strong as well. It makes you more attractive to girls and can scare off other guys as well. If there were guys coming up to fight you, you might be able to frighten them off by looking strong and they wouldn't even attempt it.

GREG

I WOULD LIKE TO be stronger. I guess all my friends are stronger than me. So I would like to be able to beat them in arm wrestles and stuff and be more competitive. Looking stronger is always important for guys.

MURRAY

BODIES BOYS LIKE

I THINK BODY-BUILDERS are a bit excessive, but I think muscles are good. Maybe just not that big. Guys certainly need to have muscles that people can see.

MATEO

I THINK SPRINTERS HAVE got the best bodies. You know, like 100 metres runners. They have great muscles and they can use them really well too. I think it's important to have a body that looks good as well as one that you can use.

RAMI

Working out

For many guys having a muscular body is seen as a positive thing: it's associated with being able to attract girls. It's also about being powerful. But some guys also think that taking an active interest in your body and appearance is associated with being gay! What do you think?

A GUY WHO WORKS out is strong and can do anything he likes. He will get a lot of girls who will absolutely die at the sight of his muscles.

JACOB 14

IT'S FINE FOR A guy to work out at the gym if he wants to make himself fit—good on him. It's good also because at the gym there are heaps of chicks to meet.

KEVIN 15

A GUY WHO WORKS out at the gym is someone who probably got bashed and wants to wreak havoc and revenge on the person that bashed him up or else he is someone who loves himself and thinks he looks good in the mirror, and probably thinks that he is a hunk. Probably has a tendency to be a fag or maybe a ponce.

ADRIAN 15

IT'S PERFECTLY NORMAL TO work out—provided you don't go to the gym to engage in friendly contact with other males.

JUSTIN 14

Girls and boys' bodies

I'VE NOTICED THAT GUYS want to lose weight so they'll be able to attract the girls. I think I'm okay, there's nothing wrong with me, I'm a bit overweight.

CHRIS 16

GIRLS CAN BE QUITE picky about the way that they judge guys. Like girls will say, 'Oh my God, he's got a pimply face, he's probably a real prick'. They sort of grade the guys from their looks instead of their personality.

MICHAEL 13

I THINK WATCHING 'BAYWATCH' and programs like that you see a lot of guys with great bodies. You generally don't want to be seen as the ugly one. I think with friends you don't really care because there's a couple of friends of mine who are rather podgy and when we go swimming or go to the beach we always pick on each other's belly flab, but we don't really care so much. But I think beneath it we sort of say we'd better get rid of that before next summer. I think girls experience the same thing, they don't want to see fat. They don't really mind being extremely thin whereas guys do. With girls, even if they don't have much body fat, even if they're very thin, they still consider themselves fat. Girls are really conscious about their bodies and we don't pick on them as much because we know that they'll make a big thing out of it.

JOHNNY 17

MANY YOUNG GAY GUYS are obsessed with their body. They want to have a masculine body because that's the accepted norm in urban gay ghettos.

JONARD 18

Boys in change rooms

BOYS HAVE TO DEAL with the size of their dicks.

JOSH 15

BOBBY IN THE CHANGE ROOM

IF PEOPLE HIDE IN the change rooms to get changed and people begin to notice it, then that person is called pin dick or is given crap. If they are fat, then people start talking about them having big tits and a fat arse.

JEREMY 15

I USED TO WORRY about going into the change rooms and taking off my top because of my chubby stomach while other boys were blissfully unaware and would whip off their tops. I used to think, 'How come you're not embarrassed, how come you're not ashamed of your body and how can you not try to cover up or do it in the corner?'.

DANIEL 23

MINE'S BIGGER THAN YOURS!

Jokes or comments are often made about penis size and for some guys there can be a lot of anxiety around this. Some boys might worry that their penis isn't big enough and feel inadequate or are afraid of being targeted. It might only be a joke but behind joking there can often be a lot of anxiety. It's important to remember that we can't control the size of our penis, the way the balls hang, the amount of hair on our chest, backs, underarms and legs. It's the way we are physically. But what we can control and change is:

- **LEARNING TO ACCEPT OUR BODIES AS THEY ARE.**

- **THE WAY WE SEE OR PERCEIVE OUR BODIES.**

- **THE WAY WE USE OUR BODIES.**

- **HOW WE TREAT OUR BODIES AND OTHER PEOPLE'S BODIES.**

- **HOW MUCH INFORMATION WE GET ABOUT OUR BODIES AND OTHER PEOPLE'S BODIES.**

Body targets

ONE GUY WHO'S TREMENDOUSLY overweight was hassled by some people. They don't really hassle him anymore because he hangs around with the lads, a local gang, and has become a drug dealer.

TIM 14

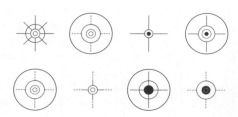

IT'S EMBARRASSING FOR SOME guys at the swimming pool or at the beach to strip down to their bathers because they get picked on by other boys and get called fat. They'll try and ignore it or get angry. One guy used to get very angry and a couple of times he kicked the toilet door off the hinges or he'd run out of school because people used to tease him.

ZACH 14

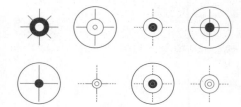

Change rooms and toilets can indeed be scary places. Maybe the kinds of fears these guys have told us about and this kind of bullying needs to be talked more about at school. Let's hear from Nathan below who we think has a very healthy attitude to his body.

I DON'T CARE HOW I look as long as I just get on with my life the way I am. It's just how I was born and how God created us.

NATHAN 13

MARK AND MICHAEL WITH THEIR TALKING BODIES

YOUR BODY TALKS!

DID YOU KNOW YOUR BODY 'TALKS' TO YOU ABOUT ITS HEALTH, ITS FEELINGS, ITS NEEDS? DO YOU UNDERSTAND ITS LANGUAGE? DO YOU LISTEN TO IT?

DO YOU:

- GET TO KNOW THE LIMITS AND BOUNDARIES OF YOUR BODY, RECOGNISE THE SPECIFIC WARNING SIGNALS YOUR BODY SENDS YOU? WHEN YOU'VE BEEN PUSHING YOURSELF TOO HARD, RECOGNISE YOUR BODY'S SIGNS FOR TENSION, ILLNESS, EXHAUSTION AND ANYTHING ELSE THAT STOPS YOU FEELING EMOTIONALLY AND PHYSICALLY WELL?

- LEARN HOW TO TALK BACK TO YOUR BODY, RELAXING AND RELEASING PRESSURE ON YOURSELF?

IF YOU CAN'T UNDERSTAND YOUR BODY'S LANGUAGE OR DON'T KNOW HOW TO RESPOND TO IT, DEVELOP THE COURAGE TO SEEK HELP ABOUT DIFFICULT FEELINGS AND BODILY EXPERIENCES WHEN YOU NEED TO.

GUYS NEED TO KNOW ABOUT THEIR BODIES

THE WHOLE MASTURBATION THING, I don't talk about it seriously with my friends. They all joke about it but I was talking to my friend Mel about it and she was saying, 'Oh, yes, I do sometimes, but don't say anything'. Everyone is like, 'Okay, yes, I do but sh, sh'. Everyone is too embarrassed. I'm kind of embarrassed as well because you don't want to say 'Oh, yes, I masturbate'. It's something you don't want to say. If it were socially okay to talk about it, then I wouldn't be embarrassed about it.

ROB 16

GUYS NEED TO KNOW about their bodies, about masturbating and things like that. It's important.

SIMON 13

Talking about masturbation

 Many guys don't feel really comfortable talking about masturbation. But did you know that in the past there were a lot of myths about masturbation? It was thought that masturbation caused guys to go blind or crazy and that it made hair grow on your palms. It was also thought that if you did too much of it that you would go infertile and that it might affect your ability to have sex in the future. We know now that this is just a lot of nonsense!

It's important to be well informed and to talk about these kinds of things but understandably many guys might just feel too embarrassed. Guys don't talk about this kind of stuff unless they're joking, right? Joking can be a way of dealing with really scary feelings.

Masturbation can be a healthy way of learning about your own body. But it can also be used to avoid or escape actually dealing with your sexual feelings. Some guys use porn magazines, videos and websites without being cluey about the rules that are imposed on men by porn.

Porn's an industry making money from people. Think about the images. The women and men are models and in the minority of body shapes compared to real women and men. Think about the lighting, photography techniques, costume, make-up, facial expressions, plastic surgery, computer changes to images, the fact that it's the models' career so they work out all day for a five-minute photo shoot and get touch ups in between photos. Think about the fact that what you're seeing and hearing has been scripted, edited, dubbed and choreographed hundreds of times. And looking at a magazine of naked figures who can't talk back or challenge you is a lot easier than talking to and relating sexually with real people.

Masculine bodies

It's not only having a biologically male body that makes you a man, as both the following boys point out. It's the way you walk, talk, act and use your body. Did you know that there was a time when it was considered 'normal' for guys to wear make-up and to wear fancy clothing? And in some cultures it is acceptable for guys to wear a range of clothes. Have a read of what these guys say makes a masculine body.

SHORT HAIR, HAIRY FACE, muscles around your chest, and abs, and your penis—I guess, hairy body, that's mainly what men are meant to be like.

MARK 12

NO LIMP WRISTS

THERE ARE EXPECTATIONS for a guy: no limp wrists, has to walk like a guy, has to talk like a guy, has to dress like a guy. Some people, not all gay people, but some heterosexual people, may walk a bit feminine and they might get targeted because people might think they're gay just because they walk like a woman, or because they talk like a woman, or they do not have a deep voice. It's hard and it's sort of scary in a way. You feel nervous, sometimes you get depressed, 'Why can't I be normal?'.

There's just so many restrictions, it's just so hard. The people who are the gay bashers make people feel like that.

I feel threatened because I travel to and from Rockingham to Fremantle by myself all the time. I walk from home to the bus station and back again. I'm worried that someone will come out and get me. There's always that in the back of my mind. But

SOMEONE MIGHT IDENTIFY YOU AS GAY JUST BY LOOKING AT YOU OR BY THE WAY THAT YOU'RE WALKING.

most of the time I just try and forget it. I just walk along and I might sing to myself to try and take my mind off it. Someone might identify you as gay just by looking at you or by the way that you're walking.

But there are a couple of places where I can dress up, do the limp wrist, wear the necklaces and the hair, and do a bit of a dance move. I mainly do it at home in my room because outside of home if someone sees you and they feel really threatened or they just don't like the sight of you, they'll walk straight over to you and beat the crap out of you.

VINCE 17

Guys with physical disabilities

Let's hear what guys with physical disabilities have to say about what it's like growing up in the male culture that so values sport and physical prowess.

REGARDLESS OF WHETHER I look like Tom Cruise or not, you know, disability will always be there. It will be a sticker in front of my head that says, 'He is disabled, so whatever he looks like won't matter'.

ANDREW 16

I LOOK NOTHING LIKE BRAD PITT BUT IF HE HAD MY DISABILITY NEITHER WOULD HE!

HAVE YOU EVER THOUGHT about what a male 'sex symbol' would look like if he had a severe disability that impacted on his physical appearance? Would the ladies still swoon over him? Would the photographers still be jostling for images? Would he still be paid millions of dollars to appear in a motion picture and, most importantly, would people still think of him as sexy? An example of this is Christopher Reeve, his accident changed our perceptions of him from 'superMan' to 'superCrip'!

How do our social attitudes and dominant standards of masculinity affect boys who are growing up with bodies that are affected by disability? I can only speak from my own perspective but other guys with congenital physical disabilities probably share some of my experiences. Allow me to set the scene.

I was thirteen years old at a mainstream school in suburbia. I used a motorised wheelchair and started noticing how other boys' bodies were attaining masculine characteristics, big muscles and long legs and torsos while I was just getting thinner. I also noticed that these boys with more masculine physiques were the most popular and had an air of confidence that I wished I shared. These were difficult times for me and with hindsight I can see that I went through a grieving process for a body that I would've had if it weren't for my mutant gene. I was also grieving for the life that this body would have given me: a life of independence, confidence, health and physical strength. Although I had never had this 'masculine' body, I still felt a loss from not developing a masculine physique like the other boys. Of course, I had the body hair and the genital growth, but the height, broad shoulders and muscular strength would always elude me.

I believe that for most boys, puberty is an exciting time. I imagine that boys without physical disabilities enjoy this time and feel pride about the changes that are taking place—the physical evidence that they are becoming a 'man'. These changes are visual cues for the boy, telling him that the time of transition has come. Although boys with disabilities will certainly have some of these cues, missing out on the major ones is possibly going to interfere with our self-esteem and the development of a masculine identity. We are probably more likely to focus on the developmental changes that we haven't attained, such as height and strength, than on those that we have, such as hair growth and a deeper voice.

At the age of 25, I still wish for strength and stamina. My bodily concerns now relate more to health rather than aesthetics. I focus more on staying well and alive than being concerned about how my body looks to other people.

I know that my physicality cannot impress or allure but I also know that there are other things about me that can.

GEORGE TALEPOROS 25

GROWING AND DEVELOPING AS A DISABLED PERSON

I'M AT THE POINT now where I am really growing and developing as a disabled person. I feel I can talk about my disability constantly, I can actually go up to other people with disabilities and feel comfortable. I remember feeling ashamed, scared and intimidated being around people with disabilities and now I'm really claiming that identity back.

The shame with being disabled is everywhere, like when you aren't able to lift a cup and you're in a restaurant and you can't pick up a fork, when you're in a lift and you need someone to press the button for you, when you need someone to wipe your arse, all these things, these are in your daily life. You constantly feel ashamed about not being able to do things for yourself because that's what society is all about, you know, being independent and being able to be your own person and self-sufficient.

I'm trying to come to terms with my disability and realising that being dependent is not a bad thing necessarily and we all depend on one another in society, generally. People with disabilities just have this different, more obvious kind of dependence. Having a disability is totally opposed to the main concept of masculinity. If you have a disability your body is helpless, weak, my muscles are wasted, and what it means to be a man is being strong, tall, able, lifting heavy things. I have weakness of the limbs, of the arms, my whole body is physically weak. It's a condition that I've had all my life that continues to become progressively worse, yet very, very slowly.

How do disabled guys reinforce that they're men? They pick on someone who's a little bit different and that's how you feel better. I remember there was this girl we used to pick on and make fun of and I remember her crying and me thinking I'm sorry I didn't mean to upset you but I'd say something nasty. I remember I'd start singing songs in the maths lesson because I just wanted the attention. And people thought I was really funny. Since I had a disability, obviously there was a novelty factor and I played that up a bit. I appreciated they paid attention to me. I was also traumatised and I'd cry at lunchtime because the school had stairs and I'd have to stay in class during lunchtime and recess. I was just the freak. There was no one else there with disabilities as obvious as me and I remember being really traumatised and crying myself asleep at night not wanting to go. When you're a kid you just want to really blend in.

I'm not ashamed of my disability anymore.

TONY 24

WHEN YOU'RE IN A LIFT AND YOU NEED SOMEONE TO PRESS THE BUTTON FOR YOU, WHEN YOU NEED SOMEONE TO WIPE YOUR ARSE, ALL THESE THINGS, THESE ARE IN YOUR DAILY LIFE.

Sexuality and the body

A LOT OF MY FRIENDS have only just started shaving and we'll talk about things like that. Like they'll say, 'Gee you've got a lot of hair around your belly, I haven't got anything yet'. They talk about how they'd like to have sex with girls, but I don't think many of them actually have had sex with anyone. So it's more like they're wanting to and they're saying jokes like, 'If I don't have it by the time I'm 21, I'm going to cut it off and become a monk'.

JOHNNY 17

MY MALE FRIENDS AND I were at a party one night in Year 9 and we all sat down discussing puberty and what was happening with us, who was at what stage, and what they'd experienced, and what they actually thought about it all. I don't see that as being a regular conversation between most fourteen-year-old males. But we all had this closeness where we could actually sit down and discuss what was going on.

XANDER 19

I REMEMBER ONE TIME this Anglo-Saxon boy asked me, 'Do you think Chinese guys have pubic hair? He doesn't have much hair on his legs.' The Anglo-Saxon guy was being ridiculous because a Chinese male may have less hair on his body. Some Asian guys want to look more European so they can seem more masculine. I know a Chinese guy who wants to change his nose, he wants to have a nose job. He doesn't have high self-esteem. He's always comparing himself to Australian men, blond guys, footy players. But then I said I would rather have a person who likes me personally than a person who has these physical expectations of me. One guy in my school advised me to build my body so that I can become straight. That was so naive.

JONARD 18

PEOPLE WITH DISABILITIES ARE seen as 'asexy'. They're not considered attractive and I think that's different from being seen as asexual. A person with disabilities does not match with the image we have of someone that is sexy. I have always been a really sexual person but for a long time I never had any sex.

TONY 24

INNER BEAUTY

THE WORLD IS HOOKED on aesthetics and external beauty. We are a society that seeks out the unblemished and settle for the least blemished among those who will accept us. This is a weakness that we all share and people who do not meet the physical ideal are the first and most obvious casualties. However in the end, we all suffer as we reject our soul mates and secure our trophies.

We need to become a society where inner beauty determines our sexual choices and where human relations are guided by self-cultivated pleasing compositions of kindness, love and compassion.

GEORGE TALEPOROS 25

What George says about inner beauty applies to everyone.

SOME DAYS I JUST don't want to go out. Teenagers place so much importance on image and how you look. I get teased so badly by strangers who don't even know me and I can't help but feel that it's because I don't look like Brad Pitt. It's not as bad as it used to be. My skin has started to clear up, but it used to be really bad. I hate my complexion, my teeth, my tiny build, yuck, yuck, yuck.

BEN 17

'INNER BEAUTY', BEN GERRARD 17

If we could dream of a world where people weren't judged on their appearance but on what was on the inside, imagine what a different place it would be. Guys wouldn't feel so yuck about themselves. It's important to get a perspective on our bodies. There are so many different bodies but so much energy and advertising goes into creating the ideal guy who has that slim gym-toned muscular body. Healthy bodies matter but it is not healthy to get carried away with this ideal because it can be destructive and prevent us from growing and developing as people.

FEELING SEXUAL

- WHAT KIND OF PERSON ARE YOU ATTRACTED TO?

- WHAT IS YOUR IMAGE OF SOMEONE WHO IS SEXY?

- IS THERE A DIFFERENCE BETWEEN PHYSICAL SEXUAL ATTRACTION AND FEELING INTIMATE WITH SOMEONE?

- WHAT HAPPENS IN YOUR BODY WHEN YOU ARE ATTRACTED TO SOMEONE?

- WHAT EMOTIONS DO YOU FEEL? DO THESE EMOTIONS GET EXPRESSED THROUGH YOUR BODY, IN WHAT IT DOES, THE WAY IT MOVES, THE WAY IT SMELLS, THE WAY YOU CLOTHE IT AND 'AFTERSHAVE' IT, ETC.

CHAPTER THREE
TAKING RISKS

NOT A WORRY IN THE WORLD . . .

WHAT A WEEK! Work finished on Wednesday so my cousin Nathan and I had some extra time to catch up with each other. We worked together on the farms and we were like best mates, like brothers. We decided to visit Nath's girlfriend. Before we left the farm, we had a black and white photo taken of us. I now keep that photo framed beside my bed.

As we headed off back to Nath's place in his new, hotted up car, with Jackson Browne as loud as it could go and singing at the top of our lungs, there was not a worry in the world. Nath's house was only five minutes through the backroads, but the way he drives, it was only two minutes away.

Should I have said something as we did speeds in excess of 140 kilometres per hour in a 60 kilometre zone? But over the last hill and we would be home.

That was not to be the case.

A car was coming the other way with his high beams on, and at that speed Nath was blinded, swerved, lost control and careered into a pole. Nath's door hit the pole and we were both knocked unconscious by the impact. I awoke first to see my cousin, my best mate, with a lump on the side of his head, the size of his head.

I flagged down a car, went to Nath's and called an ambulance. There could have been an ambulance there and he still wouldn't have survived. What if I had said something? Why didn't I have a mark on me? This couldn't be happening.

A couple of days went by and I was too scared to sleep. Sleeping pill after sleeping pill and bourbon after bourbon was the only way to put me to sleep. All I dreamed was the car spinning and spinning and coming to a huge halt. I pushed my

SLEEPING PILL AFTER SLEEPING PILL AND **BOURBON** AFTER **BOURBON** WAS THE **ONLY** WAY TO PUT ME TO SLEEP.

girlfriend out of my life to avoid anyone trying to help me by talking about it. Nath was her friend too, but I didn't care. I was the one in the accident. My family all bonded together to help each other with the torment of the accident. Mum and Dad were devastated by the death of their favourite nephew, but on the other hand relieved that their son was still alive.

The funeral came not long after. To see so many hundreds of friends gather together, some people travelling from interstate just to pay their respects, would've made Nath happy. The support given to me and my family by the community was great, but they did not have the graphics in their head like I did, and still have. Whenever I was in someone's passenger seat, I was against any sort of speeding. I was fine behind the wheel but not in the passenger seat. Every time I would hear Jackson Browne, or see a car similar to Nath's, I would 'lose it' through both endless tears and sometimes aggression. I felt so guilty. If only I'd said something, I should've said something. But fast cars and driving fast were considered 'cool'.

I really needed my friends to cheer me up. They were good, as good as they could

LEE DRIVING

be anyway. My spirit was crushed. I felt like the whole world was against me. I began to not care about anything. There was nothing to live for. I was unaware of how to handle all this. The best way I found was the grog. On numerous occasions it made me become aggressive and I found myself in many fights, but it made me feel better too. I also got into smoking drugs. I found myself a job and all the blokes there smoked. I thought this was all great: I got trashed, forgot about everything, and passed out until the morning.

A year later, not long ago, I met a girl who made me wake up to myself. Her younger brother was killed in a car accident too. She seemed to be the only person I thought could understand. I had someone that I wanted to talk to who actually understood.

I realised what I was doing with drugs and drink was wrong and that Nath would not want to see me like this. I got off the drugs and started to look on the up side of life a bit more.

Sure, I still grieve and can still 'lose the plot' sometimes, but my life is now back on track. And anyone who talks about getting a 'hotted up' car, I tell them not to bother.

MATT 18

So this chapter is about guys taking risks. Why do they take so many risks? Did you know that one of the major causes of death for 15- to 24-year-old males is motor vehicle accidents? Why do you think this is? Matt kind of gives us some answers to these questions. It's cool to drive fast cars! It's cool to act tough! But there can be tragic consequences as he reveals. And like many of us after something happens, Matt thinks about the 'if only' scenario—maybe if he had just said something to his cousin it might have been different. But life's never that simple, is it? What we can learn from Matt's experience, though, is that it is helpful to think about the consequences of what might happen when we are in certain situations with friends because this is one way of keeping safe and living a longer, healthy life. We also learn from Matt that sometimes taking drugs and drinking alcohol is about trying to avoid a problem or the feelings associated with a painful experience. But we also know that many guys just think it's cool to do these kinds of things. Have a read of what these guys have to say about smoking, taking drugs and drinking.

I ALWAYS SMOKE IF I'M DEPRESSED

I'VE BEEN SMOKING CIGARETTES for about a year. I didn't start because I wanted to be really cool. I don't know why I started. I suppose my friends started smoking so I thought I might as well try it. I didn't do it much, only when I felt like it. People say life's less stressful if you smoke, and that's a lot of crap. It's less stressful only because it gives me something else to think about for a while.

ROB 16

I QUIT SMOKING FOR maybe a year or so, but for the last few months I've been smoking maybe one a day. At the most, I'll go four days without one. If someone is smoking, I'll have a few drags but that's it. I think I may have started for the image and to feel better about myself because I was quite depressed when I was thirteen. I was confused about life and I didn't know whether I wanted to live or not. I slowly got out of that but I can't stop smoking now.

KIERAN 16

'SMOKING DUCK', MICHAEL BOKODY 13

IT'S ABOUT IMAGE AND PEER PRESSURE!

IT'S IMAGE. I DON'T THINK half of them ever wanted to do drugs. I think it's peer group pressure. Because their friends were doing it, they felt obliged to. I've done it as well. I started smoking because it was a social thing and then I realised that I'd made a mistake. But that's how it starts, that image thing: 'I'm cool, I've got a joint hanging out of my mouth, look at me.'
LUCIANO 19

IT ALWAYS COMES BACK to the same issue, peer pressure. Even though you say, 'No, I don't smoke because they tell me to', it always ends up being the same issue: peer pressure. If you don't go out on the weekend you're a geek, if you don't drink you're a geek, if you don't talk about the same things as them you're a geek. Those kinds of things make you more popular.
JULIO 17

'I'm cool, I've got a joint hanging out of my mouth, look at me.'

IN MY FIRST YEAR of high school I got involved with some bad people and got in trouble for doing marijuana at school. I was a bit disappointed in myself. It was because of peer pressure, wanting to be accepted. From when I was little I've always wanted to be accepted, but I always felt different. I had to do something or say something for people to like me, although my mother and friends said that I was really popular. But I could never see that, I never understood that. I always felt alone. In Year 8 I actually got addicted to cigarettes and I was smoking a lot every day and it took a lot for me to stop. Cold turkey, but it was very difficult. It sounds really weird but smoking made me feel good. I thought I was cool, I was doing something with my hands, I thought I wasn't fiddling around and looking really stupid twisting my fingers. I had a cigarette in my hand which didn't make me look as nervous as I felt. When I'm with my friends at work I might have an occasional cigarette but afterwards I feel pretty silly and I don't do it much anymore.
JORDAN 16

SOME GUYS SEE THAT they've got to prove themselves by drinking silly. Some people sit there and they go to every party and they just get totally drunk. They think, 'Hey it's masculine to drink. I mean I don't like the taste of it but it's something I've got to do because I'm a guy and everyone else is drinking, so I mean I should drink too.' So he does and he doesn't like the taste, he's sitting there and it's probably not the alcohol that makes him throw up, it's probably the taste because he didn't like it so much. But I mean he sits there 'yerking' his guts up and he's lying on the floor in a pile of spew everywhere. I probably see less females do it than guys. I drink quite a bit but I don't feel I have to. Sometimes I don't drink because I just don't feel like it whereas other people will say, 'Hey, everyone else is drinking'. Then they might think, 'Well these two people are already drunk, they're lying on the floor. Hey, I've got to catch up.' So it's like they're sitting there all night going, 'Don't even like the taste of it. It's a masculine thing to do so I've got to do it.'
PAUL 17

It should be about drinking sensibly but it's like, 'If you drink and drive you're a bloody legend!'.

IT'S LIKE IT'S COOL getting pissed and having a good 'yerk', you know, puking. At a party it's like, get really blotto and it's always the guys doing it, have a drink and puke your guts, yeah. It's like you've had a good time and then you're congratulating someone—'You've done it, you've drunk yourself into an absolute blotto state, killed half your brain cells and then 'yerked' it all back up again'. It should be about drinking sensibly but it's like, 'If you drink and drive you're a bloody legend!'. That's how it's viewed. And the more you consume, the bigger legend you are as well. So it's like a competition. It's just bizarre, yeah.
NEIL 17

AT PARTIES GUYS JUST DRINK, joke around and laugh. There's a lot of drinking, a lot of smoking pot. I drink but I don't smoke. Guys probably drink because of the peer pressure but girls drink too, a lot of the girls drink.
JULIO 17

GUYS LIKE TO GO TO PARTIES and get pissed. It's also considered fairly acceptable to smoke a little dope in today's adolescent society. They had some statistics at school on how many people do alcohol or do drugs and it was just really, really high for people my age. Because you've got the statistics it's more of a reality. I don't usually get pissed at parties but I'll just have maybe one or two beers.

The first time I got pissed was with my nextdoor neighbour. We went out of our way to get drunk one night just to see what it was like and to see what our limits were. It was really funny because it was just next door to my house when my mum was home and we were out on the lawn going, 'Whoa!'. But it was sort of like, 'It's not that good'.

We don't do it because we think it's cool to get pissed. We do it more because it just frees you up a bit. You're not so tense in party situations, I suppose. Like last Saturday we just had a few friends over and we were all just playing cards and everyone had something to drink. I had three beers but then I stopped. I won't drink a lot because I know what it's like. But I suppose some people find it hard to communicate with others, so maybe if they want to free themselves up a bit, such as when a guy likes a girl or a girl likes a guy, they might find it a bit hard to talk to each other. So if you're just 'under the influence' it's a bit easier for them. You're not so conscious of what you're doing so you're more likely to be more open and just more able to speak freely and stuff, so that's pretty good.
JEREMY 16

AFTERMATH

It's three a.m. on a Sunday morning
I'm throwing up cheap wine
beer
pizza
McDonald's burgers
French fries
a medium Coke
carrots
and what remains of my dignity.
PETER BALL 21

MICHAEL SPEWING AFTER DRINKING ON HIS SIXTEENTH BIRTHDAY—NEVER AGAIN!

A KINDA DEPRESSING DRUG POEM

SICK
I'm making myself sick again
For what I need and where I've been
I'm feeling weak I'm feeling sick
I'm such a fucking hypocrite

How did I let myself fall
So far from anything at all
A vision of what I used to despise
The smoke in my head clouds my eyes

I swear I never wanted this
Pathetically perfect, twisted bliss
I can't be what I have become
Drowning in my sunken lung

I'm tearing everything apart
I'm wishing for another start
I am making myself sick again
I'm such a fucking hypocrite

MAXO 17

'SELF-PORTRAIT', MAXO 17

IT'S NOT WORTH THE RISK!

I DID MARIJUANA IN YEAR 7 but I'm over it now. It doesn't really give you that much of a high, it's really not worth the risk. My dad used to grow it in the backyard, he doesn't anymore.

TIM 14

THERE ARE A LOT OF drugs being taken at our school. I observe that peer pressure has had a grave effect on many people's lives. Many very smart people have chosen a different direction for their life with their friends and wasted all their potential. Example, one boy came in Year 8—he was quite smart but very shy—was made miserable for two years, did a lot of drugs. Six months ago he died of a heroin overdose.

MATT 16

Doing drink

While you think you're being cool, funny, sexy, the life of the party, if you filmed yourself, you'd see this desperate guy passing out, chucking up, smelling bad, looking dead, stumbling around, unable to get two words out, groping girls like a real sleaze, having a beer gut. Alcohol isn't a magic potion that turns an unhappy and insecure guy into a happy and confident one. When reality hits, you find yourself feeling sicker and maybe with a whole lot more problems to deal with like: having less money, wondering who you got with and whether you had safe sex, why you got into that fight, how you're going to pay for the busted car, someone's torn clothes, your friend's parents' furniture, etc. etc. Sure, alcohol can be fun and okay, but there's something wrong if you're drinking because you can't face a problem or you think it's cool.

Doing smokes

You know about the cancers, and you've seen the unfit older guys struggling to breathe. What's so cool about having stained fingers, stained teeth, bad breath, smelling like an ashtray, coughing up slime?

Doing drugs

No one can stop you experimenting with drugs . . . and no one can stop the addictions forming. Make sure you get informed, and don't fool yourself about what doing drugs is going to mean in your life. Don't believe all that boring old stuff about drugs making you happy, drugs giving you some amazing insight into the mysteries of existence, making you so creative, being good for your soul. The price you pay in the long run is: you lose money, you lose precious brain cells, you spiral down, and as you feel worse you do more drugs, and so it goes. And they can leave you dead.

By the way, as you know, this isn't just a boy problem. Let's hear what Jenny has to say about taking these kinds of risks.

INFLUENCES LEAD TO CONSEQUENCES!

I DEAL WITH FRIENDS who have been introduced to and influenced by drugs. People know of the influence of these substances, though they haven't heard it from young people themselves. Year 8 it was alcohol, Year 9 cigarettes and marijuana, now it's all, plus more hard core substances. As an individual it's quite scary to even think why you actually do it. I could honestly say that I'm easily led, I follow the flock, but it's hard for a female, because in today's society it's expected from your peers, especially from guys. Not all, but the majority.

I reckon that not enough is talked about drugs and alcohol at school. Nothing is done until it's too late. Personally, I get furious when I hear of teenagers killed in road accidents, either in a car or hit by them etc. Then you hear of fourteen- and thirteen-year-olds under the influence and dying, and that's when I have to sit back and think is this really worth it? Is it worth the fatal consequences? If and when it happens?

> I HAVE A FRIEND WHO HAD SEX UNDER THE INFLUENCE, NOW SHE'S SEVENTEEN WITH A CHILD AND HER EDUCATION IS BASICALLY DOWN THE DRAIN.

Influences lead to consequences. I have a friend who had sex under the influence, now she's seventeen with a child and her education is basically down the drain. She screwed up! That's hard for girls. Our fear is 'rape' and I also know girls who have been. And this whole issue is related back to school!! It's basically peer pressure—it's absolutely ridiculous, what we have to do for a position on the ladder. But by knowing the facts we can solve problems before it's too late!!

JENNY 15

Taking care of yourself

So how do you take care of yourself? It takes courage and real guts to walk away from risky situations, to put up with stirring from your so-called friends. But if they're your friends and they're forcing you to do something then think about what kind of friends they really are. Think about why they might be taking risks with drugs, alcohol, smokes and driving? Why might they want you to be a part of this? Have you ever forced a friend to take these kinds of risks with you? What was going on? Why did you feel the need to do this?

Boys who don't and why they don't

I WOULDN'T KNOW ANYTHING about drugs. I've never been involved in them. I mean, I know people who have, who could say, 'Hey, smoke this', but I wouldn't know. I've seen them made, I've seen them lying around after they've been made and used but I wouldn't have the faintest idea. I've had friends offer it to me before but I'll pass and I'm quite happy.
PAUL 17

I GO OUT ON the weekend to a party and just see people who are so drunk making fools of themselves. I just look and think, 'I'm not going to get like that'. Yesterday in the street, for example, I was going to work and there were all these drunk footy heads playing with each other's dicks. I was just like, 'Nah, this isn't my scene'. Being so drunk that they're falling everywhere. Then throwing up, ending up in the gutter, and saying, 'Oh, I've got a really good hangover', in the morning. For me, everything is all together, life's good. Some people are so drugged out, they spend all their money, they spend all their time, and

they just can't be bothered getting their life together.
JOSH 15

I DON'T SMOKE BECAUSE I don't want to shorten my life. Every time we come back to school on a Monday, we get the story of, 'I was drunk on the weekend, I went to this place on Saturday night, this Friday night and Sunday night, and I got drunk every night'. I go out but I never drink to the extent that I would throw up or get drunk. Some people want to just get away sometimes so they get drunk. Sometimes you've got to get away from knowing what you're doing and you feel bored and you just go to yourself, 'Well, what am I doing here tonight? Nothing. I just need to make it exciting. I want to be in that group, I want to be cool.' I think it's more pathetic because they want to fit in by smoking with their friends and they don't really need to have it at all and they don't enjoy it. They just do it to be social and they're looking pathetic.
PAUL 16

DAD'S WARNED ME. He said, 'I don't mind if you drink but if I ever catch you smoking weed or anything you'll be out of the house'. He's seen what weed has done to people for a long time. Like his friends who he knew when he was 20 have totally changed by now that they're 40. It actually does poison your insides. Drinking's all right, but Dad's never been into heavy spirits. He mainly drinks a bit of beer.
WAYNE 16

MY DAD SMOKES and I've seen how it affects him. All his fingers are going yellow and his hair is all smoky too. I don't really want to go like that if I can help it.
BRENDON 14

BUYING DRUGS and smokes is a waste of money.
JACOB 15

JUST A FEW WEEKS AGO I was involved in a special training course on tobacco and then went and taught primary school students in the area. I felt good passing on the information about tobacco and smoking, what the effects are and what it's like at high school, and how easy it is to get pushed into smoking. I've never tried smoking. It's a deliberate decision I've made. In science class we asked one of the teachers if he smoked and we got a cigarette off him, set up some experiments that smoked the cigarette by itself via water, and in that water we put chemicals to see what smoking does. The smoke turned the water into a different colour. We put a white collar bone in and that came

out black. I could tell that's what my lungs would be like.
MARK 14

SMOKING SMELLS DISGUSTING. It's sort of scary to know that your lungs are rotten with all this stuff. I might have a bit of alcohol occasionally but it's not like I'm going to drink a bottle of Scotch a day or anything like that. I think drugs are stupid as well. Most people just smoke or take drugs to look good and you don't get happiness out of taking drugs. You could die with most of the stuff that's going around these days.
JASON 14

I'M CHICKEN, OF COURSE, WHY ELSE WOULDN'T I WANT TO SMOKE?

I'VE NEVER DRUNK ALCOHOL in my life because in my Muslim religion it's not allowed. A little bit of alcohol, but there are so many that can't control it so they don't drink at all because you're damaging yourself and others as well. In Australia, for some reason alcohol is allowed to have commercials on TV but I think alcohol is worse than a cigarette because with a cigarette you damage yourself and a couple of people around you, but with alcohol, if you drink too much, no one knows what you'll do. You might actually kill a person.
ABDU 16

ABOUT A MONTH BACK I was faced with some peer pressure about smoking and I didn't take up the offer, and then they were teasing me for about a few weeks after that. They asked me if I wanted to smoke after school and a friend of mine did and he said that it was fine and nothing happened to him. I just didn't want to smoke and then they said I could get with four girls if I had a smoke. I didn't take up the offer and they just started teasing me. They were calling me chicken and saying that I was 'uncool'. I just agreed to it and so they stopped doing it to me. I said, 'Of course, I'm chicken, of course, why else wouldn't I want to smoke?'. I talked to Mum about it and she said, 'You made the right choice'. It gave me a sense of confidence that I could stand up to it.
MICHAEL 13

I WOULD NEVER DO DRUGS and I would probably never start drinking or start smoking, and that's only because my father and my friends have seen people die. I've heard of people dying because of drug overdoses. Health education about drugs would've gone straight over their heads because they're just too set on being popular; they don't do it because they want to do it, they do it because they think it's popular.
ANDREW 16

I WALKED INTO HER ROOM AND FOUND HER DEAD

I HAVE NEVER DONE DRUGS and never will. My father had a fiancee who was a heroin user. One morning I walked into her room and found her dead. I was only fourteen at the time. I was in so much shock that I left her there and sat in the lounge room for fifteen minutes trying to convince myself that she was just asleep. When reality set in I walked back in and saw that she was surrounded by syringes. She'd overdosed on heroin. I called the ambulance and was instructed to attempt mouth-to-mouth. I had to try and revive someone who was already dead. I was only fourteen and was home by myself.

I fooled myself into thinking it didn't affect me but it really did. I never got help or spoke to any sort of professional about it. The pain became really insular. I was writing poetry by the pageful and cried so much. But I felt a responsibility to be strong for others so I made others think that I didn't care and in the process fooled myself. I never felt I could turn to someone and say, 'This affected me'. It wasn't that people were insensitive, there was just a lack of understanding. It wasn't something that someone my age could relate to unless they'd gone through it.

A few months after her death it finally began to manifest as I started to punish myself. I'd just cut myself with scissors, blades and knives. It became such a habit that I'd carry them in my wallet and hide them under my pillow. I'd just get so angry at who I was and would slash away. I just wished I could disappear. Other times I desperately wanted someone to hold me and make it all better. It was a cry for help.

Every day we all have to wake up, wash up and go back into the world. Having gone through so much so young has put me out of touch with those my own age.

BEN GERRARD 17

I'D JUST CUT MYSELF WITH SCISSORS, BLADES AND KNIVES.

BEN GERRARD WHEN HE WAS FOURTEEN

I WANT TO BE HEALTHY AND STRONG

A LOT OF BOYS I know are into heaps of drugs. I can just imagine if I were an undercover cop I would catch so many boys and girls. You get stories about some of them when they go for their sessions like, 'Oh he only had one cone and he was game and acting like he was wrecked and really out of it'. People see it as cool. Like you're cool if you've got dopey looking eyes and your eyes are red and really glassy! That's just what some people think. I can honestly say that in our group none of our boys smoke, we don't smoke cigarettes, gunge or anything like that. We just don't do that stuff, it's something we don't do.

I said to one of my mates who's already quit, 'Look, it's good you've quit', and he goes, 'But I want to be strong like you. See you haven't even tried it.' I said, 'Yes, but see man, you were already addicted to that stuff and you had the mind power to pull yourself out. So you're just as strong as me, so don't think that I'm better than you because I'm not, man. Some people just wreck their whole lives with doing something like that, but see man you've stopped.' Then he said, 'Yeah!', and he felt really good about himself and I was happy that he understood that it was a real good thing.

A lot of guys drink but I don't do all that stuff. I just don't see it as cool. I just don't want to do it. I don't want to see myself in the mirror with my eyes shut or staggering around smelling of grog. It's something I don't admire. I want to be healthy and strong. A lot of kids at school drink at parties and smoke. Even if their parents don't do it, they still do it because their friends do it. I think it's got to do with the people you hang around with. If you hang in this group and all of them smoke, you'll end up smoking too. It's just like any other little thing, if you hang with the group and they wear Nike shoes, or Adidas shoes, you're going to go out and buy the new-fashioned shoes, or if they smoke, you're going to smoke too. I think of myself as being so lucky these days, because I have the mind power not to do any of that stuff.

NIGEL 17

Risky sex

There's another risk for guys and that's unsafe sex. Here's what Beade has to say.

YOUNG PEOPLE GET their information about sex and stuff probably from their friends. Some boys think it's cool to have sex and to have sex without a condom. They go on about having sex without a condom because they think it's cool, you're taking a chance. They say, 'It feels better, just do it without a condom'. If a boy talks to his mate and says he had sex with this one girl, the first question he'll get asked is, 'Did you do it with a condom?'. And if the person says 'Yes', they'll say, 'Oh you should have done it without a condom it feels better', so they get influenced by that.

But they just sort of ignore the stuff they get from teachers at school. They usually just give out pamphlets and that's about it. If teachers talked about it and did more stuff at school to do with sex, I think boys would keep it in their head a bit more.

I think I've got a strong heart because I've been in that situation where I wasn't cool because I didn't smoke drugs and have sex without condoms, so I just took the name calling and still talked to those people but don't really hang around with them.

BEADE 17

In the following story, James Wall takes us into the life of Harry, a young man slowly descending into the solitary confinement of an alcoholic. He seems blind to where he's heading as he borrows money from neighbours to meet a girl and yes, pay for drinks. Yet right in front of him, he can see where he is heading as he thinks about and hears his older, unhealthy and violent neighbour Donald abusing his wife. The last line of James's story reads, 'That was all there would be'.

What does Harry need to do now to get out of Solitary? How can he break out of the inevitability of becoming Donald? What can you do right now to make sure you don't end up in or get further into the lonely and unhappy drug-induced, drink-induced cage of solitary confinement?

SOLITARY

HARRY ALWAYS FOUND the last dregs—the few drops left at the bottom of the bottle—the worst. They were the last ones, which meant he had no more, none for tomorrow, none until the money came in. It always did, but it was just a matter of when. Sometimes it was days, weeks, sometimes months. It would be there, but not as soon as he wanted it to be. All he asked for was enough money for another bottle of wine, port, whisky, whatever, maybe a six-pack. Maybe some cigarettes or a good cigar. Everything was getting more and more costly, but people weren't getting more money to make up for it.

Sometimes he got a job, a few days work picking mangoes, other kinds of fruit, some hard labour here and there. He had never held a position for more than six months, and that suited him fine. He would rather not have to deal with it, the monotony, the timetables and schedules, the bosses breathing their stinking yellow-toothed breath down his neck. He preferred his freedom, isolation, self-comfort. He listened to music. He sat in the darkness. He took a swallow of wine. That was all he wanted. Peace, solitude.

When he finished his last bottle of port, sucked the bottle dry, Harry got up and got dressed. He would head to the bar across the road. He had no money, but he was a decent hustler, could usually get a couple of beers out of people. As he was pulling on his shoes, the phone rang. He didn't want to answer it, but what if it was something good, he had won the lottery? He couldn't take the chance of not picking up. He picked up.

'Hello?' he said.

'Hello, this is Alison from Shades Co.'

'Yeah?'

'We were wondering if you were interested in buying some fine shades. We have a special on this month.'

'What kind of shades, Alison?'

'Shades for your windows, sir. They compliment any surrounds, they keep the sunlight out, ensure privacy.'

'That sounds like a good idea, Alison. How much for a set of shades?'

'We have a special on this month. The price of a set of shades is only $170.99.'

'I don't have that sort of money, I'm afraid. But I sure could use a set of shades. Sorry.'

'We also have an instalment plan, sir. Nineteen dollars a week over ten weeks, plus an ultra-low $22.95 for delivery and installation.'

'But that ends up costing more than the original price.'

'This isn't a charity, sir. Do you want the shades or not?'

'I don't think so.'

'Perhaps you would like to pass our phone number on to a friend or relative who is looking at buying some shades?'

'I don't have any friends or relatives.'

'So you aren't interested?'

'I'm afraid not. Tell me something, Alison . . .'

'What, sir?'

'How come you do shit like this? Pick a name at random out of the white pages, ring it up, ask people if they want to buy shades on an instalment plan, call them sir and madam. Is the money good?'

'Oh, yes, sir! Our hourly rates are quite excellent!'

'And you enjoy your work?'

'Most certainly.'

'You can tell me the truth. You really get job satisfaction out of crap like this?'

'Well, honestly, sir, I have to tell you . . . no. I'm a nursing graduate, I spent four of the best years of my life at some nursing school, and I end up selling shades over the phone.'

'You sound down, Alison. Perhaps you'd like to meet up somewhere with me, get a drink?'

'I finish at 10.30. You can meet me at Bill's Bar and Grill. You know the place?'

'Surely.'

HE EXITED HIS APARTMENT, DIDN'T BOTHER TO LOCK THE DOOR. NOTHING WORTH STEALING IN THERE.

Harry put the receiver down. He went into the bathroom, took a shit, washed his face. It was nine. He still had time to get to the bar for a few beers. But he needed money if he was going to show this Alison a good time. He had to get money. He exited his apartment, didn't bother to lock the door. Nothing worth stealing in there. He knocked on the door to the apartment across the hall, knew the people there, an elderly married couple, perhaps they would lend him a few bucks. The door opened. There stood the wife, a kindly white-haired person with bad hearing, stooped over. She shuffled about in a torn pink nightie. Harry had counted on just her being home.

'Hello?' she said, squinting up at Harry. She also had bad eyesight.

'Hi, Marge,' Harry said, 'How you doing?'

'Oh, Harry! So nice to see you! Come in, come in!' Marge had taken to yelling because of her hearing. Harry went on in. 'Sit down, Harry! Donald is out doing the shopping. Won't you have a cup of tea? The kettle just finished boiling.'

'I'm sorry, Marge, but I can't stay long. I hate to ask you a thing like this, but . . . could I borrow some money? Ten or fifteen dollars?'

'Oh, Harry, you know that any time you need anything, to just come and see us! We're always so happy to see you, Donald and I! Why, just this morning Donald said to me, "That Harry is such a nice young man".'

Harry knew this was a lie. Donald was a son

of a bitch, hated Harry's guts, he would smack Marge around, was always screaming. Sitting in his room at nights, Harry could hear Marge's head thumping against the wall. Right now, she had a black eye, bruises on her neck, up and down her arms. Harry felt guilty. He should be helping Marge out, getting that loser off her back. But all he did was say, 'Thanks, Marge. That would be a great help.'

He watched Marge shuffle into the bedroom and shuffle back with her purse. She rummaged around in it, smiling at Harry, and pulled out some notes. She handed them over.

'Oh, Marge, this is too much. I can't take all this.'

'No, no, Harry! I want you to have it! I want you to have a good time! Why don't you have a girlfriend, Harry? Handsome young man like you, should find himself a nice girl, settle down.'

'Thanks, Marge. Yes, maybe I will, one day. Is there anything I can do, anything I can get you?'

DONALD WAS A SON OF A BITCH

'No, no, it's fine! Fine! Donald will be back soon with the shopping! Have you eaten yet? I was just about to cook some dinner!'

'It's okay, Marge, thanks. I'll pay you back as soon as I can.'

'No rush! Stay a while!'

'I really have to go. I'll visit you again soon.'

Harry walked out, shut the door. Walking down the hall towards the stairs, he saw Donald coming up. Donald was a huge, obscene, fat man, bald, angry eyes with thick, dark eyebrows, constantly scowling. He wheezed as he made his way up the stairs, carrying the shopping in some plastic bags, bottles sitting in there going clink, clink, clink. Harry ignored him and brushed past. Near the bottom of the stairs he heard Donald start yelling, then the smacks, the thumping, Marge wailing.

Harry put his hands in his coat pockets, went across to the bar. That was all there would be.

JAMES WALL 21

CHAPTER *FOUR*
FRIENDSHIPS & RELATIONSHIPS

In this chapter you'll hear from guys talking about their friendships and other relationships, and about being in love. Boys value deep and meaningful relationships with other guys and girls but can feel restrained because it's not seen to be cool to talk about what you're feeling—especially with another guy!

Friendships

YOU JUST HAVE TO FIND out who your real friends are and stick with them, either black, yellow or white. Once you find your real friends then you will be set for life. Real friends will stand by each other.
STEVE 13

FRIENDS TALK TO EACH other and relate their experiences to each other because it's all about sharing and being trustworthy and having someone there for you to talk about things.
ANDREW 16

YOU CAN ASK FOR a couple of bucks from a good friend, if you're short, to buy lunch and he gives it to you. He helps you out in class if you've got trouble.
PETER 14

FRIENDSHIP IS ABOUT loyalty. It's when people don't talk about you and they don't tease you and they're always nice to you. I think it's ridiculous that boys can't be good friends to other boys because there are a lot of kind boys out there who just want to be friends with other boys.
JASON 14

WE HAVE HEAPS IN COMMON. If I'm thinking something he knows what I'm thinking. We've only fought once. And it was a serious fight, but we didn't fight as in a physical way. We were walking to the shop and we started arguing about girls. He just went too far, and then I went too far, and we just got too far. Then he just walked off and didn't say anything. I got home and I thought about him and I thought it's not worth fighting over. I rang him up and I just apologised and we were friends again. And from that day on we haven't ever fought again, and if we did, we'd probably make up.
NIGEL 17

PHOTO COURTESY OF INDIGENOUS YOUNG FATHERS SUPPORT GROUP, QLD

I WAS STAYING AT my best friend's house one night and I just had to tell him that I was gay, so I told him and it was okay, he was cool with it. The worst part was telling him that I actually liked him as well. He was really understanding so it was cool. My other friend was totally surprised when I told him. He didn't expect it. But they're both pretty cool, they understand and I can talk to them about it.

VINCE 17

I THINK SOME GUYS find it hard to talk openly with another, like it's not their thing. I know my friend James wouldn't. It's hard to talk openly to him—he's just got a one-minded view. You try and talk to him about a problem and he'll just go, 'Oh, just get over it, get over it'. And I've seen other friends go up to him and they've gone, 'James said I'll just get over it'. He can't relate to anything. I don't know why but some guys find it hard.

PAUL 17

WE DON'T REALLY OPEN up like girls. If we've got a problem we don't really talk about it. We just deal with it because they'll think you're weak and stupid. You're supposed to be strong.

TIM 14

WE CLAIM EACH OTHER AS BROTHERS

WE DO A LOT TOGETHER, we claim each other as brothers. He knows that I'll always be there for him and he'll always be there for me. It's happened a few times, like if someone is calling him names, I'll just automatically react to it and stick up for him. It's a thing that just happens, you don't have to think about it or anything. You don't think about, 'Oh, what if this fellow hits me?'. It's just sort of like, 'If he hits him I'm going to be there for him'. If I say something bad to people, he'll say, 'Oh, I don't think you should have said that because he wouldn't have liked that'. And if I say, 'So who cares?', he'd say, 'You wouldn't like to be treated like that'. And I'd just stop and have a think about it, and I'd do the same to him.

BEADE 17

I SUPPOSE I LEARNT early that I wasn't too interested in hanging with all the tough guys because I just thought they spoke a lot of shit. There was a lot of fakeness and my best friend through high school was a lot more genuine. People pretend a lot, putting on a front, getting very macho and aggressive. It wasn't something that I really appreciated, all that fakeness. You just didn't really understand where they were coming from. One moment they might be your friend and within a split second they wouldn't be and I didn't want to deal with it.
DANIEL WITTHAUS 23

THERE'S THIS ONE GUY that I tell everything to. We don't care what it is, we just tell each other everything and I think that makes you a really, really good friend. But at the moment he's going out with this girl and he spends more time with her than with the group of friends that we have, and I've just gone up to him and told him about it and I'm saying, 'Look, you're going to lose friends if you keep doing this'.
PAUL 16

I OFTEN FEEL UPSET about what my friends not only say about me but also other people or other issues. Especially when what they have said has just come out of the top of their head and they probably haven't given two seconds to think about it. The worst thing is that I too sometimes laugh and join in.
PETER 13

I'VE GOT A GOOD group of friends. They're not exactly the popular group of the school but they're very quiet, very understanding guys and they don't care that I've got a disability or that I don't play sport.
ANDREW 16

ONE MOMENT THEY MIGHT BE YOUR FRIEND AND WITHIN A SPLIT SECOND THEY WOULDN'T BE

IT DOESN'T MATTER WHAT COLOUR YOUR SKIN IS

ROY IS A FRIEND who's just come into our group. We're all dark-coloured skin and Roy is the only white-coloured skin. He had things in common with us, he listened to the same music, liked the same sport. The white group sort of left him out and started saying stuff like, 'Oh, you're a big homey G boy because you listen to rap'. We thought that he was pretty cool, so we just said, 'You can come and sit with us, hang in with us, you're welcome'. I said, 'Roy you know that we will never ever exclude you from our group just because of the colour of your skin. Roy I call you "bro" like bros.' I call all the boys brother. Roy's a little overweight but we don't say he can't hang around with us because he's overweight or because he's white, he's just with us because we get along together. That's why I love it like this so much because all my friends get along real well, we're really open.

NIGEL 17

Do you have to be 'cool' to be a good friend?

What's a 'cool' friend? Is it about the 'cool' image or acting 'cool'? Is it about being too scared to be who you really are for fear that you won't be accepted? But is that what friendship is really about—pretending to be someone you're not so that your mates will accept you and not treat you as an outcast? Let's hear what guys have to say about 'cool' friends and issues like conformity and control.

STEVEN AND MICHAEL ACTING COOL

NOWADAYS IMAGE IS EVERYTHING and it's the biggest joke ever. Some guys wear all the exact same clothes. They all look the same and you see them looking around to see what everyone else is looking at. No one is himself, everyone is just a sheep.

MIKE 17

SOME PEOPLE GET INTO the cool group and it's something like an exam and you've got to pass. So when you're in the cool group and you're not good enough they'll sort of say go away or something like that. The exam's something like being cool and going out with good girls, stuff like that, and not doing much work.

BRYCE 13

TO BE COOL AND in the 'in' group you're supposed to play football, be really rough and talk about the size of your dick!

Stay away from the people you don't get on with and hang around with the people who are real friends. Don't try to be one of the popular ones. At times I've found myself trying to blend in with them but it doesn't tend to work. I'd hang around in certain areas and talk about certain things like how much they smoke. I'd hang around with certain girls and dislike other girls, some of whom are fairly good friends of mine now. Now I'm asked, 'Oh, who would you choose, this girl or that girl?'. I'm like, 'Oh I'm not going to answer that question, they're friends of mine'.

SIMON 13

IT'S NOT REALLY AUSTRALIAN TO TALK ABOUT FEELINGS

I THINK IT'S JUST the 'blokey' attitude, being Australian, that holds male feelings inside. All they talk about is sport, cars and women. It's the cliche that defines these attitudes. It's not really Australian to talk about feelings, especially for blokes. Diversifying is the key to understanding. Everyone should really talk a lot and find out things about each other, find new friendships and hang out with different guys—make friends with different groups who they never thought they would socialise with.

SCOTT 17

WE'RE CLOSE MATES AND WE LOVE EACH OTHER

ONE GUY IN OUR GROUP, he's all open and he goes, 'Oh, I love you man', like that, and he hugs us in front of everyone. The girls look at us in a funny way. They know that this guy is an open person and we're all close mates and, yeah, we do love each other.

NIGEL 17

MICHAEL, MICHAEL AND TONY

Maybe it's the homophobia that prevents guys from getting close to one another. Have a read about what Tom has to say about this. In his first piece he talks about blowing kisses at other guys in order to stir up their homophobia. But in his second piece, Tom is honest about being uncomfortable around guys who he thinks might be gay. It's like he's scared that any body contact with a gay guy might be interpreted as an open invitation to some kind of sexual involvement. But just think about it. Is a straight guy attracted to every single girl he sees? Maybe if people talked more openly about sexuality, fear and ignorance would break down and maybe we could see the stereotypes of gay people for what they are—false. You know there's that stereotype about gay guys being predators but it just isn't true.

HUGGING ANOTHER MALE WOULD DEFINITELY HAVE TO BE A DISPLAY OF HOMOSEXUALITY

HUGGING A FRIEND—if a male hugged another male, straight away they'd be on to that, they'd be trying to intimidate and they'd pick on that. I actually blew a kiss at some guys once because they were looking at me and making fun of me. I didn't really care, I just thought I'd do a little experiment and see what happened. They really reacted to that and retaliated and the foul language came pouring out—all the words associated to homosexuality, 'faggot', 'poofter', 'gay', 'bum-jabber', all that kind of stuff. They just said anything they could to get to you. I just shrugged and talked to one of my mates and that really annoyed them. They just walked away still making their comments as if they had to prove to one another that they had totally rejected the fact that they had just had a kiss blown to them from another male. They had to prove to one another that they didn't accept because there isn't that much power associated with being gay.

TOM 16

AS SOON AS THAT BODY CONTACT IS MADE . . .

SAY IF ONE OF my friends, who I didn't consider to be homosexual, put their arm around me or patted me on the leg or something, I'd be fine with that because I know they're heterosexual and that there's nothing to it, it's all platonic. There's nothing suggesting any sexual behaviour, but the idea of sexual bonding with another male—I've been brought up to reject that. Straight away if there's any sexual connotation at all with another male, I will reject that. I don't know why it should bother me but sometimes where just everyday body contact has been made, which I would do with heaps of guys, I just think about it because in my mind I've constructed this guy as possibly fitting that gay image. It makes me very uncomfortable.

TOM 16

BEN GERRARD AND SEAN

Girls as friends

WELL WHEN YOU ONLY have girls as friends, you've got some serious problems!
RORY 13

A GOOD FRIEND IS SOMEONE you can trust, someone you can tell secrets to and they won't go and blabber them to someone else. Someone who cares about your feelings and what you have to say, your point of view. They're really caring, really sensitive. They're just really good friends. They're girls. Boys are really immature, they just swear, they're just stupid with each other, like they punch each other when the girls are around. They always treat them really rudely. Boys can't talk about personal stuff. Being friends with girls, you can say a lot of stuff and they'll just listen and won't stir you. I think that's really good.
JACOB 15

BEN GERRARD AND EM

GIRLS ARE JUST EASY to get along with. They accept me for who I am. They don't care that I'm a guy and that I'm a bit chubby. They don't give me shit. If any one of us has a trouble we meet and talk. A friend of mine got pregnant accidentally and she didn't know what to do because her boyfriend said that he was not going to have anything to do with her. She was devastated and we met in town one weekend to try and help her feel better. Whenever one of us needs the others we're always there.

One thing that makes me laugh a lot is the way guys walk in front of girls, wiggling their bums or some shit like that. I'd be sitting there with my friends and we'll be picking them out. We laugh because it's so funny. It's like a mating ritual like birds or something. The girls also get hassled for not wearing the in things or for being chubby.
JORDAN 16

I'VE GOT LOTS of friends who are girls. I can talk to them about my girlfriend having her period and how she's in a bit of pain so that I can find out what I can do.
GLENN 16

It's great that girls are such good friends to guys—they offer boys terrific emotional support. But don't you think boys need to offer one another this kind of support as well? Do boys offer girls this kind of emotional support in their friendships? Maybe if there wasn't so much homophobia guys might feel more comfortable about getting closer to other guys and offering them this kind of support. What do you think?

Gay friends are okay

I HAVE A FRIEND who's gay. I didn't know he was gay until he told me and I thought, who cares, he's my friend and if I really value him as my friend I'm not going to care if he's gay.
JORDAN 16

I DIDN'T HAVE MALE friends who were straight because a close friend is someone who you share emotions with and who you feel strongly about and you can talk to about things that happen to you. I think that's quite discouraged among a lot of straight guys. They weren't really friends, they were just guys I would spend time with whom I didn't really like very much and who would tease me and be nasty to me about my sexuality.
ROWAN 19

I STILL WANT TO be friends with my gay friends, talk and have fun rock climbing and going out. Just because of their relationships with males, I'm not going to change my point of view of them. I've always liked them. I tell them what I did

with my girlfriend and if I'm having a hard time, they can relate to it with their perspective of going out with a male. Just because they went out with a male and I've gone out with a female, nothing changes and it's something we can talk about. All straight guys talk about is girlfriends, girlfriends, girlfriends. You get sick and tired of it, and they're really up themselves, 'Oh, I had this person on the weekend', and it gets annoying and you don't want to talk about it anymore, you don't want to hear about it.

Gay people talk about what they do and it's pretty interesting. You're learning about what gay people do, because you don't hear about it here at school. They go out, they have fun, they go to parties, so what's the difference with my girlfriend and us and them going out with their boyfriend? There's no difference. One of my gay friends was the first person to show me around the school and to introduce me to other students and we've stayed friends, we're all good friends. Friendships are friendships, I got a decent friendship with them and I'm not giving it away because of their sexuality.
GLENN 16

I ACTUALLY HAD A male friend who started being really aggressive towards me. I got really sick of it and I pulled him aside and said, 'Look what's the problem, what's going on?'. He said that other people had started assuming he was a homosexual because he talked to me and he was starting to get harassed about it. I said, 'Look, I'm really sorry but it's not my fault. They're going to say whatever they want to say regardless of whether you talk to me or not.' So we had a big long chat about it and he was fine after that. He would tell them all to go and get stuffed. He went back to how he was before which was good.
LUCIANO 19

I FIGURED I COULD tell my friends I was gay. I asked them a question first, 'How do you feel about gay people?'. That's what I asked. My best friend sort of assumed, he thought I might be anyway, so it kind of made it a bit easier. But my other friend, I asked him and he goes, 'I don't have a problem with it'. So I told him and that was it. I think it was a mixture of trust and the fact that I was sick and tired of lying to them, covering it up. So I just thought yes, it was about time I told them.
VINCE 17

I HAVE A GAY FRIEND. He was an older guy, he was 24 or something and we had a really good time. We went out all the time on the weekends and we had a lot of fun.
PAUL 17

I HAVE A FRIEND who is a grandmother and she's very active in gay activism. I'm aware that many young gay men do not want to be around her because of her age. I went to a function with her and saw how people deliberately ignore her. It's a shame that some gay males of my generation are somehow shallow.
JONARD 18

JOHN AND BRETT

When a friend dies † † † † †

JOHN WAS DOING HIS casual job, working in a family gardening business. He was using a tree-mulcher, and was cleaning up fallen branches and leaves. Somehow he fell into the mulcher. Hours later I was informed. I wouldn't believe it and I had to ring a friend to confirm this shattering news. Four days later, it was the first day of the school term. It really hit me. We had an assembly in tribute of John. A candle was blown out to symbolise his death and then re-lit to symbolise his life after death. They spoke about him and the many things he did at our school. Just hearing his name read out started me crying. I cried and cried, practically for the whole assembly. Everyone could see I wasn't coping, but none of the guys really knew what to do. They kept their heads looking forward, avoiding eye contact completely. The support I received from the staff was amazing. I was told not to go to school and stay at the school hospital instead (I boarded at school) for however long it took. Teachers would come and chat with me—to see how I was coping.

I am too young to fully understand death, and I'm not sure if any of the adults do either. Emotionally I survived and from what I've learnt, don't hide your emotions—let them out. For some reason, most guys want to seem 'strong' and able to handle everything, the old 'I'm a man' sort of thing. I believe that by talking to John's family/friends and my family/friends, they really helped me come to terms with his death. Don't be afraid to open up.

I love my friends and it took a terrible tragedy for me to realise this. Don't ever take your friends for granted and never forget to tell them how much you appreciate them.

GAVIN NICKLETTE 15

> *A candle was blown out to symbolise his death and then re-lit to symbolise his life after death.*

CRYING IS REALLY IMPORTANT

I THINK CRYING IS really important and you have to do it. I talked about John's death a fair bit with other people. I didn't try to ignore it. I faced it and let myself think about it. I didn't put it out of my mind. When a friend dies or something bad happens, definitely talk about it and let yourself think about it, let yourself cry. Don't feel ashamed to ask for help because everyone wants to grieve in their own way and they shouldn't be stopped by anything in any way. You should talk, especially to your other close friends and reminisce.

It may be faith, but I'm sure it's not as simple as that, that has let me accept John's death. I don't want to give the impression I'm cold-hearted, but honestly, when I do feel pangs of sadness, I'm able to focus on things that really need doing. Later, usually alone, I'll reawaken these thoughts and deal with them; that is when I'll cry. Of course, if I'm at a friend's place, and something makes us all remember at the same time, I'll gladly cry with them, and I'm sure this is some of the best therapy, for them and for me. I understand when other friends need to go away and cry, but also when myself and others should go and be with that person. Sometimes, everyone needs to do what they feel they need to do, though at other times, friends can really help your mood.

Next year we're all going to pursue different studies, some of us not even in the same state, and although we're certain to make new, close friends, I worry that when they're really hurting, they/we won't have the 'rest of the group' around to be there for them.

I'm not willing to 'forget' about John.

I think it would be stupid to say anyone really could. But I'm willing to get on with life and be there for others and make this a strengthening experience, in the knowledge that John is with us, just not in body, but in soul.
MICK EVANS 16

ONE OF THE WORST times in my life was when my friend died of a diabetic attack. I was shocked. I saw him a week before. I kept myself busy, going boating, fishing, computers, anything I could do.
DARREN 16

When a friend dies or something bad happens, definitely talk about it and let yourself think about it, let yourself cry.

Why do some guys feel that it is okay to cry only when something tragic happens like the death of a friend or a loved one? It's important to remember that being able to cry—when we are feeling upset or even when we are angry and frustrated—is a sign of good mental health! It means that we are actually dealing with what we are feeling rather than trying to cover it up and pretending that we are coping. In fact, crying is a sign that we are actually coping with what we are feeling. It is important to acknowledge what we feel. The problem is that guys learn from a young age that it is not something that men should do.

The following true story by Craig is a powerful one. He writes about how he was kicked out of his friendship group when he was in Year 8. But eleven years later he runs into one of the guys at a pub. Have a read and see what happens. Craig still hadn't forgotten how he had been treated and neither had his ex-friend. Maybe the most important lesson to learn from this story is that the memories of what you do to others at school can haunt you for the rest of your life. And it's all in the name of 'acting cool' or trying to 'stay cool'. Sometimes the costs of not being yourself and doing what you know is right can be too great.

Note: In Canberra 'high school' refers to Years 7 to 10. Years 11 and 12 are called 'college'. It's like the junior and senior high school arrangement in Canada (see 'Degrassi Junior High' and 'Degrassi High'—ABC TV).

WHERE DID MY FRIENDS GO?

IN YEAR 8 I WAS KICKED out of my friendship group. I had been hanging with my friends, Jamie, Adam and Speros, since the beginning of Year 7. Our group had gone through changes before, but when five others, Todd, Elliot, Mark, Alex and Nick, joined our group, everything changed for me.

It all happened while I was away from school for a week. When I came back I was suddenly the butt of every joke. While playing sport at lunch I'd either be the last person picked for a side, or they'd say if I played there would be uneven numbers so I'd have to watch. So I watched. I knew what was going on, but I didn't know what to do about it.

I would lie awake at night until 4.00 or 5.00 in the morning. (School started at 8.30.) I felt sick all the time and I could hardly eat. For weeks I didn't tell anyone what was happening. My parents found out one morning. After struggling through breakfast I threw up onto the table. I didn't even have time to get out of my seat. My parents wanted to take me to a doctor. When I told them what was going on at school they wanted to call the principal and tell my teachers and the counsellor. I told them not to. Whenever anyone said anything to the counsellor the entire school knew about it five minutes later. I had to deal with it on my own.

I remember coming into class once and sitting down. All the desks were arranged in rows. Jamie, Speros, Elliot and Adam came in together and purposefully sat next to me. Then they moved their desks away so I was sitting on my own. They spent the entire class chanting a bastardised version of my name: 'Craig Garrar, Craig Garrar'. Every time the teacher asked me a question they would chant louder. Even though they were disrupting the class the teacher ignored them. I felt so alone and abandoned. At the end of class a girl asked why I was sitting on my own. I didn't know what to say, so I said I was sitting with my friends. One of them overheard me and told the others. They laughed in my face. They never gave me shit while they were on their own.

I was very confused. They were supposed to be my friends, but they weren't acting very friendly. I thought it would stop. I thought they would see I was a good person. I believed they still liked me and would be my friends again. I thought all I had to do was hang out with them and pretend that what they were doing wasn't affecting me and it'd be okay. It took weeks for me to understand that they wouldn't treat me like a friend again. I found it hard to break away.

I did break away—eventually. I was wary about making new friends, but high school's hard enough with friends, let alone being on your own. My new friends didn't care what was going on with the others. The taunts continued for about three or four months, but finally the group forgot about me. The next person cast out was Speros (he left school). Then it was Elliot's turn. Finally Todd hooked up with some others. No one else received the taunts and shit-stirring I took.

For a while I hated them a lot. Slowly they became inconsequential to my life. We were rarely in the same classes ever again. They ignored me and I ignored them.

Eleven years later I ran into Jamie at a pub. When he recognised me he came up and re-introduced himself.

We talked for a while. The sort of unimportant stuff you tell people you have nothing in common with. He told me he was an electrician and I told him I'd been to uni and was a writer and editor. Then he looked at me and said, 'You know what happened at school. I'm sorry about that. I didn't know what was going on. One minute we were friends and the next I wasn't allowed to be your friend. I knew it was wrong, but I was confused so I went along with the group. I always liked you and thought you were a top bloke. I still don't understand what happened. Even though I still had my friends, I felt funny about the whole thing. I had to tell you that. It's been on my mind for ages.'

I hadn't thought about that for years. I couldn't believe it had played on his mind for so long. While I didn't understand what was going on at the time either, at least I had a context and I knew I was the victim; I knew who was wrong and who was right (I thought I did).

Talking to Jamie made me realise I'd stopped hating them years ago. His apology reinforced how fucking weird high school is and showed me what happened to me wasn't as black and white as I thought. He had been a victim as well. He endured a really subtle and bizarre form of peer pressure. In the end though, our conversation raised more questions than it answered. How could we both be victims in that situation? Why me? If everyone was doing it because that's what was being done, who decided it? Why did it last for four months? Why didn't someone (Jamie?) stop it?

In 1999 it was ten years since I finished Year 10. I was invited to the reunion. I didn't go. I didn't have to.

CRAIG GARRETT

> **I WAS WARY ABOUT MAKING NEW FRIENDS, BUT HIGH SCHOOL'S HARD ENOUGH WITH FRIENDS, LET ALONE BEING ON YOUR OWN.**

Love and sex

IT'S THE WAY we're brought up. You learn that a male is supposed to be with a female, not a male with another male. That's just life.
NIGEL 17

GIRLS AREN'T REALLY into studs anymore!
I'm not the best looking guy but I don't think girls are really into studs anymore. They are to a certain extent but if you've got a really good personality and you're really open and talk really well I think girls find that equally as attractive as what looks are, but I'm not ugly or anything. I'm just not a full-on stud. Because I break bones easy, guys go, 'Does your dick break in half?', and all of that stuff. I feel like saying you're an idiot because you don't have a bone in there. They're very insecure about their own problems. As soon as they get a girlfriend they start the, 'Oh, why haven't you got a girlfriend?', because they want you to ask them if they've got a girlfriend so that they can tell you, 'Yes, I've just got one', because they want to be appreciated by their peers for achieving that goal. It is a goal when you're at high school to have your first girlfriend.
MARC 18

SOME FEMALES LIKE scruffy looking guys and big muscle guys, but then some of the other girls like neat looking guys with big muscles, then other girls don't really care. Other girls want someone who they feel safe with, a protective guy.
GLENN 16

ANIA AND BEN

I JUST FEEL THAT because I really like her and she likes me, you shouldn't have sex if you don't want to. A boy should have a girlfriend if he likes her, not for the sake of having one. Like a lot of boys at my school do that just to be popular.
DAMIEN 14

A boy should have a girlfriend if he likes her, not for the sake of having one.

SAY A GIRL AND a boy hit it off at a party and they went off and talked in private and everyone thought they were kissing, the next day at school nearly everyone would know it and it would be really awkward for them. Eventually it sort of disappears but I think for those few days it's really stressful for them and they prefer not to be at school at all. I liked this new girl who came into the school. At first we were just friends and then I must have been too friendly to her or something because suddenly everyone thought that I liked her. Word got to her and she didn't like that idea and so she pretty much avoided me for two months. That was really annoying because after a couple of days I really did like her and I wanted to talk to her more or ask her out and she just wasn't around.

Things never happen as easily as on TV. But pretty soon guys catch on to how it all works, what type of girl they go for and adjust themselves accordingly. For example, there are materialistic girls who dress up in designer brands and only go for guys like that. You will see guys at parties who wouldn't normally dress up now all dressed up, their hair slicked back, aftershave all over them. Smell is a big thing for guys. Only certain types of deodorant are used and girls know it when you wear it.
JOHNNY 17

I WANT TO LOOK good when I'm going out to a disco because I might meet this girl and she might ask me to dance or something. I've had that done to me a couple of times. I feel pretty cool, 'Oh someone wants to dance with me', and my other friends are around and like I go, 'Oh, yeah, okay'. I try to wear my best clothes for the discos.
MARK 12

GIRLS HAVE BEEN CONDITIONED TO BE CAREFUL

WHEN A GUY LOOKS a girl up and down, that's very intimidating because in the back of her mind there's always the thought that this man's physically stronger than her: 'He could try and do something to me and I couldn't stop it'. Whereas if a girl looks a guy up and down, the guy just thinks, 'Hey, she's checking me out', he doesn't care 'cause she can't do anything about it. I've talked to girls about it. They were saying that they find that kind of thing really intimidating and it's scary. Girls have to be really careful because guys could interpret something as an invitation to violate, so they don't make eye contact sometimes. They've been conditioned to be careful, they've taught themselves.
TOM 16

THERE'S ONE GUY that's going out with a girl and she's Greek and she's got a bit of a moustache and he gets a lot of shit from other guys about her. He's going out with her, he likes her, so what's other guys' problems? He's Australian and sometimes he pays her out to other guys. He goes out with her at weekends but comes to school on Monday and pays her out. I don't know why he does that. He's totally different around her. He tries to fit in with the guys here. I know the girl myself and I wouldn't pay her out. He's saying he's just using her to get a root but I know that he's not. He's just full of crap. He's just saying that in front of everyone else so he doesn't get paid out.

WAYNE 16

THIS GUY I KNOW went out with a girl. He was very horny and was calling her a slut and all this other stuff because he wanted to sleep with her. She hadn't but he called her a slut.

JASON 14

I'M COPPING A LOT of shit from other guys because I've just started seeing a girl who's three years younger than me and who I am not ready to have sex with. Before I started going out with my girlfriend, we were chatting about this girl who goes out with another girl because she's bisexual, and now she knows that I am bisexual too. I will only have sex with a condom on and I refuse to have sex with anyone until I plan things with them.

There was an incident at this school where a guy went around saying that he had sex with a girl and when she confronted him about it, she said, 'Why did you say you did?'. He's like, 'Oh because, you know, I'm a guy and I have to prove to my friends and blah, blah, blah'. She said, 'You're an idiot'. I didn't start having sex until this year and I got paid out a lot about being a virgin. I've knocked it back plenty of times. I'm not someone who says you all have to be totally in love with the other person, but that's just me and my preference. It has to be someone I feel comfortable with.

JASON 17

THROUGHOUT YEAR 10 AND 11, I was madly in love with this one guy and it really affected my work. I didn't talk to anyone about it because it was, 'Oh, don't be stupid, you've got a crush on someone, deal with it, how can it affect your work'. But when you're that young and naive, that kind of emotional stress does affect you.

LUCIANO 19

I GET DEPRESSED at weddings because I feel like I'm not going to be able to get married. And just the whole thing of getting married and having kids, I still want to do that. But I can't do that in an Italian culture. My parents would think it is gross because it's two guys.

ROB 16

IF I REALLY LIKE SOMEONE and I wanted to marry, I don't see that my disability is going to be a problem for me. I do see myself, at some stage, having a wife and having children. I do see one problem, that

is if I like someone from Australia then it would be very difficult to accept it in terms of cultural background and I think that is much more of a problem than my leg. I think that if I'm married and I was wanting my wife to go to the beach and she was taking off her clothes in front of another man, this would make me feel very strange because in Muslim Pakistani culture it is not done. It would be very difficult for me to accept.
HASEEB 21

THERE WAS A LOT of gossip about sex when I was going out with Sandra. People were always asking how far we'd gone. Sandra and I mutually agreed that it was no one's business and that we wouldn't discuss that sort of thing with others. When we said nothing it was to be expected, in hindsight, for people to assume all sorts of crap. Sandra and I didn't think that just because we were going out we had to do everything that our peers expected us to. At the time we loved and respected each other as human beings—not 'good gets'.
BEN 17

SEXUAL HARASSMENT OR SEXUAL COMPLIMENT?

There are differences between showing a girl you find her attractive and sexually harassing her. For example, privately going up and saying she looks great, or you like her hair or outfit, is not the same as yelling out 'Show us your tits' across the schoolyard in order to prove something to your male friends who, of course, you make sure are standing there to hear you. Or saying hello in a friendly and interested way as you walk past her is one thing, but making some comment about her body to your friends so she hears you as she walks by is another.

The following are forms of sexual harassment.

▶ **Guys in a car wolf whistle and shout out stuff about a girl's body as she walks by but don't actually talk to her.**

▶ **Guys at school making jokes about the size of a girl's breasts as she walks past.**

▶ **A guy touching up a girl in a crowded queue for the tuckshop.**

▶ **A guy insisting his girlfriend have sex with him because it's his right.**

▶ **A guy making heavy breathing phone calls to a girl in his class for a joke.**

▶ **A guy showing porn pictures of women to a girl.**

■ *What do you think leads guys to behave in this way?*
■ *Do you think girls who seem to enjoy or don't mind this attention are being entirely truthful? What else might they be saying? Could they be under some kind of pressure to pretend to like it or to go along with it?*
■ *If you find someone attractive what are some of the things you could do to compliment them?*
■ *Can boys be sexually harassed?*

So now you've heard from a range of guys talking about all sorts of issues to do with sex, love and relationships. Daniel below also explores some of this stuff. Imagine you're at a party, you've had something to drink and you're with a girl you really like. In fact you have really strong feelings for her but are scared because you're not sure what her feelings are for you. Relationships can feel quite scary especially at the beginning. This is because we all fear rejection. He takes us inside the head of a seventeen-year-old guy who is confused but settles for a relationship that has the potential to fulfil his emotional needs and desire for love as well as the capacity to destroy him. Have a read.

LOVERS AND FRIENDS

THE NIGHT WAS HOT and the alcohol made it hotter. Cheap vodka flowed into an endless cup as we sat around the pool or listened to some music. My friend was locking lips with some girl in a corner and the couples were merrily celebrating their happiness, which grew under the influence. I sat with my feet in the water and watched my reflection stare back at me. The ripples presented a distorted vision of my features until I started to believe that that was what I looked like, rippled and translucent. It's amazing what alcohol can do.

Sarah came and sat next to me, nearly spilling my fluorescent blue plastic cup filled with orange and vodka and so I grabbed it and sculled the lot. Once you get to a certain stage, alcohol loses its taste. With my cup now empty I turned to her, swaying slightly. She smiled at me and said, 'Hello', and her eyes were drooping from the alcohol. She looked so cute. I murmured back a greeting. Even if I wasn't drunk I would find it difficult to talk to her. You find it hard to talk to the one you love and in my present state it was even harder.

I turned my attention back to my reflection in the pool. It was easier and the motion of the water combated the spinning in my head.

'Do you like me, Alex?', Sarah whispered in my ear. I was stunned . . . I was a contradiction of feelings. To speak or not to speak, the truth or the lie, which is better? Was this the opportunity that I had been waiting for, for so long?

I had known Sarah for a few years already and the gradual increase of a proper friendship started to fuel my desire for her. Often the most love is generated through a friendship. I had tried to keep my feelings hidden from her. These days nobody wants someone who is needy. I believe that most people have a masochistic incline. They like people who treat them badly and ever since my feelings for Sarah had started to come out, she treated me worse and worse.

I didn't actually tell her how I felt but she'd catch me looking at her and I'd try to find some way to be close to her or touch her and all these things gave me away.

Why didn't I ever ask her out before? Fear, cowardice, these are the main reasons. Sarah enjoyed her unfettered life, a life where she didn't have to worry about a relationship and I respected it. We're adolescents and we should be having fun. But I never felt that she'd like me as well. I like to wait and see if I get the okay from a girl, if there is some interest or possibility there for me. I never got that from her, so I never asked her out.

I TURNED MY HEAD TO HER AND KISSED HER ON THE LIPS.

But now, when the moment of truth arrived and I was given the chance to say how I felt I found that the words stuck in my throat. If I said, 'Yes', then in the morning I could pass it off as drunken rambling and still retain some semblance of dignity. Everything would be okay.

I was about to say 'Yes' when I felt her soft lips kiss the back of my neck and her hands slid down my arms. The answer remained in my mouth as I turned my head to her and kissed her on the lips. Would talking really be necessary? Maybe physical language would suffice.

I lifted my feet out of the pool and turned my body to face her properly, taking her face in my hands and once again kissing her. She started to stand up and my mouth followed hers for as far as I could reach. She stood straight and looked down at me whilst I stared back at her, want and need and desire showing in both our eyes. Sarah held her hand out to me and I took it in mine. She pulled me inside and we found a quiet room where darkness fell over us and concealed us from the wandering eyes of our friends.

After half an hour of making out and exploring she abruptly separated herself from me and stared at me in the darkness. I could hardly see her face but I knew that something was wrong. She stood up, bent down and touched my face. She whispered, 'Sorry', and left the room. Without thinking I jumped up and followed her. I needed to know what was going on, why she left so soon. I ran down the hall and found her sitting in an armchair in the living room with her head in her hands and her eyes wide in disbelief.

'Sarah?', I said from behind her but she didn't turn around and instantly I was afraid of the situation. What would happen now? Was it just a drunken affair that meant nothing? Had I done something wrong? Was there some emotion, some feeling that I was missing? As I have said it is terribly difficult to know what Sarah is feeling.

I leant forward and placed my hand on her shoulder. She reached up with her left hand and took mine in hers, kissed it once and let me go. I knelt down beside her and said, 'What's wrong?'. It was at this moment that I heard her crying softly. I couldn't say anything. What words would comfort a drunk person especially when you don't know what was wrong to begin with?

I sat there in the awkwardness of her emotions wondering what to do and, shamefully, where I stood in all this. A short time later she brushed the hair away from her face, turned to me and said with all sadness, 'I'm sorry, Alex, I don't know how I feel'. With those last soft words she stood up and left me there with a pain that ripped through my very existence.

I watched her walk away. I sat on the chair just thinking of what had happened and then I fell asleep. The pain had overwhelmed me and a few hours of drunken sleep would be part of the only real peace I would have for a while.

LOVERS & FRIENDS

My emotional stability went from bad to worse after that. We still talked to each other, a few short words every now and then to perpetuate the lie that we were okay. However, every time we were alone, even for a few moments, the memory of that night hung around us so we stood in silence trying to find something else to look at. I was wrestling with myself to say something, to force the moment to its crisis but it's a stupid thing to do and so I shut my mouth.

Things were never the same again, they never are after such a thing and what strikes me is that it's so insignificant. It was only few drunken words and actions that altered a friendship forever. But reason can never enter into these things.

Then the truly tragic thing happened. Every time there was a party, the same thing would happen and each time we would get further and further and the pain would cut deeper and deeper. This went on for five months until friends started to assume that whenever there was a party Sarah and I would be together.

WHAT I HAD DONE WAS VERY RARELY DONE, ESPECIALLY WITH HER.

Each time she would say that she didn't know how she felt and I would be left to die a little more. I tried to think about why it always happened and why there was the sudden departure with those words that had become her motto.

Another party was to be had but this time I had to find the reason behind it all: what she didn't know and why it had to keep happening. These were questions that must be asked.

I needed to know what was happening, where we were going and if we were going together. I couldn't take the accidents that meant nothing but really did. Meaninglessness didn't exist in this and one or both of us usually got hurt.

LOVERS & FRIENDS

I had come to learn something about Sarah. She was most open and easy to talk to when she was drunk. I had to wait until she'd passed the high stage of her drunkenness and had slipped into the depressive and calm stage.

I went up to her, in my own equally depressive state, and asked to speak with her. She agreed so we went around the corner where no one was. It was a quiet place where I could hear my heart pounding inside my chest and my head screaming at me to retreat from this confrontation. I persisted. She was quite happy pretending to live in ignorance of my feelings for her. It was fine with me, most of the time, but when things started to happen it cut me deep and she knew it. That's why she said 'sorry' whenever she stopped and realised she was with me. But I had to speak.

'This is going to sound very bad and completely wrong but . . . but', and she knew where I was headed but didn't stop me, 'do you ever see an "us"?'

There I'd said it. I'd bared my soul and shown how much I needed an answer, how much I needed her, and how much pain I was in. She looked to the floor, as frightened of the words as I was. What I had done was very rarely done, especially with her. No one spoke of their feelings or a situation unless they were strong enough to find out what was really there.

She looked at my face and said, 'I've already

told you, I don't know how I feel'. She was almost in tears when she said this, either from the alcohol or from some emotion she had hidden deep within her. I hated hearing those words, the indecision and the fact that my heart was hanging in the balance.

'Please, please, don't say that. What don't you know?' I was nearly in tears myself. The crux had been reached and now that I had breached it I wouldn't stop, not until a proper answer had been reached, I wouldn't allow it. 'Is it that you don't know if you hate me or like me or love me? Or is it that you don't know if you should love me? Please, please, I need an answer. I can't take it anymore.'

'Why does everything have to change? Why can't we just be friends?'

'We've tried it, it doesn't work. We always end up getting with each other and each time it happens it pulls us further and further apart. Please tell me, can there ever be an "us"?'

She turned away, her face in her hands, crying, softly, remorsefully and I felt my heart sink. I would never get an answer; she would never allow her feelings to come forward, especially if they were for me. We would never be together and she would never love me. I came to this conclusion in the blink of an eye and I felt my heart heave and my stomach clench. The pain, the never-ending pain.

I couldn't stand watching her cry so I put my arm around her. I tried to comfort her. 'It's all right. I shouldn't have brought it up. I'm sorry. I'm so sorry. Can you forgive me?' She nodded in between the sobs.

I sat her down on the steps that were nearby and sat next to her, with my arm still around her shoulder. She turned to me and clung to me, hugged me and wouldn't let me leave. I didn't mind. I wanted her near me so I stayed there for her. I held her as she sat crying when all I wanted to do was cry myself. I didn't feel angry, just

I PULLED HER HAND AWAY FROM MY MOUTH AND SAT HER UP AND SAID, 'WE CAN'T, NOT NOW, NOT LIKE THIS, NOT WITHOUT MEANING'.

empty, devoid of faith or hope for us ever being together.

But while I sat there holding her and thinking about nothing, she had stopped crying and started rubbing my chest, her hand moving slowly up and down causing fire on my skin. Her hand moved further up my body to my chin and she put her fingers over my lips. I was surprised to say the least, and immensely saddened. How could this be happening? I didn't know how but it was. I couldn't take it, I had to stop it or else we would just fall back into the same pattern as always.

I pulled her hand away from my mouth and sat her up and said, 'We can't, not now, not like this, not without meaning'.

She understood and she leant closer to my ear, and whispered, 'I know, but who said there wasn't a meaning?'. She drew back and looked at me with a slight smile on her face. I didn't know what to think.

'What do you mean?'

'I've made my decision.'

'And what is it?' I whispered back.

Instead of answering, she leant towards me and kissed me. I enjoyed it but I still hadn't heard the answer. I pulled her away again, 'We've kissed before and it's all been for nothing. What does it mean this time?'

'I want to be with you, like you want to be with me', and she kissed me and I kissed back.

After we'd finished I realised that it didn't mean anything. All my hopes and faith in us ever really being an actual item were fantasy. When I meant I wanted us to be together, I meant as a couple. She just wanted to be together, a warm body next to her so that she could lose herself in someone else and forget all the problems that were facing her own life about which she never spoke to me, or to anyone. When she said she wanted to be with me the way I wanted to be with her, maybe it was how I wanted it. Two warm bodies, devoid of emotion or compassion, just the need to let go and forget.

Had I deluded myself that I actually loved her? Or did I just need someone near me, a warm body that wanted just what I wanted? The next morning I thought about the whole situation. We could never be together. She wanted her life of freedom where she could lose herself so many times and never be tied to any of them. I respected it and I saw no reason why she couldn't have that. But she would never be with me except in the throws of some alien passion

TWO WARM BODIES, DEVOID OF EMOTION OR COMPASSION, JUST THE NEED TO LET GO AND FORGET.

that was never sweet or gentle on any emotional or physical level. I felt it when she dug her nails into the yielding flesh of my back. But there was no emotion and there was no 'us'. There was nothing.

The morning after is always awkward and no conversation is ever had. A hello or a goodbye but now that we're sober no words will flow like the cheap vodka that had the night before. All emotions and anger and sadness are locked away until the next time we inevitably find each other's skin and start ripping each other apart.

We will go on doing what we always do until something snaps and we either refuse to see each other ever again or we end up together. But we're both strong and stubborn and needy and it will be a long time before that happens. Time may distance us before our actions do. As long as we come out rather unscathed, but that seems implausible so we'll end up having some emotional catharsis that will either bind us together or destroy us.

DANIEL SCARPAROLO 17

So what's going on in this story? Do you agree with what the following guys have to say?

- **THE GUY IN THE STORY** has strong feelings for the girl but the girl just seems to want sex or really doesn't know what she wants.
PASQUALE 17

- **THIS GUY REALLY LOVES** this girl but she's just playing with his heart and stringing him along.
CHARIS 16

- **IF THE GIRL** was telling the story, we'd get a different picture of what was going on.
FRANK 16

- **BOTH THE GUY** and the girl can't cope with what they're feeling and drinking just gives them a kind of way out—they can do what they want and then use the alcohol as an excuse.
BOB 17

- **THIS STORY SHOWS** how relationships can be rocky and complicated—they should just sit down and talk about what they're feeling.
MICHAEL 16

'LOVERS AND FRIENDS', BEN GERRARD 17

One of the keys to having healthy, loving and exciting relationships, as Michael below points out, is to honestly communicate about what you're feeling and what you really want. Understanding and listening to the other person are the other side of this and that's what decision-making in a relationship is all about.

HOT AND HEALTHY SEX

I FIRST HAD INTERCOURSE at eighteen, about six months into one of my first long-term relationships. Now I'm 33, I've had six lovely relationships, and I'm with a woman I'd love to stay with for life. But I think back to when I was first wandering through the exciting, complicated world of sex and relationships, and I wish I'd known then some of the things I know now. Things which have helped me have sexy, blissful, loving sex and good, healthy relationships. I've made mistakes, and I've learnt crucial lessons.

1 HOT SEX IS CONSENTING SEX.

Maybe the biggest mistake some guys make is to pressure or force a girl into sex. I did this once to a woman who was my girlfriend at the time. I didn't hold a knife to her throat or physically attack her. But I pressured her. I made her feel guilty that we hadn't had sex in a while and I really wanted to, and I kept showing her that I wanted to have sex (by touching her) even though I knew she didn't want to do anything sexual, until she gave in. My actions hurt her and hurt our relationship.

She said later that she felt 'used' and treated 'like an object', and she didn't trust or like me as much after that.

These days, I make absolutely sure that what I and my girlfriend do in bed is fine with her. I check out whether or not she is consenting—whether she is happy with and agrees to whatever sexual activity we're about to do. I don't just go on her body language, as it's easy to get this wrong. I say what I'd like to do (in cute, playful or sexy ways) and I ask what she'd like to do. And I take no for an answer.

Consent—both person's agreement to sex—is the bottom line of good sex and a healthy sexual relationship. Consenting sex is hot sex. You're both into it, you both want it, and you both feel safe and in control of your choices. And this builds sexual closeness and intimacy.

2 THERE'S MORE TO SEX THAN PENISES IN VAGINAS.

One of the best things I've learnt about sex is that there's a delicious range of sexual and sensual acts you can get into with your partner. Lots of guys focus on penis-in-vagina intercourse as the best kind of sex, as the ultimate goal of all other sexual activities, and as the very definition of 'sex'. But most women don't have orgasms from intercourse.

In my experience, women get 'turned on' by lots of kissing, sensual touching and caressing, as well as by being masturbated or oral-sexed—or doing these things to you. So one good reason to broaden your definition of 'sex' is to enhance your partner's pleasure and enjoyment of what you're both doing. Another is to expand your sexual appreciation of your whole body, not just your dick.

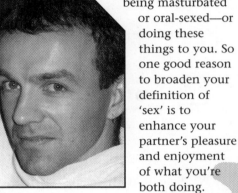

MICHAEL FLOOD

3 GO FOR QUALITY, NOT QUANTITY.

Some guys at my high school used to talk about 'how far they'd got' with such and such a girl. They'd say they'd 'squeezed her tits' or 'gone all the way'. I never knew if they were bullshitting or not. But I knew that some guys exaggerated and some guys boasted, and I felt pressure to do the same.

Some guys think that it's important to lose your virginity as quickly as you can, and to have sex with as many girls as you can. There is pressure on guys to gain sexual experience, and some guys get status from doing so. There are two problems

with this stuff. First, it treats girls just as notches on a guy's bedpost. Men's sexual 'conquests' become proof of macho status. Second, this stuff limits guys' choices. Some guys want to have sex early on, others want to wait until they're older or in a relationship or in love or with the right girl (or boy), and either choice is fine.

If a girl has had sex with a few guys (or people say she has), sometimes she gets called a 'slut'. But if a guy has had sex with a few girls (or he says he has), sometimes he gets called a 'stud', 'legend' or 'player'. The girl gets criticised, but the guy gets praised. Why is there one standard for guys and another one for girls? This is sexism, pure and simple.

The way some guys talk about girls, it's obvious that they don't give a shit about them. Some guys are happy to discuss girls as collections of body parts rather than people with minds and feelings. Some guys are happy to use put-downs about girls like 'whore', 'bitch' and 'slut'. Unless these guys change their attitudes, they're not going to have good relationships with girls. Because a good relationship depends on each person respecting, trusting and liking the other. Disrespect, sexism and inequality are the enemies of good sex.

I've learnt that the most effective way to have hot sex, whether one-off casual sex or as part of a relationship, is to show respect, make sure there is consent, communicate about your desires and listen to hers, and build trust and closeness.

MICHAEL FLOOD 33

But as Michael has said above and experienced himself, guys feel pressured to have sex or boast about sex to feel accepted by their mates. Peter Ball takes us right into that culture where there are powerful rules which dictate what guys need to do to prove themselves. In the poem it's like there's a pounding voice in the guy's head telling him what to do and what to think. But is it only in his head? Where do all these rules come from? Where has he heard them before? Could some guys be actually saying this stuff in the nightclub to him?

Go on, Fuck her
Ignore your fucking conscience
Ignore all the shit going on in your head
Ignore anything that's going on in your heart
Just follow your dick

Fuck her
Fuck her now
You know that you aren't really complete till you do
That you aren't going to be good for anything
That you aren't really a man
Not in our eyes

Just Fuck her
Fuck her now
You aren't gay or anything, are you mate?
It seems like it sometimes
You don't seem to like sex as much as the rest of us
You won't fuck the chicks that we find for you

Fuck her
Fuck her now
It's not like it's against your religion or something, is it?
You're not some upright, uptight Catholic?
You don't have to marry her or anything

Just Fuck her
Fuck anything that's female and moves
We don't care if you want to or not
We just want you to prove something to us
That's why you're here isn't it?
These are the rules

Fuck her
And Fuck her now
PETER BALL 22

Have a read of these. All three guys write about their experiences of love and relationships. Relationships can be painful especially if the other person doesn't feel the same way or if feelings change and relationships break down. For guys who are gay it can also be difficult because they have to hide what they feel and it can be quite traumatic and devastating leading them to the edge. But Luc, who never thought love was possible, discovers that it is really a 'wonderful thing'.

A KINDA DEPRESSING BROKEN-HEART POEM

I gave you everything
Never took a bit
I treated you like a queen
You treated me like shit
I could never see
What was in front of me
But that's all I have seen
Since you called it quits

Found a false security
Made it my home
How could you so lie to me
Tell me you were my own
I'll go one day at a time
Never look between the lines
But now I'm lost for words
And I'm drinking all alone

I really thought that I knew
Thought that all was well
Now I hurt myself for you
And wish that you could tell
I loved you, you hurt me
That does not seem fair
I don't think that I'll pull through
I'm just a fucking shell

MAXO 17

ON THE EDGE

IRONIC HOW IT'S COME to this, I think to myself as the icy wind sliced by. Me, the most popular guy in school, standing on the edge of a bridge looking down as the cars cruise unknowingly by below. Amazing how much everything has changed, and in such little time. I can't even remember what it was like being me back then, so happy and carefree, each day better then the one before it.

I've always known I was somehow different, dancing to the beat of a different drum, if you will. But I'd never really thought much of it. A grim smile spreads slowly across my face, ignorance is happiness, as the saying goes, I just wish I could have stayed stupid. But no, reality can't be ignored forever. The funny thing is, I can't remember what day it was when I realised the truth, or even the month for that matter, but the memory of it seems seared into my mind.

'YEAH! WE KICKED THEIR SORRY ARSES!!!!', screamed Ben, one of my team mates, as we charged into the change rooms. 'Beat the living shit out of 'em!', shouted another at the top of his lungs.

'Yeah, but we would've beaten 'em by even more if *fumble-fingers* here hadn't dropped so many damn passes', declared our quarterback as he tossed his cast-off shirt at me with a smile.

I began to twist up my towel slowly and deliberately, 'Well if *someone* had thrown straight

CRUNCH!
I HIT THE SIDE OF THE BRIDGE.
I HANG HERE AND LISTEN TO THE BLOOD POUNDING IN MY TEMPLES AND THE CARS SCREECHING TO A HALT BELOW ME.

maybe I'd have caught more,' I retorted as I flicked my towel at his bare legs.

CRACK! He yelped and jumped back in pain. 'Now I'm gonna have'ta kick your arse bitch!', he yelled as he too began to roll up his towel. And Ben was just standing there in the background looking on with those kind of knowing eyes that could see right through you.

I muttered something to the effect of 'In your dreams little man', but my eyes were locked on his left arse cheek where a red mark from my towel was growing.

'Check it out', said one of the other guys 'homeboy's turnin' queer on us'. This got a laugh from everybody, including Ben, and the QB made a show of being afraid of me, quickly wrapping his towel around his waist and backing up warily.

I smiled and laughed along with the rest of them, but something inside of me stopped. It would make sense, I thought to myself in a moment of clarity, I'd never

been that attracted to chicks, and I preferred the company of my buddies to that of my girlfriends. I kept thinking about Ben and the way we often caught each other's eye if only fleetingly at times.

No way! I told myself and forced the thought from my mind. I'm not a fucking poofter! Not a chance!

How often I'd told myself that, trying in vain to deny what I deep down knew to be the truth. I'd even slept with as many girls as I could to convince myself I wasn't a fag. But now that I had the idea in my head, I knew I wasn't really enjoying it. And then I'd think of Ben, those eyes, that glance he often gave me and I knew deep down inside he knew what I never wanted to acknowledge about myself. The fear gripped me and I felt my head spinning.

I look back down at the road and try to gather my nerves. It'll all be over soon. Over, totally over. No, I don't want it to be over. But what other way is there? What

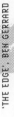
'THE EDGE', BEN GERRARD 17

else can I do? I can live. Live. Fuck this, find another way to deal with it, not death.

Slowly I begin to turn around, but a blast of wind hits me and rips me from my perch. I hang in midair, suspended in time it seems. NO! NO NO NO NO NO!!! I don't want to die! My hand shoots out of it's own accord and catches . . . something.

Crunch! I hit the side of the bridge. I hang here and listen to the blood pounding in my temples and the cars screeching to a halt below me. Breathe, breathe, look up. Argh, my eyes watering, I can see a young man silhouetted against the sun, straining to keep a hold of me. I guess angels *are* real after all. I feel myself laughing hysterically, so this is what the touch of an angel feels like. 'Hold on', the angel whispers coarsely, 'I won't let you go'.

But gravity has other ideas, my hand's slipping through his. 'NOOOOO!!!', I hear him screaming as I tumble downwards. The sky so blue above me, I'm alone in the world as I descend.

I don't feel the impact, but I know I've stopped falling. People running towards me. My angel looking over the bridge, a look of horror on his face and his arm still outstretched, as if trying to reach me, touch me, the strange touch of an angel.

My vision dimming.

Ben came to visit me every single day I was in hospital. Turns out he was on the bridge that day for the exact same reason as me, a one in a billion chance. Maybe, just maybe, he was meant to be there, maybe God sent him, maybe he really is an angel—though the touch of his hand is no longer strange.

KEVIN HUNT 17

I GUESS ANGELS *ARE* REAL AFTER ALL.

LOVE IS A WONDERFUL THING

IT'S A SIMPLE EQUATION. I'm sitting on the park lawns with my friends, soaking up the hot sun, staring lazily into the distance—anything to escape the blabber coming out of my friend's mouth. Last night, she prattles, she heard a song. It went like this: ' . . . *love is a wonderful, wonderful, wonderful thing . . .* '

And as she listened dreamily to the song, she tells me, she decided she loved him. It is at this point that I decide I am having a hard time keeping my eyes from rolling so far back into my head I'll soon be staring at my brain.

What she feels for him, she tells me, makes her want to melt into him like the snow melts under a hot sun. My nostrils begin to flare as I attempt to stifle a roaring laugh. Love, she continues, feels like . . . yadda, yadda, yadda.

Three years later. The equation is not so simple. I'm sitting on the uni lawns with my friends, soaking up the hot sun—holding onto someone's hand. Somewhere in the distance I can hear my friends talking amongst themselves—this time I don't mean to escape. It just happens. The feeling of two hands together is not foreign to me except for one thing. This just feels too right.

In the distance I can see a couple hugging and chatting. I wonder what it feels like, I begin to think, to share everyday life with someone.

WOAH!

Hold on a sec. Isn't that reminiscent of . . . love? I remind myself that love is hocus pocus—that's all it is. But . . . I don't seem to be doing a good job of convincing myself.

A year and a half later. This equation doesn't have a park and a hot summer sun. It has something different—actually it has a lounge room, bedroom, study, kitchen and bathroom. It is an equation I never pictured myself in.

I am sitting in the lounge room. Or rather, *our* lounge room. It is dark and warm outside, and the spring rain is pounding on the roof and windows. My partner is sitting on the couch reading a book as I tap these keys to recall a story.

A story of a boy who never believed in love. A boy who scoffed at the very idea that people could even consider spending the rest of their lives together, scoffed at the idea of loving someone.

Now, look, God knows what I've turned into. From holding hands to sharing a house and a life. Pity I don't have a front yard: picket fences would go nicely.

Love *is* a wonderful thing. It's a strange thing that I can't explain. That no one can explain, no matter how many times they've experienced it.

Love is genderless. It doesn't have boundaries. Love is between any two human beings. Between animals even.

But one thing I do know definitely about love.

It feels goddamn good!

LUC 21

> LOVE IS BETWEEN ANY TWO HUMAN BEINGS. BETWEEN ANIMALS EVEN.

CHAPTER FIVE
SPORTING AROUND

Sport as personal best, sport as pressure

For some guys, playing a sport can be a way of really connecting with other guys, being part of a team, experiencing the highs and lows together. It can also be a way of expressing yourself through body and movement. But for other boys, playing sport can also be a time of great pressure and competition, when you can be made to feel a failure, ashamed of your body, a time when you humiliate others in order to feel good about yourself and avoid being humiliated by others. Likewise, training can be fun, but it can also be obsessive and excessive. For something meant to promote respect for your body, physical fitness and health, it can often mean getting bad injuries that some boys try to hide. Now how healthy is that? Have a read of what these guys have to say about sport.

SOCCER GUYS ARE ALWAYS ON CRUTCHES. They're always breaking their ankles because they play soccer or they're getting their knee reconstructed.
JULIO 17

I LIKE PLAYING RUGBY. I just like the physical side I guess, just running around and tackling people, running through packs and stuff like that.
TREVOR 17

I THINK THAT GUYS are expected to do stuff like football because it's more like what males have always done. You don't see any girls playing football, AFL, league or anything like that. I think families sort of point boys in that direction and because everyone else has been pushed in that direction they're going to follow it.
DAVID 15

I THINK SPORT'S the main thing that brings people together because when you go to someone's house, you don't really just sit there and talk, you want to go out and do something. So you might not invite somebody over to your house because you know they can't play basketball. You invite people that can play basketball and you get friends like that. I think sport is the main reason why people are friends.
NATHAN 15

THERE'S ABOUT 20 or 30 boys in one big group on the oval. They're all friends because of football. They all love footy, so everyone goes down there and plays footy. There's like five or six little groups and you can see at any rate who hangs around who but everyone's around there for footy.

There are guys who aren't into footy in our group but they're all right because they're into the rock bands. None of them can play football so they do the next best thing, they do the band and that's all right. The group sees it as being okay. And then there's Carl, he's into music and not football, but he goes to the parties on the weekends, so he makes up for it in different ways. It's like, okay, he doesn't play footy but he does other things that the other group does so it seems all right. He's always pretty popular with the girls as well and the group respects him. He's into basketball and basketball's sort of seen as all right as well. The group sort of knows, okay, not everyone's going to play footy. A couple of years ago, you either played footy or you weren't in a group. I think that's how it was. But as we've got older it's sort of like, okay, if you're into basketball then it doesn't really bother us anymore. So they're seeing that football is not everything and they've sort of let basketball in and music.
DAVID 15

> A couple of years ago, you either played footy or you weren't in a group.

I WASN'T INTO SPORT. When we were doing sport in Year 9, we were doing softball or T-ball. Instead of lining up, one of my mates would be teaching me how to juggle three balls in the one hand and we never batted once through that entire unit, and we would pick the furthest outfield, we would tell jokes and things rather than be serious and all that sort of sporty stuff talk. We'd just be out there having a hell of a good time and we weren't concerned about our grades in sport. Basically, it was just fun rather than, 'You have to win.' But you get other guys and they have to act macho. They definitely established that with me in Year 8 because they just beat me up. A good punch in the guts during sport. Sport's a brilliant time to target people. And they'd do it when the teacher's not looking. The geeks were targeted by everybody and the Asian kids who didn't speak Australian or speak English were targeted because they'd speak their traditional language to each other and they wouldn't bother talking to anybody else.
LEON 17

We'd just be out there having a hell of a good time

Leon has a lot more to say about sport. He believes that sport is definitely a 'cultural male thing'. He kind of rejects all of this stuff about having to prove yourself through sport.

IT'S A CULTURAL THING

SPORT IS MORE of a male thing. It's like you have to prove yourself. If you are good at sport then you're more easily accepted by other guys, maybe because you're better than them at that sport. There's this group of guys at school who hang out down under the pine tree by the basketball courts on the oval, and I've talked to them. They'll always be pushing each other around. They'll also put people down, they'll give someone shit and everyone gets a laugh out of it. It's like a game and they establish like a pecking order. They're always out to get this small guy in their group. But when they're not doing that they're kicking a bottle around or they're just throwing a frisbee or booting around a footy. For example, the last Year 12 camp we went on, the guys would often go out and kick a footy, whereas the girls would be off in the dorms talking or just going for a walk talking.

These guys are just very competitive about everything. Not all of them are like that but a lot of them were. It's like there's a need to be competitive but it's definitely a cultural thing. When the younger kids first came to the school, it was the older kids who were playing football on the lower oval at the footy goals. And when they leave, another group takes over that region.

There's another group of guys at school who usually just sit and chat and there are girls there too. Sometimes they play this game with a bouncy ball. They've pulled apart this plastic table and made three of the legs stumps and the other leg a bat and they would bounce the ball down and the person would hit it and it would bounce all around our area. It was 'cool' fun because nobody knew where the ball was going to go so you had to watch out. But it's not a conventional sort of a thing to do because they were mucking around. If you mucked up it didn't really matter because it was just a fun thing. There was no competitiveness in the whole thing at all. But with the other guys, if you stuffed up when they were kicking the bottle around, the attention was on you and everyone was bagging you for stuffing up. But with this group of guys it didn't matter if you were crap at sport or uncoordinated.

It just shows the way different groups relate and I think it's got something to do with the competitiveness of people and it's definitely a cultural thing—sport for the guys seems to be a cultural thing. Their fathers did it and now they're doing it. But, even if their fathers don't have an influence, it seems that the kid just falls into the cultural cycle, without knowing it. I mean it starts off when they're little kids—guys are expected to be into the sports that they were playing in primary school. The girls were also into playing sport but they didn't have that competitiveness. They played basketball at lunchtime but it didn't matter. There was only that competitiveness in the guys.

LEON 17

If you mucked up it didn't really matter because it was just a fun thing. There was no competitiveness in the whole thing at all.

Football

What's it like to be a football player? Can some boys play football and enjoy the culture and relationships that go with it, or does playing football have to be unhealthily competitive? Read about what Matt and Josh Carr and Trent Paulet have to say about football. Matt was formerly an AFL football player with St Kilda, but he now plays for the Fremantle Dockers. Josh plays for Port Adelaide. They give us an insider's perspective on playing professional football.

MY LOVE, MY LIFE!

AS LONG AS I remember all I wanted to do was to play AFL football. When people grow up they are constantly asked what they want to do and for me it was always simple— to be paid to play football. But it is not easy. The highs are as high as you get. The lows feel like you have hit rock bottom. I suppose because I love it so much and I work so hard at everything (that is, training, playing), it hits you hard when something goes wrong. I try to make every day count. Be as professional as I can but still enjoy myself when I can. I have left no stone unturned and when football is over, whether it's tomorrow because of injury or in ten years time, I will know I had a real go. Football to me is not a game, it's a way of life. But it will not last forever.

When you play in a team you meet some funny characters and great people from all walks of life. There are all sorts of people involved in

MATT AND JOSH CARR GROWING UP

football clubs—politicians, lawyers, labourers, people with disabilities, ex-SAS soldiers. You learn so much from all these people. I have been very privileged and heard some great stories that have helped me to become a better person.

I love nothing more than to run out onto the oval when there are forty or fifty thousand people there. To play well and to win is a real buzz. The feeling you get when you do something good and the crowd is screaming is amazing. The tingle and the adrenalin rush—the feeling is hard to put into words but the emotion involved can make you do strange things.

I remember my first game and the captain makes all the first gamers lead the side out of the tunnel onto the oval. I could hear the crowd as I walked down and as I was nearing the end

MATT AND JOSH CARR

I KNEW WHERE I WAS GOING. OTHERS SOMETIMES COULDN'T SEE IT BUT I COULD.

I could see the people—there must have been forty thousand people out there cheering. At that stage you are supposed to be straight-faced and serious. But the excitement overcame me. I had a huge smile on my face and my eyes were watering. It was that feeling I had been waiting for for my whole life and it was even better than I ever could have dreamed of.

With football I pride myself on working hard. I never take short cuts and I believe I work as hard as anyone else. I'm a pretty laid back sort of person but when it comes to playing and training I hate getting beaten. I don't like someone thinking that they are better than you but you have to believe in yourself and that you can win. I always back myself to win.

Football can be tough on the mind and the body. Some players cope with terrible injuries to knees and other parts of their bodies which ends their careers. It is a very high-risk occupation but that really is no different to life in general—something is always happening, things change, people move on and you meet different people.

Being a footballer to me is great. It's funny though how some people treat you. If you have a good game, they'll want to talk to you, but if you have a bad one they will walk straight past you without even saying hello. Some people stereotype football players as all being the same. But I have all the friends I want and I don't care too much what others think because it's the man in the mirror who counts the most.

Football has given me and my brother Josh Carr, who plays for Port Adelaide, a start in life. I remember at school how teachers would ask what I was going to make of my life. But unknown to them I have always been a very goal driven person. I knew where I was going. Others sometimes couldn't see it but I could. I remember writing down my goals for myself from the age of thirteen. I bet there weren't too many kids that age setting their sights yearly like that so that they could get where they wanted to go. But some people at school would look at you and say, 'He's a slacker! He won't do his school work. He's too laid back and doesn't care. He's just a good time boy!' But people don't see behind the scenes. They don't really see what makes a person.

I have a long way to go before I can say I've made it, but it is what I think that counts to me. I'm going to spend my life doing what I want because it's my life. Eventually, when I'm ready, I'm going to start working with boys and girls who have roughed it and help them to do what they want in their lives. Teach them some of the things I've learnt from this game and the people I've met through footy.

MATT CARR 23

PLAYING AFL: A DREAM COME TRUE

LIKE MY BROTHER Matthew, I also love the game of football. As a kid I would get home from school and the first thing my brother and I would do was ring up our two best mates who were also brothers and go over to their house for a game of footy. That went on for me until I was thirteen. But I guess having my mind set on what I wanted in life, which was footy, had an effect on other things in my life, for example, school. School always came in last behind everything else. I would get to school on a Monday and right from the first bell I'd be thinking of having a kick at recess, and then lunch, and so on, and the weeks would just go so slowly because all I would be thinking about would be the game I was going to play.

Football to me now has not changed much, except I get paid for it. I still love it as much as I did before. One thing I will make sure of is that I do not take people for granted. I will always remember who helped get me to this important stage in my life. My family has always been there to support me in whatever I did. Teachers thought I was just a bum who liked playing football but what they did not realise was how hard I would work at my football. One thing I can say is that I wish I had been able to mix my school and football a lot better than I did because now I need to go back and study to catch up. I am currently doing a course through correspondence which will hopefully help me to get something behind myself in case football does not work out how I want it to. If it did not work out it would not be the end of the world but definitely the end of a dream but I think, like all ambitions in life, if you want something bad enough and you work hard at it, your dream will come true.

JOSH CARR 21

MY FAMILY HAS ALWAYS BEEN THERE TO SUPPORT ME IN WHATEVER I DID.

JOSH CARR

ROSEDALE FOOTBALL CLUB: MY FAVOURITE PLACE

MY FAVOURITE PLACE out of everywhere I've been is the Rosedale Football Club. It's not a real posh place or a theme park or anything but it's a place where everybody knows your name and people take you for who you really are.

I first went there about one year ago to have a meeting with the ex-president Greg Mitchell about playing with the club. There were offers from richer clubs and better ones but Rosedale was where I chose to play my footy. At first I wasn't too sure if I had made the right decision, but after playing there for a year, there is nowhere else I'd rather be.

I love waking up at 7.30 in the morning, getting ready, walking to the end of the road and catching the team bus. You get to Rosedale, the sun is shining and the fog is clearing up. As you pull into the ground, you get this big feeling in your stomach and you know you're in for a big day.

You begin to get dressed and warm up and as you look around and see all these people running around for you and doing everything they can to make sure you're happy and ready to go, it's just like a big family.

Once the game is finished and the reserves start, you seem to be fighting your way past senior players and some people

PAUL AND HIS FOOTBALL

you don't even know, all telling you that you've played a great game or you tried really hard, or trying to give you money and making you feel wanted. You can't even get past the cafeteria women without them telling you what a great game you had, even if you didn't play that well.

As the day rolls on and the reserves and seniors have both finished their games and the spectators have all left, it's celebration time and everyone flocks to the bar. You'll be standing there with a 60-year-old guy, a 40-year-old guy, and a 20-year-old guy, and they treat you no different to anybody else. You might not even know these people but they'll introduce you to people and tell everyone how great you are.

I plan on playing for Rosedale for as long as my body allows, because I know I'll be playing with great people and good friends. It's just not the game I love, it's the people.

TRENT PAULET 16

You might think that circus performers and football players are at two totally different ends of a macho-meter! But as the following guys tell us, it should all be about the same stuff when you ditch the rules about what's a real sport and what isn't—about doing physical activity to stay fit and healthy, and about having fun, travelling around, making new friends, learning new skills and doing your personal best. What all these guys seem to be telling us is that, at its core, sport is about friendship, respect for others, teamwork, support, preparation, commitment, communication, healthy competition.

Spaghetti Circus boys

EDDIE

I STARTED JUGGLING when I was living in Sydney with my Dad. I came to Byron Bay to live with my Mum and I found the juggling store. In Sydney, I wasn't going well at school. I'd been getting in trouble around the neighbourhood and I needed to start a new life. I wasn't handing in homework, I was being a smart alec, making prank phone calls, the usual stuff. My dad didn't like it at all and I'm really sorry for what I did to him and I regret it a lot. I used to have fun causing trouble but now that just seems like it was really dumb. We might go to the shops and steal something and then say, 'Yeah! Look what I've done!' We were bored because we had nothing to do after school.

I played football but that got way too competitive. You couldn't talk to other people at practice, it was work, work, work. Being competitive doesn't exist in the circus. We don't even have games really, it's just like a big lesson and almost everyone is at the same level.

After I moved up to Byron Bay I changed heaps with juggling. It's just the kind of people I now hang out with, the kind of lifestyle I live, like travelling a lot, seeing new people and everyone you meet you always share something in common, which is the circus. I do well at school now. I think life just is and you've got to achieve the best you can out of it.

Being a juggler you've got the whole

stage to yourself, you can do whatever you want. You can express a different side of you. In my performances I like to look as good as I can. But I might take it to an extreme. In the last show I had to take out a costume and I replaced it with something else because it was just too weird. We were meant to be punks but it was too scary for the little kids. The make-up I had was a deep purple mask just across my eyes, black lips with a slight brown, and a spike coming from the middle of my lips. I cut stockings up and webbed them all over my chest and then had really, really baggy black jeans. The make-up is always really important.
EDDIE 11

I'M A JUGGLER and one of the tumblers. I really like performing and just being in front of a big crowd. Sometimes other guys hassle me but it's very rare. I think it's just jealousy that they don't do it. They go, 'Oh, circus boy' and stuff like that.

Sometimes, if I have to wear tights, I get hassled. You get heaps of people just whistling at you and guys trying to pay you out but you just act it up if someone does that. You just pretend to like it. Just smile and rub your chest or something like that. I'm just too busy trying to concentrate on what I'm going to do to really let it bother me. I wish schools had a bigger range of choices which all kids can choose from to do physical fitness. I can't kick or throw a football well but I'm good at circus skills. I used to play soccer and then I quit because I had to spend more time at circus and study. I'm thinking of changing schools because at my boys' school I just don't fit in. They're yobbos and very racist. I just don't like them tough people. If you don't play football or aren't in any of the school teams, they just don't really like you that much. All the kids who really tease are the big ones who play football and work out. But I don't really know what they're thinking. When they hassle me, I mainly ignore them and just don't really talk to them.
DANNY 16

> I CAN'T KICK OR THROW A FOOTBALL WELL BUT I'M GOOD AT CIRCUS SKILLS.

DANNY

1999
Albury Wodonga

Bobby, Antonio and Sash are three of the male dancers in the Ilinden Macedonian Cultural Association Folk Dancing Troupe. They dance to folk songs in traditional costumes. Let's hear what they have to say about dance as a way of keeping fit, making friends, keeping in touch with your traditional culture and learning about diversity.

Boys who folk dance

I DO MACEDONIAN DANCE to meet people and to keep fit. It's a great work-out on my legs and helps with my soccer. Friends often laugh at me but then will ask me to teach them. Girls ask me too. I don't feel uncomfortable having a gay dance teacher. In the dressing rooms, I'll get changed next to Yorgo. If I need help getting the difficult costumes on, I ask him to help me. I'm not going to turn gay by touching Yorgo. Some people just don't understand.
ANTONIO 17

DANCING IS MY LIFE. It's like breathing. I need to breathe. I need to dance. It's good exercise and a great way to make friends. You're always learning, no matter what! Guys who aren't Macedonian can laugh all they want but when they realise I'm serious about it and I don't care about them, they stop.
SASH 15

I DECIDED TO join Macedonian dancing because I wanted to meet more Macedonian teenagers. I love it as every song and dance has a meaning and tells a story. The music is very lively. A lot of my non-Macedonian friends laugh and think it's uncool but some think it's great that I'm helping preserve the Macedonian culture. I think my teacher, Yorgo, is the best and excellent at what he does.
BOBBY 17

BOBBY, ANTONIO AND SASH → → →

 Read what Chris has to say about tai-kwon-do. Just imagine if playing all sports could be like this how different it would be—the emphasis wouldn't be on winning but on supporting one another in a pressure free space.

TAI-KWON-DO IS WICKED!

IT'S THE ONLY PLACE where you go and you cannot be judged. It's not like a tournament situation or like a school scenario where people rely on you. There will always be a winner and a loser. But with tai-kwon-do there never is. You never feel the pressure of the other kids, they never laugh at you, they never tease you for what you look like, they encourage you, they say, 'That's a good technique, but you might want to do it this way'. They're always helping and they're never criticising. It's just like a free environment. It's my only escape that I can ever get away. It's my little world where I live and can be anything I want and no one cares. They support whatever I do and it's just great. I love it. They really care though. You can go to some places and they'll say, 'Okay you can come in only if you do this and this, and if you don't you're terrible, you're an outcast, go away'. Here they don't say, 'You have to', they say, 'You can try if you want to and if don't like it, we'll figure out something else for you'. They'll modify for you and it's just great, it's wicked and I love it.

CHRIS 16

it's my little world where i live and can be anything i want and no one cares.

Putting sport into perspective

IT'S FUN BEING a boy because I can do sport, I can be strong and I can be gentle.

JESSE WHINNEN 11

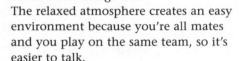

Jesse's GAY

JESSE WHINNEN 11

Why Don't I Fit in?

SPORT IS SOMETIMES the only way that boys get together and share emotions with one another. If you're getting together after a game, you talk about the sport. But you talk about other things too. The relaxed atmosphere creates an easy environment because you're all mates and you play on the same team, so it's easier to talk.

SCOTT 17

IT SEEMS TO BE every father wants their kid to play sport or something which they did themselves when they were young. Lucky my dad just wanted me to do the best that I could at what I wanted to do. It was completely up to me.

MIKE 17

I KNOW SOME COACHES don't want a player to be a hog. They think if you're going to be a hog, why are you playing in a team? You might as well go on the field by yourself and play by yourself if it's going to be just a one-man team. I like a coach who will enforce rules but won't enforce them in a harsh way. If you do something wrong they won't tell you to get off the team, they'll enforce a rule but they won't shout it at you. They'll just tell you, 'Use your best ability, I can't expect anymore'.

CHRIS 16

I CAN REMEMBER quite clearly in Year 7 my phys. ed. teacher had known my older brother who is quite athletic. The teacher was calling out the roll, and I put up my hand and he said, 'Well, you're Michael's brother', and I said, 'Yes I am'. He then says, 'You've got to be kidding me, there's no way that you could be Michael's brother', and he actually went on about it in front of the whole class.

DANIEL 23

SPORT WAS IMPORTANT to me purely because that was the way I was brought up. I think being fit and healthy is an important part of everyone's life. I don't think that it should be limited to just people who are interested in sport. I've never been a real junk food eater, I was always wanting to be fit or become fitter, and participating in physical activities, and also I was mentally capable of dealing with school life. I think that's all part of being healthy. Okay, you may be super fit but if you're not mentally able to deal with certain things, then you're not entirely healthy.

CHRISTIAN 22

MOST KIDS THAT PLAY a sport act like they're champions at the sport. There's this dude in Year 10 and he likes cricket and there's this girl in Year 11 who plays for the state cricket team and there's this other girl in Year 11, she's a state goal keeper. The teachers treat them like she's a queen and he's a king. They're popular, they've got only friends who like to do sport and people that like to talk about sport.

PETER 14

AT A SCHOOL assembly sport gets a lot of time. What about other stuff students do?

JOSH 15

The teachers treat them like she's a queen and he's a king.

BEING A GOOD SPORTS player is one thing that makes you cool but it's also being a good person, being generous and not being selfish towards other people.

PATRICK 17

BODY IMAGE IN SPORT

MY NAME IS CAMERON ELLIOTT. I am nineteen years old and have been rowing for the past five years. I began the sport when I was thirteen and originally it was the idea of getting strong that attracted me to it. Since then, I have been exposed to what I feel is a huge problem, not just in rowing, but in the wider sporting community. It seems that body image takes priority over a person's health and wellbeing.

When I began rowing at thirteen, I weighed about 65 to 70 kilos and had no trouble with the way I looked. In fact I was quite happy with how big I was. It wasn't until we had a one-month break in summer that I was told to lose some weight. In my opinion, being just thirteen and being told to lose some weight is a bit stupid, so I ignored the coach who told me to do it. When I returned from the break, I obviously hadn't lost any weight so I was demoted down to the end of the boat. I spent the rest of the season down the end.

AFTER A MONTH OF BEING IN THE BOAT, I WAS DEEMED OVERWEIGHT, AND SINCE I SHOWED NO SIGNS OF LOSING THE WEIGHT, I WAS DROPPED FROM THE CREW ALTOGETHER.

In the break between seasons I had a growth spurt and put on about 10 kilos. When it was time for try outs, I was one of the bigger kids, and it showed in my results. My strength and size placed me in the top five and the coach was pleased. Unfortunately, I broke my arm and ended up missing the season. When I was healed, I was weighing about 90 kilos which was partially due to lack of exercise, and partly to do with my growing.

By the time I was starting to exercise again, the try

outs for the school first rowing crew were taking place so naturally I jumped at the chance to be in the premier crew. After a month of being in the boat, I was deemed overweight, and since I showed no signs of losing the weight, I was dropped from the crew altogether. I was bemused as to why I could be showing signs of improved fitness and have a strength rating higher that most in the crew, but have no chance until I lost weight.

It was in the summer break that I decided to lose weight so I went on my first diet, at fifteen. It worked. I was back in the crew and I managed to drop 10 kilos by the end of the season. Rewarding me for losing weight simply made me think that I needed to be thin to be healthy, so for the next six months over winter, I remained at 78 kilos, 12 less than the same time the previous year. When the new season started, I was in great shape, or so I thought. I was instantly accepted into the crew and training began. I wasn't eating properly and soon began to feel weak. After almost passing out after a race, I had a blood test that showed I had glandular fever, made worse by a massive iron deficiency.

It took me a month to overcome the illness and get back to full health. My final

WHEN THE NEW SEASON STARTED, I WAS IN GREAT SHAPE, OR SO I THOUGHT.

year at school was ruined and my results reflected this. Every doctor I saw agreed that my diet wasn't adequate for the amount of exercise I was doing, and that my body was naturally big. Still my coach didn't agree, but the season was over, so it didn't matter.

Looking back, I am still shocked as to the amount of gibing I received from coaches, friends and fellow rowers about the size of my gut, my bum, my legs and anything else that was deemed to be fat. It doesn't surprise me then when I hear of children who are starving themselves in order to make a team. While it is obviously wrong, it is still taking place everywhere, be it with rowing, football or athletics. A girl I know is a ballerina; she weighs only 45 kilos, yet I once remarked I needed to lose weight. Her response: 'Me too . . .' When asked why, she remarked, 'My instructor told me I do'. This girl is almost eighteen and, to me, is a prime example of body image being more important than health.

My experiences with rowing led me to coaching the fourteen-to-sixteen year age group, and it is a delight to be able to coach kids and not put any pressure on them to lose weight, but to rather fulfil the potential that their bodies have, without losing weight.

We've sported around with lots of sports and physical fitness. Ultimately, whatever you do, it's about being healthy, having fun, and relating to people. Sporting around is not about stressing out!

AN EMBARRASSING MOMENT

I WENT TO THE SCHOOL swimming-team try outs. I had made it in the team once before but I really wanted to go this time. I swam my best times ever. The next two days were full of anticipation, anxiety and excitement. When we got the results about who made it and who didn't, I was relieved to find out that I was selected in the team. The interschool carnival was massive, in a gigantic indoor heated pool that smelt strongly of chlorine. There were going to be heaps of schools there.

So the day came. I got ready, packed my bag and went to school. I had to be there earlier so I could catch the school bus. The bus was late but I still got to the sports complex in time for a quick warm up but I decided not to have one. I watched the other kids swim until about fifteen minutes before my race. Then I thought I would stretch and get ready for my swim.

I started to pull my pants down. It was then when I realised that I had forgotten my togs.

I didn't know what to do. I went over to the coordinator and told him the news. 'WHAT?' he replied sharply. 'You travelled

IT WAS THEN WHEN I REALISED THAT I HAD FORGOTTEN MY TOGS.

45 kilometres from school and forgot your togs?'

'Yes,' I replied weakly. We ran around asking if anyone had a pair of board shorts or togs, but everyone said no except for one kid called Daniel. He lent me a pair of togs and I ran down to the change room and put the togs on. They were pretty tight and I could just get them on, but they had to do.

I had to run straight to my race and swam so fast that I came first. I think it was because the togs were so tight and I wanted to get them off.

As soon as I was finished I ran straight from the pool to the change room and pulled the togs off. I thought that they had stretched a bit, but I didn't care. I was just glad they were off. I got dressed and walked up to where the group was sitting and gave Daniel back his togs. I went home and told Mum and Dad all about my exciting day.

The year before this at the same event I got lost in the enormous carpark with the trophy which we had just won.

I have now been once again selected in the team. I wonder what will happen this year?

DAVID MCGUINNESS 13

CHAPTER SIX

SCHOOL

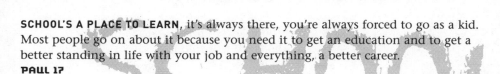

SCHOOL'S A PLACE TO LEARN, it's always there, you're always forced to go as a kid. Most people go on about it because you need it to get an education and to get a better standing in life with your job and everything, a better career.
PAUL 17

On a scale of one to ten how would you rate your life at school? School's not just a place where you go to learn and to get a good education so that you can be set for life. Many of the boys that you'll hear from in this chapter tell us that it's also about learning to be a boy and about conforming to certain expectations. Those who don't, or refuse to, find themselves in trouble. So school is often an unhappy or stressful place for many students—both boys and girls—as you'll learn from reading what they have to say. And, you'll see, one of the major problems for boys is BULLIES!

But some boys have no problem with school, especially if they have the support and respect of their friends. That seems to make all the difference. Check out what Beade and Derek have to say.

I FEEL MORE comfortable at school because I've got all my friends here and they stick up for me. Respect is a big thing for me, because all my friends respect me and I respect them. I give back what I'm given. If something happens to me, they're always there for me. But I haven't really got into any fights or anything.
BEADE 16

SCHOOL IS PRETTY COOL. I don't have any worries about going to school or my mates. There are people who I don't like and I just let them do their own thing. I do what I want around my mates because we don't care. Once me and my friend wore kilts to school and no one gave us a hard time. Everyone admired us for having the guts to do that.
DEREK 15

Boys thinking school

I'M A BOY who wants to go surfing and school is a waste of time. All it does is piss me off.
RAYMOND 16

I DON'T MIND SCHOOL but I know it is not going to help me in the long run. All the things that school has taught me I could have learnt myself at home. What I am going to do when I leave school has nothing to do with school now. Let's face it, if there weren't girls at school I don't know what I would do—that is probably the only thing that keeps me going.
RICK 16

I LEARN MORE from TV and the internet than school. The only reason I go is because I want to get a good job in the future.
GERARD 15

SCHOOL FOR ME is an unfortunate chore. I get up at 7 a.m., eat, go to school, come home, eat, sleep. That's on school weeks. In the holidays I work and I'm happy. My mum says I need a good education to get out of working at a fast food place and to get a real job.
BRIAN 15

THE TEACHERS ARE NICE and are very helpful when problems arise with school work but when it comes to other classmates picking on or annoying you they don't really care . . . Some of the other classmates are very immature and it is hard to concentrate when others are asking questions that have already been answered. The issue that does come up a lot in the boys' school is the idea about relationships and in particular the idea of everyone who is not deemed 'cool' is gay or a nerd.
SERG 16

The following guys are saying that school is different for guys and girls. What's it like for you? What kind of pressures and issues do both boys and girls face at school?

I THINK IT'S PROBABLY easier being a boy than a girl at school. It's a place where you get your identity, and a place where you learn how you'll be labelled in the future.
ADRIAN 16

BEING A GUY at the school is harder than being a girl at school because you get a lot of the smart alec people coming up to you and saying, 'Come on ya wanna fight?'. Also whenever I walk into the toilet, there's about ten guys in there having a smoke. I mean, how am I supposed to go when it's full of smoke? I know how every kid says they don't like getting up in the morning to go to school. I don't mind it but I live at least six kilometres from the school and I don't have a bike. They expect you to get there by 8.28 a.m. It's just stupid.
ROBERT 15

I THINK THAT AT SCHOOL boys have more pressure on them to do well at sports and things like that. Girls, though, have more pressure put on them to do well academically. I don't really have much to do with sport though because I am more an academic person and I do well with my school work. There is quite a lot of pressure on people who do tertiary entrance subjects as well. I do five tertiary entrance subjects myself. You sometimes think that these are the most important years of your

life because they will shape your future and you have to think about whether you want to go to uni or do something else.
LIAM 15

I'M CONSTANTLY COUNTING down the days until the end of the year. I find most of it interesting but I dislike it because of the other students. If there were a class with just me and my friends in it things would be great. The worst part about being a boy in school is that everyone thinks you are dumb. I have to put up with people calling me a nerd or a square or teasing me because I've not taken drugs or had alcohol.

My main problem would be trying to concentrate at school and coming here to learn. With the pressure of other students it isn't always easy. Then I would like to think that I didn't care what others thought, but I do. I'm always trying to do things to impress other people. Luckily for me I do well at school. My other problem at school is being able to do well while having a part-time job at a fast food place where I work about 20 hours a week. That is really hard. I always find myself doing my homework at midnight, before school, at recess and lunchtime. I have to choose whether or not to work next year, I'm thinking I shouldn't because it will be too much pressure.
BRIAN 15

Why isn't it cool for guys to be into study and to achieve well at school?

I THINK THAT the popular guys are the people who hate school. I think they should start liking school even if they might get pressured. School is a good place to go when you haven't got any bullies.
GLEN 13

SCHOOL IS NOT considered a safe place. In our lunch breaks there's nothing to do and because of this we have the lunchtime 'entertainment': people smashing (fighting) each other, which is fine if you're not on the receiving end of it all.
JOHN 15

I WAS EXPELLED FROM my other school for fighting but ever since I left my other school I've been quiet, trying to keep out of fighting, trying to get my life back. I've lost interest in school though. I keep telling myself that I better pull my weight,

do something about it. I think if there were some more people I got along with, I'd find it more interesting, I'd have a positive attitude about going to school. In the mornings I'd get up happier, I'd think, 'Yes, I'm going to meet some friends at school'. But every time I have to go to the same people, the same attitudes, that's why I think I've lost my self-esteem at this school. I'm from El Salvador and even though we get along with the Aussies it's still hard. Maybe it's because there's not much of my nationality here in Western Australia. I think that's why. But I've adjusted to a lot of things, I'm beginning to fit into their group. You try and do the things they do. Talk about the things they do, what they did on the weekend. So obviously you have to go to their parties. So I started doing that.
JULIO 17

I KEEP TELLING MYSELF THAT I BETTER PULL MY WEIGHT, DO SOMETHING ABOUT IT.

What makes someone popular at school? Does it depend on which group you're in? How does it all work?

I'VE NEVER ACTUALLY heard anyone say, 'That girl's a nice person because of her personality'. Around school, talk's mostly about their bodies.
PAUL 16

AT SCHOOL, girls have the pressure of staying clean, i.e. being a virgin.
HABEEB 15

 Why do you think that some boys feel the need to talk about girls' bodies in this way? Do girls talk about boys' bodies in this way?

'GIRL AT SCHOOL', BEN GERRARD 17

What girls say about guys at school

BEING A GIRL at school is hard as guys tease you about the size of your body, and when you get your period they say, 'Oh is it that time of the month?'.
NICOLE 15

 Are periods a problem for girls or is it the boys who have the real problem with girls' periods?

THE MAIN ISSUE FOR BOYS IS TO GET SEX AND ALSO BE COOL AND PARTY.

SAYING SOMETHING WRONG in class for a female can be embarrassing because all the boys tease and laugh. It's all right for boys to say something wrong because everyone accepts that most boys are just immature.
SIMONE 15

 Are guys really that immature or do they feel they have to act that way to prove something?

AS A GIRL I AM pressured by boys for sex. For boys the number one issue is 'sex from girls'! Fitting into the group and being cool is the main issue for girls, and the main issue for boys is to get sex and also be cool and party.
EVELINA 16

I HATE THE WAY that in school if a boy fucks a girl, he's just a typical male but if a girl has sex she's the biggest slut around. If a boy does anything he's a hero, if a girl does, she's a whore. It's really unfair.
JANE 14

IT'S OKAY BEING an Aboriginal girl at school but we have to deal with being called a slut, being treated like shit. It's not just who's going out with who but who got with who.
CATHY 15

FRIENDS: MATTHEW, LAURA, ADAM, AARON, AND MICHAEL

Why are decisions about having sex a pressure rather than a choice? What is it that guys have to prove through saying that they've had sex with girls? Why does it seem to be okay for guys to get with girls but it doesn't work the other way?

SCHOOL IS SUPPOSED to be a time for learning but we turn lunch and recess into a drug period. The toilets are forever smelling of smoke and your friends are in there saying, 'Come have a drag, it won't kill', when really it does. Peer pressure is why most of us smoke pot, smoke cigarettes, take a variety of different drugs etc. You can just about say that every teenager is having under-age sex, taking illegal drugs and smoking cigarettes.
SARAH 15

THE BOYS, they're too busy discussing what alcohol they're going to drink on the weekend, how they're going to get it, where they're going to drink it etc.
MARIA 16

Why do drugs, drink and smokes go to school?

GIRL LIFE AT SCHOOL SUCKS. My school is so sexist. People pick guys to do all the jobs and to get out of class. Also, it's considered cool for guys to yell out and to interrupt and not do work but it's not all right for girls. The bitchiness and moodiness of the females is evident in the never-ending bitch fights as well as their extreme edginess. Also the pressure put on girls to comply to society's standards, we are expected to go on a never-ending diet, always look thin yet exercise is considered 'uncool'. The pressure to keep up with fashion brought my bank account from $1100 to $29 in two years!
STEPHANIE 14

I HATE HOW MALE teachers at school patronise the girls and get away with it. Because they're adults. Democracy is dead, and I'm not happy. Boys have it easy. Being a chick sucks. If you don't participate in sport, boys reckon you've got your period and they're so immature about everything. I can't do automotive workshop because I'm a chick and it really sucks. I have lots of male friends though. They do treat me well. I think guys treat me with more respect than other chicks 'cause I don't let people walk all over me.
DANA 15

Bitching, bullying, fighting—are they all about the same things? Don't boys bitch too?

Why are some subjects seen to be more appropriate for boys or girls?

I WISH I WAS A boy so I could hang around and muck around without being called butch.
LEONA 16

So there's also pressure on girls at school. Maybe it's time for guys to break the rules about how guys treat girls. Think about the ways both guys and girls could break out of the gender straitjackets?

Guys talk teachers

What makes a good teacher? Have a read of what these guys have to say.

GOOD TEACHERS act like friends, not just teachers.
ABDU 16

I GET ALONG WELL with mostly teachers who are interested in my Aboriginal background and where I can ask them questions about their background as well. Miss X is a really excellent example of that. She wants to know what's wrong when I'm having a bad day. So I talk to her all the time. She really understands what it's like for a black person. She's white and she's still learning and she's got a lot to learn, but she's really interested. I think she thinks the way indigenous people teach and look at things is a good way of teaching and understanding people.

When Miss X has a bad day I ask her about it and she has a better day, she really does. A few weeks ago she had a whole week full of bad days. I think something personal happened at home but I had a talk to her about it and she was okay that day. We hug sometimes. We hugged one time and this teacher said, 'You know you can get into big trouble because of that'. But I love giving teachers hugs. Miss X hugs all of us students. I think other teachers are jealous or they just don't like it because teaching is just a job for them.
BEADE 17

SOME TEACHERS JUST teach and want to get it over and done with. Some of them would be better suited in a police station than a school.
SIMON 13

> SHE REALLY UNDERSTANDS WHAT IT'S LIKE FOR A BLACK PERSON.

'SHE'S A PROSTITUTE, ALL SHE NEEDS IS GOOD SEX WITH A MAN'

WHEN WE WERE ON one of those student council camps we had a fake student council meeting. Someone brought up the topic of hair and I stood up straight away and said, 'You know, instead of making two different rules for boys and girls, why don't we just have one rule to tie it up in a ponytail?'. A male teacher stood up straight away and said, 'If you're going to have long hair and you're going to put it up in a ponytail, obviously you've got something wrong with your head, obviously you're gay or something like that'. And this teacher said it outright and I suppose that's how the problem starts with boys and girls being set apart.

SHAUN 16

WE HAD A SCHOOL counsellor who was a very right-wing conservative sort of woman. I remember once going to see her about something that was happening at home. I mentioned in passing that I was gay and she goes, 'This is what you've come to see me about!'. I said no but she went on to ask, 'Are you really gay?'. She recommended me going to see priests and confessing my sins. Her words were, 'You really should go to confession'. I laughed and said, 'Look I have to go to class now, I've got to go'. I cracked up laughing when I walked out of there.

LUCIANO 19

SOME GUYS THINK, 'I'm a big tough man, I'm going to make a woman teacher cry, we've got an upper hand, let's make her feel like crap'. Just to show off in front of their mates.

GLENN 16

WE HAD THIS TEACHER who taught us that women do have a right to live freely just as men do, to speak freely just as men do, to work freely just as men do. Whatever issues there may be, homosexuality, equality, women's issues, we need to be made aware of them. There was mixed reaction to her from the guys. Some had a knee-jerk reaction because she was saying something that they wouldn't have heard before or weren't used to hearing. Instead of actually debating the issues with her, behind her back they would say things like, 'She's a slut or frigid or a lesbian. She's a prostitute, all she needs is good sex with a man', things like that. The stupid thing was they were so adamant that she had a good body but was so strong and wouldn't tolerate abuse from any students. So it was just a way of dealing with feeling threatened. You could see inside of them it was making inroads, but I think with peer group pressure, they felt they couldn't voice their opinion. They would've been condemned by others.

CHRISTIAN 22

What do you learn at school?

What are you learning at school and how relevant is it to your lives? Let's see what some guys think about 'getting educated'.

I DO THINK THAT schools are too much about learning facts and using formulas and not enough about really thinking.
GLYNN 16

I WASN'T GIVEN the chance to explore as much as what I wanted to. I didn't know that there were so many different cultures around the world and that those different cultures lived with different morals and different ideas. I did like the environment that the school gave the students, but some people involved in the hierarchy were a little bit narrow-minded and very fixed in their ways and didn't want to step outside the nine dots. If I was to challenge a teacher, I was generally shut off before I was given the chance to really engage in a proper discussion about issues like homosexuality, being a boy, individuality, sex. I got the impression that teachers weren't comfortable talking about these things and therefore in turn weren't capable of giving me any direction.
CHRISTIAN 22

YOU NEED TO GET TAUGHT SEX EDUCATION AT A YOUNGER AGE

WE NEED TO LEARN ABOUT MENTAL ILLNESS!

WE HAVE MENTAL ILLNESS in my family and I've noticed that most people are really ignorant about it and I'd love to see that taught in schools. My brother's got schizophrenia and my mum's got a mild depression, and I've never heard anything about mental illness in my whole time at school. There definitely should be because even to talk about it is shocking and that's one of the reasons I can't talk about it at school.
MAX 16

SEX EDUCATION

I THINK YOU NEED to get taught sex education at a younger age because often by the time guys actually get taught about it, a lot of people have already experienced it.
JOSH 15

I THINK A LOT of guys can't handle talking about girls' periods so they just act as if something's funny. The same with wet dreams. Everyone just starts laughing and won't take the teacher seriously. Maybe they're escaping reality. Just being little kids. But I think the teachers sometimes found it more uncomfortable than we did. With contraception, the teacher would bring a big box of everything, scaring the hell out of us, saying how easy it is to get a sexually transmitted disease or to get a girl pregnant.
MIKE 17

IN SEX EDUCATION boys start laughing and snorting.
PETER 14

Why do you think some guys laugh, snort and act 'immature' during sex education? Do you think they're trying to cover up other feelings? What could those feelings be? What could they do instead in order to handle those feelings?

Reading and writing at school

I HATED READING OUT ALOUD. Whenever the class was taking it in turns to read from a novel, I'd be dreading it when it was my turn. I would start getting nervous for some reason, having all the attention on me. Most of the time I just kept thinking, 'Please, please, please may I not have to read. Please don't make me have to read.' Most of the time it worked! I don't think I like the sound of my own voice and having everyone focussed on me, even though it's not on me because everyone has still got their heads in their books and they're following along with you. It was weird that I felt a lot more comfortable doing a presentation because I can just stand up there with a few notes and speak and it feels a lot more comfortable.
MIKE 17

READING ISN'T SEEN as masculine. Reading a book is seen by some people as gay.
MARIO 16

> I WOULD START GETTING NERVOUS FOR SOME REASON, HAVING ALL THE ATTENTION ON ME.

Do you think that the stuff you are given to read at school is relevant?
How did you get a hold of this book? Why are you reading it?

School cultures

IT'S ALWAYS THE SAME guys getting the
sports awards. At our school it's really
unfair because unless you play sport and
unless you're all macho then no one knows
you. I think they're probably very narrow-
minded people if all they all think about is
sports.
ROB 16

THIS STUFFED UP SCHOOL spends so much
money on its sporting facilities that drama
and other classes end up with substandard
equipment.
TROY 16

STEVEN HODGE AT SCHOOL

What's important in your school culture? Why do you think some schools
place so much emphasis on sport? Are drama, art, debating, writers'
clubs etc. given equal attention?

We had a black South African student who
had dreadlocks when he first came to our
school. He was told he wasn't allowed to
have dreadlocks so he had to shave it.

When school rules just beg to be broken!

There are some important rules that schools need to have in order to promote learning, equity, a hassle-free and socially just environment that you can feel safe and strong in. What do you think are useful rules and what would you think are rules begging to be broken?

SCHOOL IS ALL RIGHT for me but lately it's getting shit because of the compulsory uniforms. They put up a barbwire fence that goes all around the school like a prison. I'm holding my girlfriend's hand or hugging her and a teacher would walk past and say, 'Split up. Not at school please.' I mean c'mon it's recess and lunch, our break from school work and you can't even spend time with your girlfriend. It's bullshit!
GUY 16

I COULDN'T EVEN HAVE an earring because I was a boy. If I did wear one, I'd have to cover it up with a bandaid. I think it's just plain sexism because we're boys. Girls are allowed to have one earring in each earlobe. Also, you couldn't have necklaces unless it was a religious symbol.

We had a black South African student who had dreadlocks when he first came to our school. He was told he wasn't allowed to have dreadlocks so he had to shave it. He saw it as a racist thing. He was saying that he should be able to have dreadlocks because of the way his hair is and his culture.

I also got into heaps of trouble over my green hair. I got suspended for it. It was the first day back at school. In the holidays I had dyed my hair green but it was partly blond as well. So there was only a little bit of green left when I came to school. In the first five minutes of the first lesson, this teacher sent me straight over to the front office to speak to the principal about my hair. He said that I was going to be suspended for three days. They rang up mum and she gave them an earful. She said that it's just so ridiculous to exclude me from learning because of the colour of my hair. It would be like saying I'm not going to let your kid learn because he's black. So I stayed home on suspension and mum wrote many letters of complaint just saying how ridiculous she thought it was. Things like that just turn you off school. It makes you think how ridiculous and pointless it is to try and control people. If you try and complain to the teachers, they just say, 'Hey I don't write the rules'.
MIKE 17

THERE HAVE TO BE RULES about piercings and rings so people don't have metal all over their face.
ZACH 14

Getting into school politics

So there are some things guys would like to change about school. Guys can be leaders with a strong sense of determination and desire to bring about these changes. But it can sometimes feel like banging your head against a brick wall if your school does not support or only pays lip service to students having a voice. But it is important to remember that dreaming of a better world is the first step to positive action.

NOW I'M PRESIDENT of the SRC I'm determined to make things different for students. I really want to make an effort so that students can actually have a say in how they want to learn and how their school is run. I think it's really good being a leader. I think I'm more of a leader than a follower. It's really good doing something about problems. When people come to you with a lot of problems and a lot of issues and they just throw them at you, you have to sort through what's rubbish and what's accomplishable, make decisions and then talk about how you're going to do it, and then you go out and do it. You delegate other people to do some roles and you know everything that's happening.
JOHNNY 17

MANY BELIEVE YOUNG people are not interested in politics. I think this is nonsensical. Young people want the opportunity to help and make their lives productive. Last year I desperately tried to represent young gay and lesbian people at a political convention. I mailed the convention's coordinator so many times but received no reply. I am a member of Amnesty International and the Australian Conservation Foundation. I'm also a union delegate at my workplace. At school I was involved in the SRC and tried my best to eliminate homophobia. I advocated for GLBT [gay, lesbian, bisexual, transgender] books to be placed in the library and to have seminars on homophobia.
JONARD 18

I WAS BOOTED OFF my student council. I think it was the fact that they thought I was going to be a little bit more daring than other people, that I was going to challenge them in a lot of things that they were teaching. Whether I was a councillor or not I was still going to do it. By having a student councillor's badge I don't think that I would have thought I was any better or any higher or had any authority over other students, but I think that's what the teachers anticipated and that this status would give me too much influence over other students. So if Christian was wearing this badge and he was to challenge the teachers then it would be a ticket for the others to jump on the bandwagon and challenge as well.
CHRISTIAN 22

Fitting in or pushed out?

Bullying at school

BEING A BOY at school you are sometimes faced with bullies.

ALAN 16

I DON'T GET PICKED ON that much anymore at school. In primary school I was the one the so called cool guys would make fun of and hit. Once when I was alone with one of these guys I asked him why he did it and he said that you were supposed to act like that at school. When I think about this I realise that he was in fact the weaker of us because he couldn't be himself. He was one of the leaders and could have made a difference to how other people behaved. Other people would be mean, so their group would say how cool it was. I think being mean to people is the easy way out, so that is why people take it. If it was cool to be nice then they would be nice. I think a lot of the so called losers are strong because they don't just follow the crowd. They can be themselves and do what they want to do, not what the people around them want to do.

SHANE 13

I GET PICKED ON because I sing. The guys call me Poofter and Gay Boy because it's just something that boys don't usually do. The girls don't hassle me. They always come up to me and congratulate me if I sing well. I'm really good friends with the

FRANKIE FANTASIA (PHOTO COURTESY THE LOOK STUDIO)

girls. And that's another reason why the boys hassle me as well. Because they can't really socialise with the girls. They are really immature and rude to them all the time. Sometimes it gets me down but I tell myself I'm a bigger person. Be strong and ignore it. School is only a small part of your life. When you get older you won't have to see them ever again if you choose not to. Boost your self-esteem and continue what you're doing like singing or ballet. And if you are gay, you're a stronger person than anyone bullying you. To the bullies: everyone else is a stronger person than you. You're only doing it to bring your self-esteem up and ours down so give up.

JACOB 15

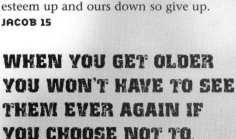

WHEN YOU GET OLDER YOU WON'T HAVE TO SEE THEM EVER AGAIN IF YOU CHOOSE NOT TO.

THEY TEASE ME because of my pacemaker. I told them they should thank their lucky stars that they haven't got one. I can't do most things that they can. Contact sports, drugs, well I wouldn't want to do that anyway. I can't drink much alcohol, one beer is the limit when I'm older, and I can't smoke, but I don't want to do that either. And it's my glasses too. They tease me about them and push me around. They just call me Battery Boy, Little Heart, Dead Heart. If I get hit, the pacemaker can get dislodged and then I could die. Sometimes they punch me. I get chest pains sometimes. My friends stick up for me, they help me, and make them stop.
AARON 13

So students who don't fit in at school are often given a hard time and pushed out. Schools should be places where boys and girls can express themselves in a whole range of respectful ways. Let's face it. Not all boys are the same!.

Maybe it's just that they feel they have to live up to certain expectations about how typical guys should act and think in order to avoid being pushed out. Before reading the following boys' experiences and opinions, think about what makes someone at school 'different':

- *The way they talk.*
- *Their sexuality.*
- *The way they look.*
- *What they say.*
- *Their disability.*
- *That they don't like sport or do what most guys like to do.*
- *Their cultural or racial background.*

Who decides what is a typical or 'normal' way of behaving for a guy at your school? Who sets the rules for judging these kinds of things? Read what Beade and other boys have to say about this.

Students who don't fit in

THERE'S THIS ONE KID, Adrian, who's Greek and doesn't really fit in well. I think he's a pretty quiet person and soft-hearted. He always sits by himself but one day, my friends and I asked him if he wanted to sit with us and eat lunch, so he did. We asked how his weekend was and he actually had a bit of a smile on his face. Now if I see him by himself I'll go sit next to him and talk to him.

Everyone thinks that he's a nerd. When he did his oral in class, someone laughed and he got really hurt by that so he went out of the classroom and cried. I reckon they laughed because they were trying to be cool in front of their friends, egging each other on, 'I bet you can't make him cry'. I just thought they were idiots for doing that.

In primary school I thought I had to be cool to be in a group of friends. If I saw someone sitting by themselves it would be cool to call them names. But in high school I just sort of go over and sit with them and talk to them so they don't feel left out. My mum always says, 'Don't treat other people how you wouldn't like to be treated', and I wouldn't like to be treated like that.

BEADE 16

I LIVE IN A BEAUTIFUL SUBURB, nice parks, great clean beaches, nice people, you get the picture? The greater population of boys in my year surf and body-board. I'm lucky I can body-board, but if you can't you're in big trouble. You'll get left out of conversations.

FRANK 15

'BEING COOL', MAXO 17

'Don't treat other people how you wouldn't like to be treated'

RACISM PUSHES YOU OUT!

AS A MALAYSIAN Chinese Australian it's hard for me to make good friends here. It could be because I'm Asian and it causes people to have a different view point about me. Or it could be because I am not as 'cool' as some of them. I have been trying to figure out for the past nine months why people don't seem to give a damn about me. It could also be due to the fact that I'm not very good in soccer, which the group of guys I am with are very good at. Or it could simply be just me—I might be too sensitive and over-reacting. It hurts when you don't get invited to parties or even get told that a party was on. I don't know how long it's going to take before I finally settle in. It sucks, and it's pathetic. I wish my own good friends from Malaysia were here. They are the people whom I can truly call 'friends'. Not the boys here. All I want is a bit of respect, attention and being treated as a newcomer who needs help in settling in. I wish they could see how badly I need friends. I am so lonely and bored.
SENG 15

I'M GERMAN, my dad's German, my mum's an Aussie. At school I get people calling me Nazi Boy and writing these symbols on their hand. I guess it annoys me but I'm used to it.
MARTIN 13

RACISM'S JUST one of the main problems. You may not see it straight away but it's hidden. There's tension between the Indigenous boys like me and the white boys, but it's hidden. They don't realise it but it's there.
NIGEL 17

MORE THAN HALF the fights usually involve an Indigenous person against a white person. Racism is what starts fights. Last week I wasn't at school but I've heard that some kids came into the school ground. They were Grade 12 students, non–Indigenous and from another school. They said that they could take on any black fella from X High. So they started pushing guys around and cops broke it up.
BEADE 17

AT SCHOOL I GET PEOPLE CALLING ME NAZI BOY AND WRITING THESE SYMBOLS ON THEIR HAND.

No room for disabilities?

I HAVE NFI [neurofibromatosis type 1], dyspraxia and epilepsy. I have trouble learning new things, I can't read very well and have trouble writing things down. I get frustrated and sometimes I can lose my temper. I'm not very good at things like swimming and sport and games although I like to have a go at things. I can't ride a bike properly. I have aides that help me with most of my work. The school has arranged a visiting teacher to come and do extra work with me especially with reading. Most of the time I get on pretty well with the other students. I don't really get teased or bullied very often. If I do I usually try to ignore it. I have been bullied in the past.

Suggestions if you're being bullied:

▶ Don't hit or argue back.

▶ Don't argue with your teachers and try to explain your side.

▶ Try and make a group of friends you can rely on and stay with them, you are less likely to be teased in a group.

▶ If you have a peer support person, you can seek them out.

▶ Use the library or computer rooms if you can at break times.

▶ Talk to a teacher or other adult if there is a problem, find a teacher who will listen to you.

▶ Try to do an activity outside school to make other friends.

▶ Try not to get angry and lose your temper.

TIM HARRISON 14

TIM HARRISON 14

OTHER BOYS are usually interested in the wheelchair, how fast it can go and what the buttons do. I get a bit annoyed with them because I have to keep answering questions. I get a bit sick of it.
SAM 16

EVERYONE TEASES GIRLS with disabilities. There's two girls who just came recently and they wave to me and I'm just being nice to them. But you get people that think they're dumb and treat them dumb. They tease them and keep them out of their groups.
DANIEL 14

I'VE GOT ARTHRITIS in my joints from my waist down and it's so hard for me to walk and I have to take medication. I'm very lucky to have good friends. I used to get teased about my disability and they'd say, 'Oh, here comes the retard', and sometimes I'd get scared and just try to ignore them. One of the bullies actually pissed on me and my friend at the pool.

Some guys think teasing makes them happy but in the end they're going to look back and say, 'What have I done?'. I don't care if they tease me about sport and if they're going to do that it just shows that they're mindless people who don't care about other people's disabilities and what's going on in their head. When I had to wear a knee brace over one of my knees, they started teasing me and laughing. At one point I started packing up and just walking out of school but then I noticed that that's not a very positive attitude and it's just giving them what they want. So I thought the positive thing to do was just to go on with what I'm doing, just lock them out and just get on with how I feel and everything.

In Grade 6 my teacher used to call me ferret legs. I found that very distressing. I just picked up my bag, walked out of class and said to her, 'I don't have to take this', and walked all the way home. I had to have the rest of that entire week off school because I couldn't just go back there. I remember the day I had to go back to a meeting with her and the principal, and the principal was actually on her side. She didn't even let me give my side of the story and I believe that was because I walked out and they couldn't see how distressed I was.
NICK 13

AT ONE POINT I STARTED PACKING UP AND JUST WALKING OUT OF SCHOOL BUT THEN I NOTICED THAT THAT'S NOT A VERY POSITIVE ATTITUDE AND IT'S JUST GIVING THEM WHAT THEY WANT.

Homophobia pushes you out

MY SCHOOL'S CALLED the faggot school or gay school by guys from other schools on the buses because we're all guys.
WAYNE 16

I REALLY LIKE the idea of a support group because gay kids are alienated at their school. It's such a bad idea for a person to be alone, to be isolated.
JONARD 18

THE TYPICAL WALK down the hallway and there'd be, 'Stick your arses to the wall', and all that sort of stuff. I was told that I should go to a poofter school because I didn't belong there. That I should 'fucking get out' like I'm 'just a faggot'. Most of them clung to the strict stereotypes that if you're a homosexual male then you just want to have sex with every other male around the place, and that is all you do.
XANDER 19

I WENT TO A Catholic boys' school in the Philippines. I had two gay teachers who were already out so they helped us with gay issues. I believe that in my school there were twenty openly gay people. There's a tradition in the Philippines, a cultural tradition which is not a Western one, of accepting people who cross-dress or who are not male or not female. I thought that Australia was a Western country and more tolerant than my country which is an Asian country.

Some Australians believe that Asian countries are backward, so conservative. Yet this is Australia where one cannot act gay or else he or she will be discriminated against. So in my first year in an Australian school, somebody threw a watermelon at me, and I told the teacher who said, 'Well you have to tolerate those people'. It's just funny that I'm supposed to tolerate them, which I did. In one of my geography classes this one particular guy threw papers at me so often and I told the teacher, who I think was very homophobic. He argued that he did not see it happen, therefore he wasn't going to do anything about that.

I just didn't want to go to high school because of homophobia. Like at one time I just cried in front of the room because my maths teacher was a homophobic person. There were some students who made fun of me. I argued that you should understand people who are gay, you should not make judgments. They alienated me in my maths class, they totally alienated me and I cried. I wrote a letter to the two boys, not condemning them, but it was me wanting them to better understand gay people.

I left that school because of the harassment, I did distance education.
JONARD 18

Why do boys fight?

BOYS WHO BULLY have small penises, and they're just trying to make themselves look big, that's my theory. I just don't see the point of fighting, even if you win, you're still going to get hurt, it's easier just to stay on everyone's side. If you want to fight someone, do it yourself, don't call in heaps of your mates to do it. I've always been fascinated with how people who have to do something have to have everybody stand there.
STEPHEN 15

THEY'RE TRYING to prove that they own the school. They fight over girls, they fight over who's better, Australians or wogs. One guy told me my mum was from another country and for her to go back to her country. They try to get a reputation, like if you fight and you win the fight everyone reckons you're hard and you're cool even if you're an idiot. Girls have fights too. They start scratching and pulling hair. When boys fight, girls just stand back and watch, but when girls fight the boys go mental. They start running around and getting the girls and pushing them into the other girls.

Bullies can't look at themselves to see how they look, they just like bagging out other people. Most of the popular people pick on the least popular people. If you're popular you reckon you're good in everything, but I'd like to see a couple of popular people get bullied and see how they felt. They would probably burst because they're not used to it but they'd see how the other people feel.

Bullies release their stress on other people by bullying and hitting them. For example, some guys spend all their money on cigarettes and then they can't buy anything to eat and they hassle others. But if you don't smoke you don't have to buy cigarettes and you can buy yourself food.
PETER 14

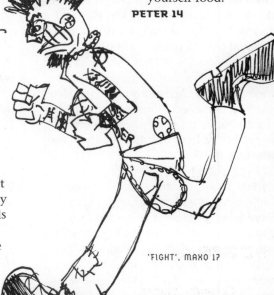

'FIGHT', MAXO 17

FIGHTING'S NOT COOL

YOU GOT TO TRY to get through to their heads, and tell them you're not a wus, you're not a little woozy if you don't hit a guy. You hear people saying the bigger man just walks away. It's harder to walk away from a fight. I think it's got to do with the people who influence you to fight. Don't bag a guy, don't exclude him from things like going out places if he has refused to fight. Somehow you've just got to get his friends to believe that fighting is not cool. It's cool to walk away. If you walk away, you're not a gig, you're not scared, you're not chicken shit. You just got to get it into their head you're stronger because it's harder to walk away than to swing a punch.
NIGEL 17

If you walk away, you're not a gig, you're not scared, you're not chicken shit.

Dealing with bullies

I JUST FEEL SORRY for bullies. They try and put you down, I just walk it out. My mum makes me strong. She always pushes me to get on with my life or come back with a smart comment that'll keep them quiet. My mum's always been there for me, so I'm really happy that she has stuck by me but the things that bullies have done are really cruel and I don't really respect them for that. People are getting bashed because they're living their lives well and bullies can't really respect that.
NATHAN 13

MY GRANDMOTHER DIED and I got teased about it. If you're getting harassed and bullied, talk to people, you've just got to let it out. I kept telling my mum, and then I'd go into the bedroom and cry a bit.
GLENN 16

Have you noticed the different roles guys play when bullying's happening at school? If the schoolyard or classroom was a stage and you had to direct your actors, you'd probably cast them in three types of roles: the bully, the target, and the bystander—other students looking on, feeling lots of feelings but not sure what to do about it, how to react. This group of people might sometimes have been called 'innocent bystanders'. But is it really that 'innocent' to watch someone getting picked on, hurt and intimidated and not do anything about it? What are the different feelings that could be going on inside them? Why don't bystanders stop the bullying? What happens if they do?

Read what the following guys have written about these three roles in a bullying situation and think about the roles you've taken at school: the bully, the bullied and the bystander. You may have been in more than one. Think about the situations in which you were in a different role. Do you think that those who are the bystanders or bullied can become bullies? Why would they? Do you think the bullies can also be bystanders and bullied? Why?

THE 'INNOCENT' BYSTANDER: 'AN AVERAGE AUSTRALIAN GUY'

I CONSIDER MYSELF to be an average Australian guy. I do not want to re-create the stereotype, but I do a lot of things society considers 'normal' or 'expected'. I play football in the winter, a bit of tennis or cricket in the summer. I have a girlfriend and enjoy spending time with my family and 'mates'.

During my years at secondary college, I never really thought of myself as someone who judges

HE WALKED IN A VERY 'GIRLIE' MANNER AND ALWAYS SPOKE WITH A LISP.

others or goes out of their way to put others down.

However, when I came across a gay student just one year younger than me, I discovered a dark part of me I did not know existed.

Let me begin by describing the situation. He was a short, stumpy character who always dressed up in business suits on 'free dress days'. I thought he could be gay, but did not really care. However, on one occasion, he came to school in leather pants, a pink shirt and sporting a bandanna. He walked in a very 'girlie' manner and always spoke with a lisp.

I could not understand why this person, this so called 'male', would act the way he did. It was beyond my comprehension. I found myself sharing the same views with people who I had always thought were mean and close minded. I thought he was weird and although I did feel sorry for him because of the crap he was getting from other guys, I was afraid to talk to him as my male friends might think that *I* was gay or was supporting his actions. It is such a powerful word . . . 'gay'. I began to realise that all I had done to create my own identity could be destroyed in a second, simply by being called one single word. It is shocking, but it is very true.

I chose to stay away from this person and go on with my own life. He left school and officially 'came out' about his sexuality and now when I think about it, I can sit back and say 'good for him'.

Why do I have such a different view?

I CHOSE TO STAY AWAY FROM THIS PERSON AND GO ON WITH MY OWN LIFE.

Education and experience are the answers. Secondary school is so isolated and confined. Everyone almost knows everyone, so if word comes out that someone is gay, then that is the 'goss' for the next week, or the week after, or the rest of the year. We can be so cruel. But many boys like myself did it to survive in our own social groups. Sharing a common view point and putting another person down only makes the unity of the group stronger. Sad but true.

University is a different story. It is a fruit salad of different cultures, sexual preferences and views. In most cases you no longer have the security of your old social group and so you begin to accept people for who they are (not joining together to bully them or watch them being bullied and doing nothing about it).

I must admit that I still feel strange if I see two men hold hands or kiss etc., but is that their problem or mine?

DAVID VAN PELT 18

THEY SKIN THEIR VICTIMS SLOWLY AND POUR CITRUS JUICE OVER THEIR WOUNDS TO MAKE THE AGONY MORE EXCRUCIATING.

THE BULLY: 'A CONFESSION'

I'M A MURDERER. I thirst for blood and I love to see slashed skin, with raw flesh exposed. The more cuts, the more bruises, the better.

I choose my victims at random although there are times when I zero in on one particular individual. At times when I feel the urge to slash someone's throat, I take hold of my weapon and gnash my teeth in frustration, trying to contain the urge to lunge forward and mercilessly reduce that someone into tiny pieces of meat. But more often than not, I search for my prey and follow the dictates of my little demons. I don't stop until I see the blood flowing in my hands. It shames me.

I am not the only murderer I know. I am a bona fide member of a murderous group, which has affiliates all over the school. I tried to avoid such people but ended up being associated with them without even noticing it. I have discovered, to my dismay, that everywhere I go they haunt me, coaxing me to feel the pleasure of dispatching someone to eternity's flames. Not long after I joined them, I belonged to them. By then I was a full-fledged killer who had mutilated a few of my victims.

There are many vicious and murderous souls lurking out there under different pretences. They skin their victims slowly and pour citrus juice over their wounds to make the agony more excruciating. Then they slice the flesh neatly, plucking every exposed vein slowly in the presence of other murderers, because an act such as this is never fulfilling enough unless it is witnessed by other bloodthirsty monsters. I should know, because I have done it and I have witnessed others do it.

I know most of you are butchers too. Like me, you have slaughtered with every lie you tell to make someone look bad, with every snippet of gossip you spread, whether true or untrue, with every judgment you pass on someone, with every curse that escapes your lips, foul and filthy, with every outburst of hurtful words, with every violent action to hurt another and with every criticism that spells destruction for another. Your tongue has committed murder for you, the same way it has turned me into a maniac, running to and fro, hunting for the next target.

But in the process of committing murder, I too have died. For as I strip someone else of his dignity in front of everybody else, I also cast away my dignity. As I bury them deep in the bowels of the earth, so did I banish my soul. My murders were also suicidal since it made others murder me viciously in retaliation.

This is what it's like for me and everyone else growing in their adolescent years. Not just guys, but girls also. A school is a giant lion pit, filled with savage animals ready to swallow you up. If you're weak and don't fight back you'll be killed along with the rest of the other 'losers', as we like to call the less popular beings.

Every day I remember and repent over all the people I have murdered mercilessly, all the people I have butchered and tortured to the point where they felt existence on earth was of zero value. I feel ashamed that at that time when I was inflicting pain on someone else, I felt no remorse whatsoever. To be accepted you have to be just like everybody else, thus you have to degrade and murder. Everyone wants to fit in. I guess it's all about conformity.

As I strive to survive in a murderous school society, I confess my murderous intent.

NICHOLAS 14

TO BE ACCEPTED YOU HAVE TO BE JUST LIKE EVERYBODY ELSE, THUS YOU HAVE TO DEGRADE AND MURDER.

THE TARGET: 'NOT FAIR'

I put on my school uniform
And make haste to get to band,
I'm running late
But
As usual, am left to set up the percussion
instruments
AGAIN.

I sit in school,
Annoying classmates disrupt my
concentration
One scribbles messily on my book
Whilst another steals a pen.

I'm fed up with the constant chant
'Don't have a teary Hodgey'
But am torn by the unfairness of it all
When the teacher's back is turned
They all turn . . .
On me.

STEVEN HODGE AND JACQUI BLANEY

At lunchtime,
It is just the same
Cruel words they chase me around
'Ballet Boy' and 'Faggot'
How I wish it would go away.

Why when I dance
Do they not understand
I work so hard; but not at football
Which makes you a man?

STEVEN HODGE 13

STEVEN HODGE

CHAPTER SEVEN
FAMILIES

I'VE GOT A GOOD FAMILY. I really love my mum, love my dad and my sister. Now and then we have our ups and downs but we're still a family.
WAYNE 16

I DO STUPID impersonations and voices. Like when my mum makes a comment I take the mickey out of her. I like taking the mickey out of my parents and I make them look stupid and I like being laughed at. I guess I'm a bit of an attention-seeker sometimes.
TOM 16

FOR ME, GROWING UP is quite easy and without hiccups since I've got great parents and an okay brother. I had no trouble at school even though I came from Poland. My mum and dad never hit us but they are quite strict and I wasn't allowed to do things my friends were allowed to do, but now that's all changed. My brother and I get along quite well most of the time but occasionally we get into a fight. My brother and I are quite close to our parents

THE HODGE FAMILY

and enjoy their company. Dad plays soccer and tennis with us and Mum helps us with homework when we need it and takes us places. But our parents have some flaws. Dad has a demanding job and is away a lot and Mum is a neatness freak.

Mum and Dad say that we are spoilt but I don't think so. One of the many things my parents have taught me is responsibility and to do my best at school. So far I have achieved this. I think that over the past year I have matured a lot, since sometimes we have to stay alone till 9 p.m. My father has urged me to play sport for as long as I remember, so now I like most sports and am pretty good at them.
RAFAL BACAJEWSKI 13

I'VE JUST BEEN brought up in a household where I can feel comfortable talking about almost anything, which makes me feel comfortable talking about anything with other students or with other adults or teachers.
MICHAEL 13

I'M VERY OPEN with my parents. A lot of kids lie to their parents all the time, but I've never lied to my parents.
JACOB 15

I REALISED I WAS GAY about two years ago and told my friends almost straight away as it didn't much worry me. My parents I haven't told yet for two reasons. The first is that the pragmatic part of my brain told me it would probably be best if I waited till I'd moved out of home in case they didn't take it too well. The second is that it annoys me that people automatically assume that their child is straight and I prefer to let them figure out for themselves that they'd assumed wrongly in order to teach them a little lesson about preconceptions.
KEVIN 17

THE WHOLE THING about being gay is that you lie to your parents, but when you're gay and disabled they know where you're going, they know where you're at, they know who your friends are, they know everything because you have no privacy, so I just realised that my mum's not stupid and she was bound to find out so I told her.
TONY 24

They want me to do some housework, stuff that an able-bodied person would do.

MUM AND DAD want me to be a good person and smart and all that but they know not to pressure me and constantly hassle me about it. Like they'll go on their spiel, but then they'll stop and just let me go. They want me to do some housework, stuff that an able-bodied person would do. I do it how they would do it. They'll make me do it because I can stand up but I can't walk. There are certain things I can't do like crawl up on a roof.
MARC 18

I GO OUT with my friends but my parents trust me. I've seen some people who have been enclosed by their parents and when they finally get that one bit of freedom it's like, 'Wow, look at all this freedom, look what they do', and then they do something really stupid that they're going to live to regret. I don't know what it's like being a parent, I probably won't for quite a few years, but it will be interesting I reckon.
PAUL 17

I DON'T WANT to fight anymore. My parents told me not to and my parents' feelings mean a lot to me.

Because my dad has worked too hard he's had two heart attacks and I don't want to cost him a third one. It means a lot that my parents are healthy. They lost a lot of family back in El Salvador in the war. My mum lost her husband and her dad and some uncles. I've got a stepdad, that's my brother's dad. He's real good, I treat him like a real dad. He was there since day one, he put me down as his son, so I really appreciate that. He's always helped out my mum, helped the family. He's really friendly to my mum's family in El Salvador. He's helped my mum's mum build a house in El Salvador. He's really friendly. My family is a big part of my life.

JULIO 17

I'M REALLY PROUD OF MY FAMILY

WE'RE FROM POLAND and we only came here fourteen years ago. We left Poland because there was a lot of stuff going on, with changes and the reforming of the government and I think my parents just wanted to get us out of there and give us a better chance. I think that my parents have done really well for us and I'm really proud of them. We're a pretty close family.

My parents have sacrificed a lot. Before we came here, we moved to Austria in 1981 and then we went from there to Australia as refugees, with no money in our pockets. My dad went out and learnt the language as quickly as he could and my mum tried to learn as well. Then my dad just went out there and started working straight away. And now my dad's a general manager and I'm really proud of him and my parents for what they've done to get me here. My dad has done well.

The first couple of years here we lived in those flats for immigrants and those were really hard places. We kind of roughed it out for a couple of years whereas other people would have been in their houses already. They would have had their jobs, they would have been secure, whereas my parents were all worried about what they were going to do next and if they were going to have enough money at the end of the week. They'd never tell me but I knew that it was going on and that type of stuff did happen.

SHAUN 16

MICHAEL'S PARENTS, MARA AND CARMINE

I WAS BORN in El Salvador, Central America. We came in 1988, in March. I was seven. We lived in flats for a while then we got to live in houses, moving around. We've always lived in, not bad areas, but not really good areas. That's probably why we're disadvantaged because my mum came without talking English and she struggled to find a job and she struggled to find confidence in going out and doing the things she does, like shopping and paying for the bills. My dad just influenced her into doing it. She finally got the courage in herself to do it. She started working after a while. My dad is a gardener. He had more confidence in himself, he knew a bit of English before he came.
JULIO 17

I LOVE MY PARENTS FOR DISCIPLINING ME

I LOVE MY PARENTS for disciplining me. If they didn't discipline me I would be swearing at everyone for no reason because my parents didn't teach me not to swear. I always respect my elders. But I only respect people who respect me. I've seen white kids swear at their mum and dad and they just don't really do anything. They don't think it's disrespectful or anything, but we consider it really disrespectful. I think it's just the way they're disciplined and the way they're taught about respect. When a white person wags it, their friends will say, 'Won't you get in trouble with your mum and dad?', and they say, 'Oh fuck them', and all this type of stuff. But I've heard Indigenous people talk and they say, 'You'll get a flogging mate'. And they say, 'Yeah, I'd better not then'.
BEADE 17

I GUESS I'VE BEEN brought up in a pretty good environment. I like my parents, they're not very prejudiced. I'm not very prejudiced and I respect women. Some guys would be brought up in environments where the father is the dominant figure, the powerful figure, he tells the wife what to do and she does it when she's told. I see that in a lot of households, what the father says goes. So the sons see this and they assume that's the way life is, you tell the woman what to do because you're the powerful figure, you're the breadwinner, you bring in the money. They see the way the father uses his power, they learn to do the same thing and they can control other guys and that's when you get leaders of groups.
TOM 16

I KNOW SOME people who have had to live with separated parents. I've been fortunate enough to have parents who stay together, but there's been a number of occasions where there's been threats of a split up and a divorce. So I've had to deal with that, especially when it got close to the break-up, it would be like, 'Oh yeah, who do I go stay with?'.
PAUL 17

LEARNING RACISM

RACISM, I THINK it's just the way a person is brought up by their parents. I reckon that if parents bring up a non-Indigenous kid always hating blacks and not mixing with blacks, of course it's going to be a problem when they're at the same school and trying to work together in the same class. That's where I reckon it all breaks down from the start—from the parents. They're brought up like that and we're brought up in another way and we just fight. When there's black against white there's a fight right there.
NIGEL 17

MY PARENTS TELL ME, 'Stick up for yourself and if anyone calls you anything racist don't let them put it over you', so I don't.
BEADE 17

WHEN THERE'S BLACK AGAINST WHITE THERE'S A FIGHT RIGHT THERE.

MY DAD KNOWS I'M REALLY BRIGHT SO THERE'S THAT EXPECTATION THAT I SHOULD SUCCEED BECAUSE I'VE GOT THE TALENT.

Family expectations

MOST GUYS ARE expected to get a good car, a good job and make lots of money. My family allow me to put my own expectations on myself.
CAMERON 13

I COME FROM a family of three boys and there are certain expectations you have to live up to. My dad knows I'm really bright so there's that expectation that I should succeed because I've got the talent. I suppose ages ago you'd have the expectation to succeed because you've got to provide for your family, whereas now it's just as much 50:50 in the husband–wife relationship, both of you contribute the same financially, so I mean it doesn't really matter as much.
PAUL 17

SINCE I CAME from a blue-collar family and went to an academically selective high school, my family saw it initially as a kind of joke, because they believed men go out and work with their hands, they don't sit down and think. Any homework I brought home I wasn't allowed to do most of the time. There were things that had to be done around the house first. Like housework and caring for my little brother on an everyday basis. If I was having difficulty with my work and I asked my stepmother, she just kind of looked at me and went, 'Oh, I don't fucking know', and then my father would come out and I'd ask him. He would kind of look at it and be a bit lost for words and go into a story about when he was in Third Form they didn't have calculators.

XANDER 19

I've seen parents who even call up their kids every two hours just to make sure they're okay

I'VE ALWAYS BEEN a shadow of my brother. He goes to a really good school, my parents pay heaps for it. He dresses nicely and respectable, with no piercings, no coloured hair and all of that. He does great sports, he travels around Australia playing football, while I'm the dreaded umpire. I've always been the black sheep of the family.

JASON 17

PARENTS ARE PROBABLY a bit more protective of females than what they are of males. I see more guys who are free to do what they want than what I see girls. There's only one girl I know of who is able to go out and do what she pleases. I've seen parents who even call up their kids every two hours just to make sure they're okay. They give them a mobile phone and they'll call them up. It's probably a protection thing, 'I like to know where the little darling daughter is', or something.

Personally if I had my parents doing that to me, I reckon it would give me the shits.

PAUL 17

Doing family history

Jim Baira, a 21-year-old Torres Strait Islander, wrote the following essay, which has been edited, when he was a Year 12 student at school in North Queensland. It is important for us to learn about our family histories. This knowledge brings understanding about how social, political and economic events have impacted on our family's past and how this affects us now. Think that how you live now will become part your future family's history. What have you learnt about relations between men and women in families in the past and how do these impact on your family's expectations of you as a boy?

MY FAMILY HISTORY

MY FAMILY ARE FROM Mabiaug on the Torres Strait. The island became overcrowded and the elders in the Baira clan decided to move to Badu Island nearby. I am a direct descendant of this family. My name is Jimmy Baira and the name Jim Baira is that of my great grandfather. 'Jim' has been handed down from my great-great-great-great grandfather, who was one of thirteen brothers and sisters of the first family to inhabit Badu Island. My immediate family branch began on Palm Island with my grandfather, Jacob Baira.

My grandfather travelled on the pearling luggers down the coast and when the boat called in at Palm Island he decided they might spend some time there. The idyllic group of islands reminded him of home and the people welcomed him into the community. Life on the island was not as idyllic as it seemed but he persevered. He fell in love with a girl, Isobel Tippo, who was eight years younger. She was sixteen years old and he asked permission to marry her. Before long they started their family, but unfortunately in the late 1960s the marriage broke up and Isobel fled to Brisbane. Isobel and Jacob remained married but lived apart for the rest of their lives.

My grandparents worked hard for the superintendent, Mr Bartlam, on Palm Island. Jacob's work involved logging, which was done to ensure materials were available to build and repair the shacks passed off as houses, sanitary detail (the removal of human waste), deckhand (on the cargo boat that travelled to and from Townsville twice a week and needed loading and unloading by hand), and for the native police. Isobel kept house for the Church of England priest, Father Bott, and Father Lawrence before him. These tasks were done in exchange for rations, which were never quite enough for their growing family. The experience Jacob had in fishing and hunting for turtles, dugong and crayfish enabled him to supplement the rations and ensure his family was fed. Often he would share the bounty with others and this helped to make him a respected and valuable member of the community. As with all other Indigenous Australians on the island, neither Jacob nor Isobel were paid for their labours.

All of the Baira children went to Palm Island Community School for residents. The school was very strict and it was a common occurrence for students to have their underwear pulled down exposing buttocks and genitals, and they were also soundly

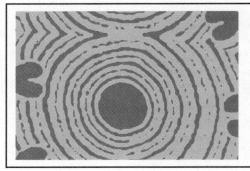

THEY KEPT SAYING THAT, 'NICE WHITE GIRLS NEVER ASSOCIATE WITH BLACK MEN, LET ALONE MARRY ONE'.

spanked with a cane by Mr Crouse, the headmaster, in front of other students in the class. All the white children of the island staff were sent to the white school. Despite the horrific treatment at the hands of the education establishment, they grew up with a close bond of shared embarrassment and never teased or tormented each other about what they witnessed. It gave the school children a strong defiant bond.

In the mid-1960s the family went to Townsville to live at a hostel in the western bushland of Aitkenvale. The men were woken up at 4.30 a.m. and loaded onto the back of a truck to work in the cane fields around Giru and Ayr as well as picking mangoes, also in the same area. The families were completely reliant on the government-run institution (hostel). They received no pay or allowances and the government also kept the social security payments and directed them into buying the land on which the hostel was built. The young men over twelve were sent to work with the older men, and the younger children attended school exclusively for residents of the hostel. The younger women helped the older women with communal cooking, washing and cleaning, as well as looking after the babies and younger children.

MY MUM AND DAD

My father, Roy, travelled extensively when he was young. After visiting Brisbane to see his mother he went to Palm Island, packed his bags and looked for work in Mount Isa. He met a girl there, Doreen, who fell pregnant and had a son, Ronson. Her family however did not approve and moved her away to the Torres Strait. Roy has not seen his son since. After that my father returned to Palm to find he was still restless, so he and his best friend and cousin, Keith Pickles, hitched to Mount Tom Price in Western Australia to work in the mines there. After working there for a while and making enough money to move on, they made their way back to North Queensland and stopped in Ayr for seasonal work in the mango season. He met a girl there of South Sea origin, but she found she was homesick and returned there some months later.

Dad returned to Palm Island where he was reunited with his brother Ralph and his cousins who had formed a band. He became the second lead singer. One night as they were playing, a nurse entered with a friend of Ralph's. Dad had seen her before and was wanting to know her better. Her name was Maria and she was of European descent.

She had come to Palm to nurse with her fiance who was a teacher. The chemistry between Maria and Dad was not to be denied and it wasn't long before Roy and Nick had a fight over Maria, who became my mum.

The white staff of the island however did not approve of the relationship and started a petition to have mum removed as an undesirable, after firing her from her job. My mum was forcibly removed from the island and with my father moved to Brisbane to live with my grandmother, Isobel. They were married in 1975 and returned to Palm Island with their oldest daughter, Rothana in 1976.

My mum and dad, though, had difficulty on Palm Island due to Maria being of European descent. The people of the community were wonderful and welcoming, while the white staff on the island labelled her. They kept saying that, 'Nice white girls never associate with black men, let alone marry one'. Mum was unable to get a job to help support her small family. This was a necessity because my father's job on the water in 1976 paid a mere $30 a week. They lived in a house that had three rooms. The walls were concrete up to waist height and asbestos to the top. There was no ceiling and guttering and the roof was made of galvanised iron. The house had one powerpoint which was used to run the fridge, TV, stereo, jug, fry-pan, heater and fan. Each house was fitted with a wood stove and outside toilet, which was manually emptied daily. There was no hot water, so showers and kitchen water were cold. Rent was charged weekly as well as electricity, and the food prices were exorbitant.

My mum became pregnant with Seneva who was born in 1977, and with two children the money became tighter. The hospital said that they didn't want an undesirable person nursing and they couldn't employ her as a nurse aide as this position was reserved for Indigenous members of the community. The store also said that they would not employ a white person as a worker as did the school. Sister Juliette who ran the old people's home though did ask Maria to work two days a week to relieve the nun so she could have two days off per week.

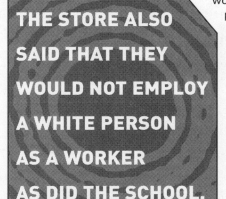

THE STORE ALSO SAID THAT THEY WOULD NOT EMPLOY A WHITE PERSON AS A WORKER AS DID THE SCHOOL.

Mum and Dad started having problems and he had an affair with another woman, Linda. Mum tried to make things work but the relationship deteriorated when Linda gave birth to Royston in 1978. Mum became pregnant with Roy and decided she had to leave the island. She got a job at a fast food outlet to support her small family. Within four months my dad made three visits to Brisbane and eventually stayed. I was born next. Sonja was born the following year and six years later Romeenah was born. My father had difficulty finding work in the city so he returned to Palm Island to run the airline office there. He had another affair and mum and dad permanently split.

JAMES BAIRA

Boys and their fathers

MY DAD'S PRETTY COOL. He gives me a lot of freedom and let's me go out because he trusts me.
TIM 14

MY DAD ALWAYS brings me to soccer matches every Saturday morning. He tries to keep his work nights free so that he can take me training. On Saturdays we watch the state team and sometimes if we're out of gas for my soccer team's barbecue, Dad goes and fills it up, and he cooks it sometimes. He's just really good. He loves soccer and he loves me playing it, he loves watching me play because I enjoy it.
ADAM CASTRECHINI 13

GOING FISHING WITH MY DAD, VINCE CHUNG 12

MY DAD LIKES carving things out of wood and working in the garden and in the backyard. He is a big help because he helps and trains me for anything that I want to do and if he can't help me, he helps me find books and other people who can help.
CAMERON 13

MY DAD'S BEEN really good, he's helped me a lot. He asks me how school's been and if I say that there's been a little bit of trouble or bullying, he just asks me questions about it. He helps me overcome things and gives me a new solution on how to act.
MARK 14

MY DAD'S A FUNNY sort of person. He makes my day happier. He tells jokes and when I tell him that I got a good mark in an assignment, he says, 'Good on you'. He encourages me. I used to tell him about being hassled sometimes for getting good marks and he would go, 'Don't worry about that'. He said there's always someone who will always be paying out others but he said just to continue and it's paid off now.

Dad's always been there because my mum works during the night and Dad's always home at night time. He works during the day and at night I can remember reading books to him and asking him for help and I suppose we got closer. I know some Italian dads who would go to work and the woman would stay home. But he's never been like that. So that's why I've followed my dad in not being a rowdy sort of character. I've always been more quiet or gentle.

MARIO 16

MY DAD HAS A very good influence over me. He doesn't tell me what to do but sometimes I think he's going to go off at me. He says, 'Sit down', and I go, 'Okay', and we'll just sit there and he'll chat to me, which is really special.

A lot of people probably don't have that relationship. It's not like a hierarchy with parents on top and kids down below. So it's like me and my dad are even. I know one person who does things that his dad wouldn't approve of. I could never do anything and not tell my dad. Some guys are afraid of their dad, probably because the father is the authoritative one, he's the one that's going to hand out the punishment. I know if any punishment's going to be handed out in my house it will be by my dad. It's just if I do something really stupid and I deserve it. I've been given the freedom to do what I want, I've been given the freedom to make my own mistakes.

PAUL 17

I'VE BEEN TO my friend's house and his dad is so sexist, and I imagine that somewhere that's come through him because I'm a firm believer that environment shapes a person. So how your parents are will basically have a lot of influence. My friend's very sexist and he always makes jokes about women as if they're an object and it's not just his father who does it. You hear of other fathers doing the same thing and on the oval with the boys, you hear it all the time.

TOM 16

WHEN WE WERE younger, my dad used to have a couple of women's clothes that he'd wear. He came to us, sat us down and said, 'You don't mind if I wear this? It doesn't offend you?' He used to say that if he won Lotto he'd have the operation but I don't think he would now. I think he's sort of changed his mind. He's got a couple of friends that have had the operation.

VINCE 17

DANIEL AND CARMINE, HIS DAD

THEIR EYES WILL BE DOWN, LIKE THEY'VE JUST BEEN SMOKING AND THEY'LL SMELL LIKE SMOKE AND I JUST CAN'T STAND IT.

I'M NOT REALLY close to my dad but an uncle of mine, that's my mum's brother, he just says to me, 'I don't want you hanging around guys who smoke and drink and fight at parties'. He sits me down, just me and him, and says, 'Look, I know that your dad is not around but I don't want you getting around like all the other boys'.

I sat down and thought about it for a long time and I looked at other guys for a while and they'll come to school and their eyes look like shit. Their eyes will be down, like they've just been smoking and they'll smell like smoke and I just can't stand it. It's just turned me off totally. And my uncle really keeps on my back and congratulates me. He sits me down and he cries, and he says, 'I'm really proud of you'. It just makes me feel all good inside. We'll just have real close talks. He means the world to me and my mum, I'll listen to everything they say.

NIGEL 17

HE DOES TAKE ME OUT EVERY WEEKEND AND HE'S A NICE PERSON TO BE WITH BUT IT HASN'T AFFECTED ME MUCH HAVING HIM LEAVE.

THE FIRST TIME I'd ever seen my dad cry was when we went for a long drive around the block for five hours, just kept encircling the block, while I talked to him about being gay and he wanted me to change. He said, 'Hold onto that minute shred of hope'. This is very funny: he was going to send me to Italy because he thought that somehow that would change me. He said, 'I'll send you to Italy, maybe you'll meet a nice girl. Go for a holiday, take a break.' My dad is an accepting man, he's got gay friends. It was just weird hearing that from him in the beginning.

LUCIANO 19

I HAVE A GOOD relationship with my dad but he is not someone I would like to emulate. He's a manipulator. He has a lot of good points but he's just not someone that I would like to hang around. I used to be really proud because he used to do a bit of weight-lifting and he was pretty good with it and I used to hang around and praise him, 'Oh, my dad's a weight-lifter, he's so good'.

But he's just very manipulative and he used a lot of emotional blackmail on people. He does take me out every weekend and he's a nice person to be with but it hasn't affected me much having him leave. I was prepared for it. If I hadn't been disabled he would have been prejudiced against disabled people. If I was 'normal', he would have been fine. On odd occasions he will tell a spastic joke in front of me. That doesn't hurt me in any way, but if I wasn't disabled and he saw a disabled person, he would probably make fun of them which is a sad thing to say, but that's just the way my father is.

I'll say this bluntly, he's prejudiced against everybody who's not Australian, any other nationality like the Japanese, Chinese, Asian, European, he will pay out. He'll be driving down the road and he'll see somebody and he'll make a racist comment, which is off-putting. He's never talked about my disability, other than bragging about the fact that he spent all that time annoying all the doctors in hospital. Whereas if I said, 'Look Mum, I'm having this problem with my disability, is there anything you can do about it?', she would probably give me a good long chat about it.

ANDREW 16

I DON'T DOUBT that my dad cares about me very much but I wish he could listen to me a bit more. He lectures me with advice when he doesn't understand the problem. He's a very intelligent man and if he could just let me get a word in edgewise then what he was saying would have more credit. It's a real 'male to male' issue. I'm a very affectionate person but I feel restrictions when it comes to expressing my love for Dad. And because of that it's difficult for us to be close. It's sad because I'm sure he wishes it wasn't that way too.

The qualities I think that make a good father are definitely communication and also to be open. Growing up in a single-mother household I've realised that the key to being close with your kids is to be a bit more . . . maternal, affectionate and gentler. When I look at my parents I'm closer to my mum because I can talk to her. I want to be able to offer that to my kids. I don't want to be

The qualities I think that make a good father are definitely communication and also to be open.

the parent that is unapproachable, I don't want to miss out on being there for my kids. He wasn't there.

If my parents had not divorced and I had been able to see my father every day in a more domestic situation then I think we would've been much closer. The potential is still there, we share a lot of interests—it's just a matter of breaking down the barriers that exist.

BOYD 16

I had been sexually molested by my grandfather from about the age of three to five.

A COUPLE OF YEARS ago things just got really, really bad for me and I ended up going into hospital because I overdosed on my antidepressants. It's a long story and every year around my birthday it's a really difficult time for me. It's really hard to get up and go to school. It's because only a little while before my birthday a few years ago I met my father for the first time in fifteen years and it wasn't what I expected. I think I had this stereotype of the perfect father in my head. He was going to be great, he was going to want to spend time with me, he was going to love me and he was going to become a part of my life. When none of that happened, it came as a big shock. I only met him for fifteen minutes and they were the worst fifteen minutes of my life. He said to my mum, 'I don't think Jordan's my son, you're lying, you're just trying to get money off of me', and that just sent me off the deep end. I couldn't believe he had said that. I was so disappointed because I haven't had many men in my life. I had been sexually molested by my grandfather from about the age of three to five. There's my uncle and one of my mum's friends and they're happy people, so I expected that's what I was going to get with my father. I built my hopes up thinking that I was going to get this fantastic person and I found my real father is a real dickhead. My mum's been getting some child support from him to help me get

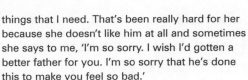

things that I need. That's been really hard for her because she doesn't like him at all and sometimes she says to me, 'I'm so sorry. I wish I'd gotten a better father for you. I'm so sorry that he's done this to make you feel so bad.'

I attempted suicide because things were getting worse and worse and I didn't know what to do. I felt it was the only thing that I could do to show people how I really felt. I needed help and it was the last resort. I usually get better at the beginning of each year until my birthday. Then to the end of the year, it's really difficult for me.

JORDAN 16

DAD USED TO LEAVE about six in the morning and get home at about eight at night so I never saw him. Mum died about ten years ago and after that, it was like, 'Hi, I'm your dad'. 'Oh, pleased to meet you'. He couldn't handle it at first so my sister and I lived with my grandparents for about six months afterwards while my dad went off and did a parenting course where he learnt things like how to cook.

STEPHEN 15

MY DAD USED TO hit my mum. When I was seven or eight it started to get really bad and then they got a separation. They're a lot better now. When Dad used to hit my mum, he used to walk into my room and say, 'Oh stop crying, stop bawling your eyes out, come on be a man'. I was four to nine years old and he's saying, 'Come on be a man', and I kept on thinking about that for years and years. I'm still thinking about it, and what I've been thinking about is how can you be a man without being a boy first?

I've made myself a personal promise. I never want to do what my father's done. He's ended up a lonely person. I want to do the opposite to what he's done. I want to make sure I never ever

act like him when he was younger. He used to get into big punch ups like you wouldn't believe with 30 to 40 other kids. I'm totally identical in looks to what he was like when he was younger. That's why I've grown a moustache, goatee and am trying to look totally different. I've dyed my hair, I've had my sideburns and had really long hair down to my shoulders but then shaved it all off. I don't want to look like him. He's my father and I love him very much but I don't want to look like him or act like him or talk like him. A lot of guys are like that. They don't want to be like what their dads have been.

AARON 14

I WANT TO BE A FATHER. I actually had a dream recently that I found a son under a bridge. I was walking with friends down a dirt track by a river when I came to an old stone bridge. We heard crying and looked under the bridge. We found three abandoned babies. I picked one up and it was a boy. I called it Diego—a name I don't remember hearing before. I was so proud to have a son and I was carrying him around in my arms. When I woke up I really wanted a son called Diego.

BEN GERRARD 17

● ● ● ● ● ● ● ● ● ● ● ● ●

I don't want to look like him. He's my father and I love him very much but I don't want to look like him or act like him or talk like him.

● ● ● ● ● ● ● ● ● ● ● ● ●

FATHER

You've been a storm
In my emotional weather
For much too long
Overshadowed my life
Darkened my doorstep
I missed what I never knew.

Now I'm going to deal with you
And when I'm finished
You're not going to hurt me anymore.

It took me a while
To find the strength
To forgive you
Even if forgiveness
Was only superficial

I let you buy me presents
Take me for rides
In your big silver Lexus
We went out to dinner
In fancy French restaurants
I took your surrogate money
And talked myself into believing
It was a substitute for love.

I remember when you
Called her a bitch
Shoved her back on a sofa
While we melted
Into the corners
Our eyes were glass circles
We watched the nuclear family
Mushroom.

I hated you for so long
It inflated my life
With a kind of poison
You have no idea
How often I cried
How you screwed up
My childhood
You were in the US
Or back at the office

After a while
I liked it better when
You were away
She made you the enemy
And I agreed
When I saw the way
You made her feel.

I learnt the mechanics
Of separation
I watched my family pulled asunder
You paid her to go to parties
I sat at home and
Watched the ship go under.

How can I love
What I don't even know
Low maintenance parenthood
You come birthday and Christmas
Bringing memories
Dripping with pain
Tears done up in wrapping paper. ▶

I remember when you
Subpoenaed
My grandfather's will
To save yourself a few dollars
In a few years
She wouldn't need child support.

I ran upstairs
And burnt a book
That you gave me
Later I threw
The charred mess
Out in the trash.

You married again
A nurse, or an air hostess
We had to visit your farm
Duty snapped her fingers
And I hated feeling like
An opportunist
And I hated you
For letting me feel that way.

Just a hobby farm
More a slap in the face
You have two houses
And we live in a duplex.

We cruised around in the Lexus
Talking irrelevancies
The cows stared
Chewing their cud
Countdown to the abattoir
Eventually we got home.

Pretending the past doesn't exist
You don't know how to relate
You were never around
To watch us grow
You weren't around
To read me stories
Or take me to school
Or teach me to shake hands
And I'm not sure
If I can forgive you
For the love
You weren't willing to give.

And you know
The one thing I can't remember
Is a time when we were happy
Painful memories interwoven
Pity families can't be chosen
Why did you get married?
Do you like inflicting pain?
And do you ever tire
Of shouldering the blame?

But I don't have to deal
With you anymore
I've reached a point
Where I can stand on my own
You can't hurt me now
I don't have to hate you now
I don't have to feel anything
I hope you like your own medicine
You'll never hurt me again.

JOHN BELL 19

MY MUM'S MY HERO

MY MUM BROUGHT me up, and my sisters and my brothers. She says stuff like, 'Put yourself in their shoes, what would you feel like? You've just got to imagine yourself being in their boots and how they would feel.' It makes you have a good think about stuff. It makes you think, 'Well, if I was in their shoes I wouldn't want all these people saying bad stuff'. Say a guy has got a disability with his face or something, Mum says stuff like, 'If you had that disability, would you like people running you down and saying bad stuff? Put yourself in their position and see what it would be like, and just don't give them such a hard time.' You get idiots these days running people down no matter what, and it's not their fault really, it's just the way they were brought up, it's just the way their parents bring them up.

In English we watched this movie called *The Mask* with Cher and that guy has a weird looking face. Maybe it's only weird

LOUISE, NIGELS'S MUM

'Nigel, you know you can come and talk to me if you ever need anyone to talk to, you can come talk to me.'

because he's different, the majority of people don't have that face. The first time I watched that movie was with Mum and I said, 'Mum, if that guy was at X High I would ask him if he wanted to hang around us, not because I feel sorry for him, but because he's like one of us, like he has a lot of things in common'. I'd let him hang around us not because I feel sorry for him but because I know deep down inside I want him to be our friend, not because of his face but because of the person he is.

I don't find it hard to talk to my mum. She says to me, 'Nigel, you know you can come and talk to me if you ever need anyone to talk to, you can come talk to me. And that will make me so happy if you come and talk to me about stuff. I won't tell no one, it's between me and you, it doesn't go to no one, none of our family, anything.' That's why I feel it's easy to talk to Mum and same as my gran. She just passed away a couple of years ago but we used to stay up until about three or four o'clock in the morning and just talk about life, the way things are and everything. And I think I just learnt from my gran, then when she passed away I feel it's easy to talk to mum.

Probably Mum and my friend are the ones that I really talk to the most. I'll talk to my friend, but if it gets really serious like if I got my girlfriend pregnant or something, that's when I'll go to my mum. I think it's because I trust them, it's all got to do with trust. I think I trust Mum the most. We're just really close.

I think it's because my mum has been there for me from the day I came out of her. When's she ever had a boyfriend, she's told them, 'Look my kids come first before anything, before you'. That really makes me and my brothers and sisters feel special. She's had the hardest life and she says stuff like, 'If it wasn't for you kids I would have already committed suicide a long time ago'. She only stayed alive for us kids. A lot of kids say Michael Jordan—and also Arnold Schwarzenegger—is my hero and all that,

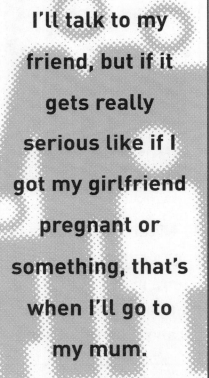

I'll talk to my friend, but if it gets really serious like if I got my girlfriend pregnant or something, that's when I'll go to my mum.

but deep down my mum is my hero.

I said to Mum, 'Look if my life was like this for the rest of my life, if I know for a fact that I'm never going to win anything else or I'm never ever going to change or anything, it's not going to bother me at all Mum because I'm happy just the way life is right now'. We aren't the richest people, but I said to Mum when she was getting a job, 'You don't really have to go and get this job. From now on if I don't get much stuff, if I don't get a basketball ring, it doesn't really worry me because I'm happy just the way my life is now'. She looked at me and she said, 'That is a real mature thing to say because a lot of people just want more and more and more no matter what'. I think right then and there she realised that I'm starting to grow up and I'm maturing and being a man. She trusts me heaps and I trust her heaps. She's really understanding. And I think that's what makes my life.

NIGEL 17

In the following poem, John, like Nigel, also writes about his relationship with his mum. With the nail polish and the rainbow bracelet that he wears, he's trying to tell her something without actually speaking to her directly.

JOHN AND HIS MUM, MARIANNE

MOTHER KNOWS

I keep
Enamel peach
On my nails
Sometimes it chips
And the
Bitten quick
Is there
For you to see

I know you
Watch them while I sleep
I know that you know
Without a word

I wear a rainbow
On my wrist
Beads clustered
On my skin
In the New World—
At home
I swallow it
Under tongue

I know you
Probe me as I sleep
I know that you know
Without a word

Your son coming out.

JOHN BELL 19

THINK ABOUT WHETHER THE FOLLOWING APPLY MAINLY TO YOUR MUM, YOUR DAD, BOTH PARENTS OR YOUR CARER:

▲ ALWAYS TAKES TIME TO LISTEN TO ME;

▲ EXPLAINS WHAT THEY ARE FEELING ESPECIALLY WHEN THEY ARE UPSET WITH ME;

▲ IS EASY TO TALK TO;

▲ SHARES THEIR OWN LIFE EXPERIENCES;

▲ ENCOURAGES ME TO MAKE DECISIONS FOR MYSELF AND TO ACCEPT RESPONSIBILITY FOR MY ACTIONS;

▲ SUPPORTS ME ESPECIALLY WHEN I AM FEELING DOWN;

▲ ENCOURAGES ME TO EXPRESS WHAT I AM FEELING;

▲ TALKS OPENLY ABOUT WHAT THEY ARE FEELING.

Families are diverse

As the guys in this book are showing you, there are many different kinds of families. But often there's this idea that there is only one proper family—the nuclear family with mum, dad and the two or three kids. There's also the opinion out there that a lot of problems that kids are experiencing are a result of the 'breakdown of the nuclear family'. Maybe there needs to be a change in the way people think about parenting. It's not so much about having a mother and a father, but about the quality of the care that's given to the child by whoever is caring for him/her as he or she is growing up. Have a read of what these guys have to say about family diversity.

MY PARENTS ARE divorced and both remarried and live on opposites sides of Australia.
MATTHEW 16

MUM AND DAD weren't married and they're not going together anymore, but they're living in separate rooms and are good friends.
SIMON A. 13

I SEE MY MUM a week and my dad a week. I have two bedrooms and I like that. I go to one place and hang out there, arrange all my stuff and then I go to another, it's cool.
CO CO 12

MUM AND DAD are separated. I see Dad every weekend and nearly every afternoon. He comes over heaps but I'm pretty much happy living with my mum.
AARON 14

I SPEND TIME with my dad who lives in Sydney. I go down there every holidays. I always get on with him really well because we don't get to see each other that much. When I'm with my mum I feel like my mum is my best friend, like I can talk about anything around her. She can ask me, 'So did you get into trouble at school?', and I'm not going to lie about it. Mum and Dad live in two very separate environments so it's almost like being in another world being in my dad's house and my mum's house. It's fun. When my dad told me they were getting a divorce, I didn't mind as long as they kept in touch. I didn't like how the first few weeks of going away they hated each other. But now that they're getting on well, my dad came up last holidays to see what life was like up here on the coast. They bonded really well.
EDDIE 11

I'VE GOT TWO DADS, my biological dad in Melbourne and my sort of stepdad who lives with my mum in the country. I get on well with both of them.
BRYCE 13

I AM THE SON of a lesbian, Maude. Now some of you might think that I have been somehow worse off because of the fact that I wasn't brought up in a 'normal' family with a mum and dad and maybe a few brothers or sisters. Contrary to that belief I have turned out as a reasonably stable child, or so people keep telling me. I don't do drugs and I don't have any issues with either my mother's sexuality or the fact that I haven't had my father around a lot for a large portion of my life.

I don't feel that my parents should have stayed together so that I could grow up in a 'normal' family because if they had then I probably would have picked up on the negativity and bad atmosphere that goes with a marriage that isn't working. Even though my father hasn't been around a lot, through no fault of his, I have always had people around who love me, whether it be my mother, a partner of hers or someone who we were sharing a house with at the time. I don't think there is necessarily a need in someone's life to have a father around, as long as there is someone loving them. A biological relation or not, whether it be a mother, a father, or both, or foster or adoptive parents, a same sex couple or three aunts, it doesn't really matter.

Now you are probably asking, 'But will you turn out gay?'. It's a question I'm commonly asked. I believe that a parent or other carer's sexuality has no impact on a child's feelings in relation to whether they are gay or not. However, it may make it more likely that if the child is gay they would be less likely to suppress their feelings, or hate themselves or even commit suicide.

My mother's sexuality has never been a major issue for me and I do not believe that it has had a major effect on my life or who I am. Many people, when they hear that someone's mother is a lesbian, only think about that aspect of who the mother is and jump to a conclusion about how the kid will turn out based on very little information. The reality is that a mother's sexuality has nothing to do with her ability as a parent.
SIMON 15

> I don't think there is necessarily a need in someone's life to have a father around, as long as there is someone loving them.

So there are all these stereotypes about non-heterosexual people but guys are saying that they can be parents too. For example, two brothers Mark and Damien talk below about being raised by gay carers. They tell us about the homophobic attitudes of their friends at school who also have particular stereotypes of gay guys as 'girlie types'. But what's wrong with that? Shouldn't it be okay for guys to express love and affection for their children? Shouldn't we just see guys and girls, regardless of their sexuality, as being able to express a whole range of emotions and actions without being classified as 'girlish' or 'butch'?

I LIVE WITH IAN and Brett. They're gay and they're my carers. I told one friend about them and he sort of teased me. I was standing up for myself at the time going, 'So what if they're gay? There's nothing wrong with being gay, it's just another type of love'. Ian's told me a lot about being gay and I can stand up to those who say things like, 'Oh, your carers will probably be girlie types'. I say, 'There's an average of 10 per cent of people who are gay so that means out of 50, five children will be gay. Watch out, it might be you'.

MARK 12

It doesn't really worry me being kissed and hugged by carers who happen to be gay.

I WAS A BIT homophobic in primary school. Then we met Brett and Ian and that helped a fair bit. Brett and Ian make me feel like I'm really special and it makes me feel good. They're kind of like role models. They tell me, 'Be yourself, believe in yourself and try not to pollute the earth'. I'll tell my friends soon because if they're my friends then they're probably going to be my friends for a fair bit longer and having gay carers shouldn't worry them. My teacher knows and she reckons they're lovely people. Ian kisses me on the cheek and it makes me feel really important. Each time I ask some boys, 'Doesn't your dad hug you?', they go, 'No, not really, it's so gayish'. And I go, 'No it's not'. And then they really disagree. It doesn't really worry me being kissed and hugged by carers who happen to be gay. It's kind of saying, 'Oh you're special'. It doesn't mean anything else, it just kind of says, 'I care about you'.

DAMIEN 14

What happens when you thought you had a home and a family but they stop being there for you? There are many young people who find themselves homeless or who find that what they thought was their home did not really give them what a home and family is meant to give you. How do you go about finding support? How do you keep strong in yourself and keep your goals so that you become your own home and family? Let's see how Haseeb, who is also in a wheelchair, lived through this situation.

HAVING NO HOME OR FAMILY

HOW DID I BECOME homeless? When I came to Australia, my father was married to another woman. In Pakistan he and my mother were always fighting, he hated her very much, and they got divorced. Since then my father wanted to get rid of everything that was related to my mother, including me.

So when I came here he was married to another woman and had his own four kids so in the first month he started telling me I needed to leave his house and his wife too. I had no place to go and yet my father

I went to a charity organisation at three o'clock in the morning and they didn't even give me a blanket although it was cold.

forced me to leave. I went to a charity organisation at three o'clock in the morning and they didn't even give me a blanket although it was cold. I waited the entire night in front of their door and I said, 'I don't want money, I want a room, I will find work and I will study'. They said, 'Go back to your father, people like you leave your homes every day and create problems for us', and I still remember his face and he looked so cynical. After that I never went to any place to get help except my school. It took me a long time before I got a shared flat and before I got money, but I kept on coming to school during the day while I slept many times in the schoolyard at night.

The Social Security teased me too much, saying I did not have a solid reason for leaving home, asking why my father didn't want me to live there. After seven months, the social worker talked to my father and he took me to the Austudy people. While I was homeless I never asked anyone for even $1 and once I remember I was eating sugar for seven days just to provide myself with energy during school holidays.
HASEEB 21

As Haseeb and other guys tell us, families can really stuff you around. But your family is also part of a community which can either support or mess your family around. In the following, Ariel talks about not only dealing with his parents' separation but dealing with it within a particular religious community and social class. Think about the community(ies) your family is part of and the ways it has made things better or worse.

MY EMOTIONAL HEALTH AND WELLBEING

THERE ARE MANY factors that have contributed towards my unstable emotional wellbeing. One such factor is my family.

I have recently been involved in my parents' own divorce. As a result I have become very confused about how my life is supposed to be led. I am up late listening to my mother or father crying after an argument. My mother puts large responsibilities on me for an eighteen-year-old teenager to handle, for example paying household bills. My father is unfortunately in a career field which is very unstable and as such has never had a stable income or job. Probably the most unlucky man in the workplace, my father continuously has pressures from my mother's side of the family to provide a stable income for the family and to get back together with my mother. My sister, being only sixteen years of age, has had a lot trouble coming to terms with the whole ordeal and the separate lives she must blend into with both parents. My sister, therefore, relies on me to be her source of strength and guidance through the whole ordeal.

I have only one set of grandparents who are on my mother's side. They came from nothing, surviving the Holocaust and immigrating to Australia, to very wealthy and prominent people in the Jewish community in Adelaide. They have different morals and ethics dating back to their past in Europe and find it very difficult to understand how or why my parents, who lived together for 21 years, can now just split up. My grandparents blame the whole ordeal on my father and

I HAVE RECENTLY BEEN INVOLVED IN MY PARENTS' OWN DIVORCE. AS A RESULT I HAVE BECOME VERY CONFUSED ABOUT HOW MY LIFE IS SUPPOSED TO BE LED.

have now severed all ties with him. This on its own is enough for emotional instability but there are many other influences that contribute to my state.

My physical environment is filled with wealth, power and snobbiness. As a Jew there are many expectations given by the religious community, which to some are extremely difficult to live up to, myself for example. I have attended a Jewish day school all my life and therefore only have wealthy Jewish friends. As a result I am bombarded with the extravagances of life, wealth, the power and snobbiness, on a regular basis. I am constantly worrying about my financial status and ways to keep up with their luxuries. This is a major burden for me since I just cannot keep up with the expectations of not only my immediate family, but my peers and the rest of the Jewish community. My father has raised me to give as much as you can because one day you will reap the rewards. This is the motto I live by. However, it is very hard to abide by this when the community you live in has everything already and someone like me has to keep up to fit in.

ARIEL 18

MY FATHER HAS RAISED ME TO GIVE AS MUCH AS YOU CAN BECAUSE ONE DAY YOU WILL REAP THE REWARDS.

No matter what happens in your family, it might be helpful to keep in mind that your parents/carers are only human beings with their own questions about love and life, unfulfilled dreams, changing dreams, disappointments and celebrations. But it can be messy. John's poem below is about divorce. The married couple is waiting for lawyers, 'the wigged wolves', to arrive so that discussion about settlement or 'feeding' can begin. Going through a divorce can be a really stressful time for a family, as John shows in his poem. During these times having a good friend or teacher or other family member who can support you can be a great help.

'WELL BROUGHT UP' AND 'IN OUTRIGHT WAR', BEN GERRARD 17

STUDIED INDIFFERENCE

The lady sits straight
But her hands reveal
The internal agitation
Coiled like a snake
At the edge of a chasm—
Her bridges were burnt long ago.

Dancing together
They play with the rings
And pick at well-manicured nails
With their pale peach enamel.

On the other side
Of the imitation potted palms
Sits her male counterpart
Studiously ignoring her
As he cheerfully whistles a tune
From some big musical.

His breath smells of money
You can see it in the lining
Of his Armani jacket
The small change
Rattles a little too loudly
In his hip pocket.

No further apart
Than when they shared a bed
Yet, the palm might have been
A wall, or a jungle
As they waited
For the wigged wolves to arrive
So that feeding could begin.

JOHN BELL 19

CHAPTER EIGHT
BOYS BEHIND THE LABELS

STICKY (SICKLY) LABELS

Why do you see
what it is that you see,
when I reveal to you,
a shade of me?

What did they tell you,
it could make you think.
You would change your world,
within a blink.

I say a word.
You see a label.
They got you babe,
straight from the cradle.

I think, therefore I am.
What do you think?
MASON CHIDGEY 29

What are the labels used to discriminate against some boys? How does a label 'stick' so that it becomes a stereotype and then some guys are only seen according to that label and prejudice? Labels can be 'sickly', they hurt and can cause harassment and violence. Where do we get our myths and labels about people from? Think about racism, heterosexism and discrimination against people with physical and emotional disabilities and how these stem from certain labels superglued to some boys because of narrow-minded and ignorant social attitudes.

In this chapter, we're going to take you into the lives of some of the boys behind certain labels. You'll get to see how much of their lives is more than the simple silly label and yet you'll see how these guys are courageously dealing with the fact that other guys, girls and even some adults, who should know better, stick sickeningly to these labels.

Being labelled disabled

I'VE GOT A NEIGHBOUR who is intellectually disabled. I stick up for him when he gets picked on because I reckon he's a really nice guy. He's 21 and he's pretty much got the mind of someone who's twelve, even younger. But I don't really see him for that, I see him for who he is.

JOSH 15

I'M ONLY 2 FEET tall but I don't think I've really got a disability. I think that everyone in this world has disadvantages and advantages, so I can say I'm one of the people who has advantages and disadvantages.

Recently, my mum told me to get some paper serviettes from the supermarket. When I gave the woman at the counter the money, she said, 'Where's your parents?'. I said, 'I'm sixteen'. She goes to me, 'You're not supposed to be here all on your own little kid'. I just got the serviettes, left the money on the counter and went out. I felt all worn out, it became a long day. But now I don't listen to any ignorance anymore.

ABDU 16

I WAS IN THE DEAF WORLD AND NOW I'M TRYING TO BE IN BOTH AS I CAN SIGN AND TALK

I THINK THAT EVERYONE IN THIS WORLD HAS DISADVANTAGES AND ADVANTAGES, SO I CAN SAY I'M ONE OF THE PEOPLE WHO HAS ADVANTAGES AND DISADVANTAGES.

IF I TAKE MY hearing aid off I would say I pretty much have a disability. If someone says that I'm deaf, I just laugh. For example, the teacher was walking in and he said, 'Don't go in the classroom', and I didn't go in the classroom but I stepped in the door and he said, 'Are you deaf or something?', and all these kids started laughing. Sometimes it's funny when someone says things like that. He didn't realise that I couldn't hear him.

But I do feel different when something's going on and it's exciting and I can't hear it. I feel out of it. Some guys try to act tough with me. They reckon they can beat me in a fight because I might not hear them come toward me. Sometimes I feel a bit different when someone treats me in a different way. If someone's teasing you,

you feel dumb, you feel deaf, but if someone treats you really nice, you feel like you're at the top.

There are deaf people in the deaf world and the hearing world. I'm in both worlds. I was in the deaf world and now I'm trying to be in both as I can sign and talk. I feel good that I can talk to deaf friends and also talk to my hearing friends. Sometimes I hate it when the hearing aids play up and I get angry with them. If the hearing aids get wet they play up and I wish I had a waterproof hearing aid. It would be great if I could hear underwater. When I go swimming, I take them off. When I put them on again, I make sure that the top part of it works, and that the hair near my ears is dry.

BRYCE 13

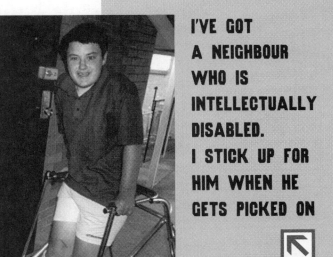

I'VE GOT A NEIGHBOUR WHO IS INTELLECTUALLY DISABLED. I STICK UP FOR HIM WHEN HE GETS PICKED ON

PHOTOS COURTESY OF FAMILY PLANNING, QLD

I BREAK BONES very easily so I chose to go into a wheelchair. I was ending up in hospital two or three times a year. Now I'm down to about once every two years. After I did a double break, I broke my lower leg on the right side and my upper leg on my left side, I was in hospital for eight weeks. I was just going into Year 7 and I thought, 'No, I'm not going to do this anymore', so I went into a wheelchair. It was much easier because on a walking stick I was finding it hard to walk all over the school. It's such a big place so it's easier in a wheelchair and gives me more protection.

Sometimes I get stirred. One guy threatened to break my arm. He was only mucking around, but you just don't muck around with stuff like that. Years 7 and 8 were not so good because students didn't know me but then I began to stand out because I'm really into music and have a band. I play lead guitar and lead vocals and from then on everyone just knew me really well and didn't treat me any different. Before that they'd say, 'Try and get up and walk, you don't need to be in a wheelchair'. I've got alopecia as well, which means losing your hair. I'd get stirred with, 'Why do you always wear a hat? We know you've got a wig on', because I've got patches of hair just around the side. I was always teased and I didn't want to tell the teachers. I didn't want to tell Mum and Dad in case they took me to another school, so I pretty much kept quiet until some guys started actually physically hurting me and it was really easy for me to break my bones.

After I did a double break, I broke my lower leg on the right side and my upper leg on my left side, I was in hospital for eight weeks.

My music is like a communication thing between me and everyone else.

The very first day of high school I remember the coordinator specifically saying, 'You've got to be careful with this boy over here because he breaks very easily, you can't physically touch him or his bones will break'. But they didn't understand. To be funny to their other mates—and it's just typical stereotyped male stuff and ignorance—they'd try to hurt me. I suppose immaturity is a big thing.

Today, I don't think many people get paid out or bagged anymore about being a nerd, being gay, being in a wheelchair. Everyone's becoming more open-minded about everything. There is more education and acceptance. If it wasn't for the disability I don't think I would have got paid out and it wouldn't have made me stronger in myself. I can handle pay outs with ease, it's like water off a duck's back.

Sometimes when I see other guys with huge arms I wish I could have that but I can't build my arms and muscles up, it's just going to snap the bone off. Even trying to lift myself up, the bone on the tip of the elbow got pulled off by my shoulder muscle, so I've just got to watch it.

My music, being the front man of the show, and having people say that you're good at something really helps your confidence. My music is like a communication thing between me and everyone else. I sit in a wheelchair and they think, 'Oh my God, he's not normal', and then as soon as I sing and play the music that I like and they know it's going to sound good, they just think, 'Oh, maybe he's not so different after all'. Then they get to know me and it's awesome.

MARC 18

In the following, Kathy introduces her son Michael and we get to read his poetry which takes you into the mind and heart of a young man who cannot speak but can certainly communicate.

NOT SPEAKING BUT COMMUNICATING

MICHAEL IS A fifteen-year-old young man with cerebral palsy and in a wheelchair. He has limited vision and is non-verbal. Michael communicates using an alphabet board. He lifts his right arm and points with his thumb to the letters.

Communication is a slow, laborious and, recently, painful process and so he will only use the time to do his schoolwork or say what is most important to him at that particular moment.

Michael spent his first four years of schooling at his local primary school where he thrived. He was a high academic achiever and had a positive self-image. Other children and their parents included Mike in social events, such as birthday parties, and he rarely felt an outsider.

Against our better judgment, we were persuaded to send Michael to another school where he would be able to learn to communicate with an electronic device. This failed to eventuate. He stopped communicating altogether during the three years he was there and he became suicidal.

He now attends his local secondary college where he is in Year 10. He listens, learns and with the help of his teachers and aide is able to do the work required to complete each year's requirements. But his physical condition is deteriorating.

Michael's dearest wish is to be able to speak. He wrote to a friend, *'What freedom, what perfect joy to communicate naturally'*. Michael is often stared at and asked inane questions by those who don't know him, and often ignored by those who do. People will talk over him (often about him) as if he has no hearing or is not present. They will also direct questions to his carer (aide or family); he is quite able to answer himself with a yes or no response. A speech therapist told me, in front of Michael, 'I would believe he had ESP before I believed he can read', when, at the age of four, he demonstrated his ability to communicate on his board. My eldest son could read at four but he was not disabled and, therefore, this ability was not thought impossible.

Michael dreams of being a writer and poet. *'I imagine my life creating marvellous works of literature.'* Although he had the following poem in his head when he started to point it out on the alphabet board, it took him sixteen hours, over several weeks, to complete.

A SONG OF TEARS AND HOPE

You usually pontificate stridently about what the 'meaning of life' issues are.
About what you think the world should feel,
and how it should behave about guilt and innocence.
About trust and mistrust.
About anger,
About pain and ruthless, unremitting frustration.
About boredom that eats at every fibre of one's being!
About caring, nurturing, loving,
unyielding knowledge about when Christ deigned to live.

Wrong!
Wrong are you to assume such an all-encompassing knowledge.
As ten great, gagged men can never understand that which I suffer,
to interpret so typically,
stupid, simplistic, supercilious and quaint wants and desires.
To be so utterly all-knowing.
To make such loquaciously extravagant comments is quite outrageous,
dangerous,
un–Christian.

How long I have depended on rare moments of communication?
Of understanding?
Are people so prejudiced against disability?
Mindless hate and ignorant pity bond irrevocably.
Tears spilt in cruel, silent monotony.
Insecurity screams.
Tortured souls.
By being disabled we endure
that which only Christ, in His persecution, could understand.

Yet joy quickly uplifts our hearts in real understanding.
God has quintessentially untied the bounds of ignorance.
Taut nerves, painful memories.
Vulnerability.
Slowly changing assumptions.
Questions asked.
Hope nigh,
You guide souls, dear Jesus,
Omnipresent.

MICHAEL NORRIS 15

MICHAEL IS IN PAIN most of the time, the pain of a dislocated hip grinding bone against bone every time he moves his leg, and severe stomach cramping. He wrote the following piece because he wants people to understand how he lives.

STOMACH PROBLEMS

Undermining pain
Dishevelling pain
Ordaining pain
Ache demanding.
Rising agony,
so great it ages the soul,
gaining control as time passes.

Pain wrenching
Why for must I suffer?
Just I?
Nothing ahead
Pain numbing
Amplifying worries
Vulnerability
God hits you where it hurts.

Weary soul
Smile gone
Pain permeates
Wizening,
Quiet suffering
Pain unremitting
No peace.

MICHAEL NORRIS 15

MICHAEL LOVES SCHOOL; it is the most important part of his life. However, as much as the teachers and aides try to include him in the school community, they cannot force friendships. He is so very lonely and in need of young friends. There is nothing available in the general community to provide peer contact for someone like Michael, and so holidays and weekends are long and boring for him. It is our dearest wish that community education will soon help people to accept that a disabled person has feelings and a need to be included in the activities around them. A little thought is all that is required.

I can't stand racism!:
Challenging the labels

RACE IS IRRELEVANT to me. I prefer to take people as individuals. When I've become friends with someone who is of Italian, Greek or Polish descent, I learn interesting facts about their family traditions and culture, but I don't then go and generalise, expecting all Italians, or Greeks or Polish to be that way.
BEN GERRARD 17

Racism comes in many forms. It's not just white versus black but more about one group picking on another group so they can be that little bit higher up some social or so-called 'racial' scale. Think about who labels who in your school and community and why they do it. You'd think that guys from migrant and refugee families who know what it's like to experience racism, would not be dishing it out to others.

Think, too, about how labels like 'wog', 'Asian', 'Muslim', 'Indigenous' and 'Australian' lump together lots of people as if they're all the same instead of allowing us to think about everyone's differences. What are the ways you are Australian, Asian, Muslim, Indigenous, Anglo-Celtic and so on? Should you have only one cultural label or can you belong to two or more cultures?

How does your cultural background affect your life as a boy? How did it shape the way you see yourself as a boy? What have you learnt about what it means to be a boy in your culture from the older men in your community?

I'M OF MIXED Italian–English background. My father's side is Italian and my mother's side is English. At school, the Italian boys had a lot of respect for each other purely because it's their culture to respect other people. But then again, they respected each other but they didn't show the same respect towards people of different descent like the Asian boys. I'm willing to participate in or have a look at different cultures and different people and the way that they operate. Whether it be gays and lesbians or whether it be Moroccan, I'm really interested in the way that other people live their lives and the culture that they live amongst.
CHRISTIAN 22

I CAN'T STAND racism, it really irks me. I have Italian friends who go off if anyone says 'wog' but they'll turn around and say hundreds of Aboriginal jokes, so it's a bit of a double standard. Maybe they don't realise how stupid it is. A lot of Italian and Lebanese people have a pride in their country and it's really cool to be proud of who you are, but it doesn't mean you have to be racist against everyone else.

MAX 16

I WENT TO THE footy with 27 international students, most of whom are from Asian countries. It was good fun. To get to know them better we decided to have an afternoon together, so we took them to the footy, and then they took us to an Asian restaurant for dinner. They helped us decipher whatever we were all being fed, some of which was really nice, some of which was really weird. Some of my friends are Asian guys. One guy's mother's Asian and his father is Australian.

We've got a couple of guys at school who are not so much racist but ignorant. There's one guy who's absolutely appalling and as much as he's a nice guy you can't talk to him about multiculturalism. He

A lot of people don't really make the effort to get to know other people from other cultures.

thinks Aboriginal reconciliation is an absolute joke. His dad is racist as well. If you sit down and explain to them about things they don't listen, that's generally their problem. They're either scared or jealous because they can't understand what people are saying in other languages, or think because they're in our country they should all be speaking English. A lot of people don't really make the effort to get to know other people from other cultures.

SIMON MOSS 16

I HAD A REALLY bad time at school with racism. I was being called 'skip', 'yobbo', 'whitey'. I copped it a lot because I umpire a lot of the football matches of guys from ethnic families. I'd come back on the Monday after a game when I'd sent a few off and they'd get stuck into me. They'd thought, 'Oh, I know him from school, he'll let me get away with doing this', but I didn't.

As a country, we all have to mix in and we're still learning to mix in. When we were doing group work at school, they'd let us pick our groups but if they could've put us in mixed groups, like put an Australian with a Lebanese and with an Asian, you'd mix in and you would have to work together. That way you could work together and think, 'Oh, you're not such a bad guy after all'. But by choosing your own group, all the Australians would get together, the Asians would get together, your Lebanese and your upper-class would get together.

JASON 17

i know my heritage, where i've come from even though i wasn't born there.

I FOUND ANTI-WHITE racism in high school. In primary school, the teachers were saying racism is horrible and just because people are Greek or Italian or whatever doesn't mean they're lesser people. I'm like, 'Yes, fair enough, everyone's the same'. I got to high school where Anglo-Australian people were seriously in the minority and we got picked on and I thought, 'Oh, well, it's not cool, a lot of racism is happening from both sides'.
STEPHEN 15

Being Italian

MY DAD IS ITALIAN but he doesn't have any Italian relatives in Australia. Mum is from Peru in South America, she's got a lot of relatives down here. I get a lot of flack from other students about our celebrations with all the South American relatives, and the food we eat. I usually call myself Australian, and then they say, 'Oh, really? You don't look Australian, you look Greek or Lebanese.' My parents always spoke English to me, so I never got to learn any other language. I know a bit of Spanish and a bit of Italian but I don't speak it that well. I like being multicultural because it's interesting seeing different cultures and what they do.
JOHNNY 17

MY PARENTS ARE Italian but I just don't see myself as hanging around in a certain group. I don't feel as though I'm a full wog or anything. I know my heritage, where I've come from even though I wasn't born there. I'm proud that I've come from an Italian background and I'm learning Italian. My parents are not arrogant about being Italian or think Italian is best. They were both born here in Australia. My parents and relatives all eat Italian food and go to Italian festivals and I've been brought up with all of that. I sort of have an Italian way of life in me. I like all the Italian food and I acknowledge all the religious festivals they have in Italy, and my nonni [grandparents] have taught me about Italian culture and I know all about the things that they did in their lives so I feel included as being an Italian.

I would call myself Australian because I wasn't born in Italy. I was born in Australia and I experience the Italian ways but also mainly the Australian ways, so I live in the Australian culture, and I've never even been to Italy. I don't think there's a barrier at all between the Italian and Australian cultures in my life. Mainly I just do more things with my family than some of my Australian friends.
ANDREW A. 16

I DO COMMUNITY work in an Italian retirement village every Wednesday. We go and help the older people, talk to them and just socialise with them. I enjoy that because some of them speak Italian and I'm doing Italian now as a subject, so it sort of gives me more of a background. Some of them were talking about the war, how they got through everything. We had a guy who was talking to us about how he left his parents, went to war, and then had to survive on his own. It was interesting because you don't really hear a lot of stories.
MARIO B. 16

Being Greek

I'M HALF GREEK but I don't mix well with the Greeks and Lebanese. I don't speak Greek and I wasn't brought up as a Greek.
KIERAN 16

MY PARENTS ARE Greeks and they don't let you have a girlfriend at a really young age. My dad forces the religion side of things so we go to church pretty much every Sunday or every fortnight. I'm not really allowed to stay out late, not really allowed to drink alcohol, but sometimes my parents will let me have a bit. I don't really like all the rules but when you really sit down and think about them, they're probably going to do something for me in the long run. If I drink too much I might get addicted to alcohol or if I go out too much I won't

study. My parents expect me to do well at school and try and get a job because that will help me in the future.

I notice some of the ethnic guys try to be really cool to females by dressing up and getting their parents to buy them hotted up cars. They mainly hang around together, they've got a lot more money, and they'll flash around the money like wearing gold chains. Some of them want to show that they've got cash and they think they're tough because they've got cash.

I think it's pushed upon us from parents that everything has to be of a good standard. For example, if I buy a watch I wouldn't buy one from the $2 shop. My parents would make me get one that would last for a while. I think they want the best for you and to get the best use out of what they spend [their money] on. If you get a watch and it only lasts you one day, it's not worth buying a watch, you might as well buy something a bit more expensive that will last you a lot longer.

Especially among the ethnics in the past generations, the females really didn't go to school. They stayed at home, they did everything for the husband, and I think some parents are still pushing that. But the female now is allowed to go to school and get a job. In my relationship in the future, my partner and I would share everything. We'd be able to talk problems out instead of hiding them. Taking care of children should be a shared job because you're both there to make the child, so you both have to look after the child as well.

When an Australian calls you 'a greasy

wog' and things like that, you turn around and say, 'Why are you paying me out, I'm just a normal person like you, I'm just Greek'. I am proud of the heritage that we have in Greece, like the oldest buildings. We invented a lot of things as well like sports and religion. In a way you do sometimes think you're more superior because you've come from a background that has done more things.

CHRIS 16

MY PARENTS ARE from Greece and I really enjoy hanging around my Greek friends and talking like a wog. It's fun to hear about parents that are really possessive and won't let their 25-year-old son move out of home. We have a good laugh about it. I remember I went to a school that was very Anglo. I was treated differently because I was Greek. But was it because I was Greek, or was it because I was in a wheelchair? The disability totally threw into chaos the Greek expectations that parents will have of you getting married, doing the whole family deal.

TONY 24

If you're a wog, you're cool

THERE'S A KIND of notion that if you're a wog you're cool. But the people from Asian backgrounds get very much picked on. People would walk past one Asian guy and slit back their eyes. I remember the public speaking competition in Year 11 where one boy who came from Cambodia spoke about the racism in our school and he won. He genuinely cried during his speech. You could actually feel his emotions and the way he'd been beaten up so badly one time by a bunch of Australian boys. Two black eyes, broken nose, missing teeth.

A lot of Asian students hung around together. You got no choice but to annexe yourself off because you have to find that place called the comfort zone. A lot of them would just speak their language in the corridor, which I think is really good, but there'd be people walking past making fun of their languages. I just thought, 'If you ever go to Japan and you're speaking English and they start going blah blbllblbl, how are you going to feel?'

I got harassed by some of the Asian boys for being gay. I said to them, 'I'm in a minority group but so are you, so what are you talking about?'. They were kind of startled when I said that. I was also abused by one group of very, very woggy boys, Greek and Italian students. I was harassed by them, and yet I kind of belong to their community as well in that I'm Italian. They said I wasn't Italian, even though I was the only one that was actually born in Italy, actually lived in Italy. But I wasn't Italian because no Italian male was supposed to be gay. I remember one Italian student saying to me, 'You're either not Italian or you're not a faggot', with that really serious look that I was making it up that I was gay.

LUCIANO 19

Being Jewish/being Muslim

THE PURIM FESTIVAL is a Jewish festival which is really fun. Everyone dresses up in costumes and at the end there's a big concert and my Jewish school bands play grunge and other music, and there's people dancing and doing fun stuff.

ZACH 14

SOMETIMES I FEEL it's very strange being in Australia. I'm from a Pakistani Muslim village culture where men live very differently and women live very differently. Sometimes if you talked to a girl in the countryside they'd get offended. Girls in Australia don't really understand this was where I came from. When I came here and I saw the girls going out when they're sixteen or seventeen, I was always thinking how different it was for girls here. I wondered how they felt but now I'm beginning to understand the reasons for the differences.

Sometimes I haven't been very good in adapting to the way girls are here. For example, when we had to do project work at school in mixed groups of girls and boys, I would hardly talk to them because I was too shy and I'd type my report very quietly. I think I treated the girls very badly. If they sat with me or came to talk to me I couldn't answer them properly. I'm from a culture where boys and girls are trained very differently. We speak very little to each other as a sign of respect. That's why when I came here, this was an absolutely new culture to me and my teachers wanted me to talk to other people. This was very strange for me at first.

Another strange thing was that I never felt as if I was being stared at in Pakistan but here in Australia I feel like people are staring at me and sometimes they look back again and again. I feel really uncomfortable when I'm doing work in the library and another person is staring at me.

I don't believe in nationalism. I don't believe I'm a Pakistani, nor do I believe I'm Australian. I don't like hearing in advertisements, this is made in Pakistan or this is made in Australia and you should buy it. I've found that I have friends in Australia and have friends in Pakistan and I love them and care about them all. I find that Australian people who come from the country or rural areas are much easier to get along with because they are more like the people I remember from home.

HASEEB 21

I feel really uncomfortable when I'm doing work in the library and another person is staring at me.

not all Turkish muslim people go by the rules. There are a few that really like their religion and go by the book, but in the main everyone does what they want.

I'M MUSLIM AND from Indonesia. I lived there for twelve years before coming to Australia. I'm not the only Muslim student at school. My school has a lot of African people, Yugoslavian, Bosnian, Vietnamese, so we basically have Muslims from different countries and different ways of being Muslim. I think we treat one another with respect and non-Muslim students don't treat us differently. The school knows that if the day is Ramadan some Muslim students won't come to school and the teacher knows the reason why.
UEN 17

I WAS BORN IN TURKEY. My auntie wanted my parents to come to Australia and so I was only about five when we came here. I think I'm more of a Turk than Australian. I've been a Turk for sixteen years and I don't want to change that, I don't want to be Australian, it's like the blood inside me is Turkish. I'm Turkish, that's it.

Not all Turkish Muslim people go by the rules. There are a few that really like their religion and go by the book, but in the main everyone does what they want. I don't go by the book all the time. But I respect my religion.
BORA 16

OUR TURKISH CULTURE is going to be different in the future because there's the older generation of Turkish people in Australia now but it's going to be the new generation in the future. In the olden times it was very hard for the older generation. They think the culture they have in Australia is always going to be like that but it's not.
MUSTAFA 15

Being Asian

I COME FROM HONG KONG. I immigrated to this country and became an Australian citizen. My cultural background is Chinese, but as far as I'm concerned I can proudly say I'm a Chinese Australian. So I think I'm a bit of a mixture. What is a real Aussie anyway? Those rugby league players who only drink beer all the time or yell at you, 'Oh, how's it going mate? Are you Australian mate?' I don't think so. I like diversity, that's just my culture.

I find the boys in Australia very different from boys in Hong Kong. For example, many of the Greek and Italian boys felt like they had to be really aggressive with Asian students. Why did they think that to show off their masculinity they had to be so violent? They thought Asian guys were weak because we were often smaller and less muscular. Why can't everyone just be themselves?

Something else that was different about Australian men is that only if you're a football or rugby player who gets a shot or a score can you hug each other and kiss each other. Other than that you just don't show your affection. Just physical contact between men in Australia immediately means they're gay. As it's not like that in Asia, I find it really interesting. Initially, I had thought Australian men would be more open-minded.

why did they think that to show off their masculinity they had to be so violent?

I have experienced racist harassment. I was waiting for the bus after school one day and this guy from another school walked by eating a sandwich. Suddenly, he threw it at me and ran away. I was so shocked and felt very bad. But I was also worried that other male students might find out I was gay.

At the age of twelve in Hong Kong I started to have crushes on guys but didn't say anything as Asian people in my country often think that homosexuality is something from a Western culture. But at school in Australia, I thought I was the only Asian gay guy around. I felt a little bit devastated. Where did I fit in? Not in the gay community, not in the Chinese community. I was an isolated student.
ERIC 22

As some guys are telling us, sometimes shifting countries means you shift in the way you think, feel and behave. Experiencing different cultures leads you to experience different facets of yourself and question where you belong and what kind of person you're going to be. For some boys this can be unsettling as what's known is exchanged for the unknown, and along with the adventure of a new country and new opportunities can come conflicts and adjustment issues. Here is one boy currently in the middle of dealing with these issues.

EVERYTHING WAS SO DIFFERENT

I CAME TO AUSTRALIA from Vietnam when I was eleven. I lived in a village in Saigon and I remember the green fields and farming. My mother, brother and sister and I lived on a farm but my father was already in Australia. When I came to Australia, everything was so different: the houses, cars, money, like stepping into a new world. I had no English so it was hard for me but I had friends who turned English into Vietnamese for me.

When I was little I had not known my father and when I came here, he expected me to be a son who was respectable and obedient. But in Australia, young people have many freedoms, their own options, their own way. Not many people listen to their parents, and I'm one of those people. Soon it was very violent at home between my father and myself. I went away and stayed out with friends, I became homeless, sleeping at the park or at a friend's house. I got into trouble with the police at one time and got a five-year good behaviour which is nearly ended now.

I was just hanging around, doing all these stupid things, stealing because I had no money, until I was sixteen and could get the unemployment, and at seventeen I changed to Austudy. I decided to go back to school to try and get a good job later. I have done Year 11 and Year 10 and I board with a young couple and their baby and pay $100 a week for food, cooking and electricity.

Sometimes it's difficult being single and living with a family but I need a place to study. I think my parents may know I've returned to school. Sometimes I see my father but we do not speak to each other. I walk on one side of the street and he on the other. I don't know if he sees me or not. I see my mum sometimes and we say a few things. She'll say, 'You are an adult, you are grown up, do what you like'. I wouldn't go back home yet as I'm in a good place to study and if I went home, it may be violent again. One day I'd like to finish studying, get a good job, and get back to my family so we can live in happiness.

DUY 18

ON THE RUN

I'M FROM SRI LANKA and arrived in Australia when I was seventeen. I lived in the north part of Jaffna in a village which was very calm, not fast like Australia. It was a beautiful place with religious temples that I would visit every day. I would go to school, visit relations, do some farming and help other people. I lived with my mother and sister as my father was a medical research technician working in Colombo.

We came to Australia because of the ethnic war. I am Tamil and the government was Sinhalese who didn't give any opportunity to the Tamils. For example, in education, every religion has a cut-off mark to enter the universities and Tamils have a higher cut-off mark so they get less students into education.

My family moved to many places as the government would send soldiers into our homes. There would be fighting and shelling of our places, shooting from helicopters. So we couldn't live near government army places. We had to move to other places to get away from the soldiers. We'd use bicycles and motorcycles and we could only carry little things with us like clothes, some food, some documents about owning a house but the government is in there now.

We moved to the city of Colombo and every day the police would come to our houses and check ID cards. They took you to the police station and you'd stay there for five days if you did not have an ID card. I always made sure I had my ID card, but they were cruel to my friends who were caught without them, kicking them and asking them if they were fighters, if they had any bombs.

We were finally allowed to leave Sri Lanka after my uncle who was living in Australia made an application for us to be accepted as refugees. I arrived in Australia at 6 a.m. and it was very cold. My uncle was there and I was very happy to be here because there is no war. I had learnt some English in Sri Lanka but I went to an English Language Centre here as my first school and found people from all over the world there because everywhere was war—Somalians, Bosnians. Even in the secondary college, a lot of them were like me.

I like going to school here but I'm not happy with the behaviour of students at school. They joke and swear—you can't do that in my country. I want it to be more strict; you can't study, you can't concentrate. Sometimes it's hard going shopping and not always understanding the language.

I would like to be an engineer, get a job, buy a house, and sponsor my uncles and their families to come and live here. They are still in Sri Lanka, the war is still happening, and when we do hear from them, they are moving and moving, again and again. They live in camps in the forest sometimes.

SIVA 18

Being Indigenous

I DON'T CARE what kind of skin colour I am, but I think being a Torres Strait Islander is best because the culture that I have is fun for me. I just go out diving, whatever, because it's fun. When you go out swimming at the Islands you just go right out into the deep blue sea, just dive down there. It's like more down-to-earth.
DAVE 13

WHITE PEOPLE NEED to just listen to Indigenous people and try to understand what they say.
SEAN 17

MY DAD TAUGHT me stuff to do with my culture. He said I need to learn to listen to other people and that we have to care for one another, and have respect, and be proud of yourself, be proud.
JIM 13

We don't ask for money or anything, we just want to hear sorry.

IF WHITE PEOPLE JUST TOOK THE TIME TO STOP AND REALISE

IF WHITE PEOPLE just took the time to stop and realise, like if they were more involved with Indigenous people it would be good. Just stop and take the time and have a look I'd say. Even if it takes you to sleep over at one of your Indigenous friend's house, even if they're not close, just to get an understanding of them would be good I think. But I don't think white people want to understand. I think about the past, how Australia got stolen from Aboriginals and Islanders. Well Aboriginals are really into saying sorry but white people just don't want to say they're sorry, that's what I see. I don't know why they don't want to but it's all we ask for. We don't ask for money or anything, we just want to hear sorry.

My parents and relations are willing to accept a sorry. That's all we want, but I can't see why white people can't say sorry for what happened in the past even though it wasn't really their fault. I think Aboriginal/Islander studies should be a compulsory subject in Grade 8. I think it should come along with maths and English and science, all that type of stuff. You're just not going to get along with people if you don't know the background of your country and what really did happen.
BEADE 17

ABORIGINALS AND TORRES Strait Islanders all stick together. If somebody gets hurt we all stick together. It's like family, we stick together. The boys mainly get in the fights and we just look after them. They fight because somebody calls them racist names. And that's why we've got to look after them while they're here. We try to stop the fights and just accept other people. We won't start anything if they don't start anything. Racism is still a major problem in most schools, not so much in this school anymore because it's tamed down a hell of a lot. But probably if we went to another school it would be a lot worse, like in the bigger schools. It's probably because of the way parents teach their children about the Indigenous people of Australia. Because of all the massacres, they probably tell them that the Indigenous people started it all.

SEAN 17

SOME WHITE BOYS pick on the black girls. They'll call them names. They'll think, 'Oh it's a girl, we might as well pick on her'. Like my friend, she got called a name a couple of days ago by a white boy and then she told me. They won't do it to the black boys because they know there's heaps of them and they're scared to do it to the boys. They've only got the guts to do it to the girls but not to boys.

ROY 14

IT'S JUST UNDER THE SKIN

WE MOVED TO this town at the end of Grade 7. It was okay at the start but I'm starting to get sick of it now because I don't really feel comfortable here. I haven't got any relations up here and I just don't feel right here. It feels like a racist town to me. My dad feels the same way and he wants to move back. It's just the impressions you get from people and it's a covert thing—it's like it's just under the skin. For example, when I go shopping and I give money to the checkout person, I always take notice of it. It's a thing I always do. I just don't like unfairness and racism and so I just take more notice of it when it happens. Like I notice what happens to the man in front of me, how they give the change to each other, or how they say hello. To the person in front of me they ask, 'Oh, hi, how are you?', and all this stuff. But to me they just say, 'Oh, hello', and that's about it. Then when they're giving change, they don't really put it in my hand, they just drop it in my hand and don't make contact, but with the people in front they put it in their hand. I just take notice of little things like that.

No one has said anything really racist to me or anything like that. So I think it's just like a covert thing, it's under the skin. Because of the law these days, I think you can't really say much or else you can just take them to court.

BEADE 17

MY DAD WAS BORN on Thursday Island and mum was born in Charters Towers. My mum is a South Sea Islander and Aboriginal. I don't know what tribe she is from. This year I learnt a lot in Aboriginal and Torres Strait Islander studies about Aboriginal people. I didn't know anything about Australia Day, about the first settlement and about how Indigenous people don't like that at all.

In ATSI I learn just about everything about Aboriginal culture. I am just starting to learn about my culture and the languages in the Islands. You just pretty much can't forget about the past, the genocide of Aboriginal, Torres Strait Islander people—the racism and Australian history, black history. Like racism, it still goes on and it hurts a lot of people and you just think of it, like you're still in the past. You can't get the past out of your head. It's like all the past is just coming back to you and just little by little just growing again.

NEIL 17

WHAT I WOULD say to white people is don't be scared of us because we don't want to fight people or anything just for the hell of it, we're friendly people. We just like talking to people and being friends with them and joining in activities. We're not out to cause trouble.

SEAN 17

My mum is a South Sea Islander and Aboriginal. I don't know what tribe she is from. This year I learnt a lot in Aboriginal and Torres Strait Islander studies about Aboriginal people.

MY MUM AND DAD are up in Mauri. I live with my dad's brother. I've learnt about the land and about my culture. I've learnt weaving and they've taught me how to build a house, how to cook and how to look after your family. Here I sort of miss that stuff. I miss the learning. Black people say we need to talk like white people talk. That's why I came here for a good education—to lift our Island up, to lift the Torres Strait up. Every time the Island songs come on the radio, it breaks my heart. I just sit there and think I should be there now. But I know school is better for me.

MARK 15

PHOTO COURTESY OF INDIGENOUS YOUNG FATHERS SUPPORT GROUP, QLD

IT'S A GOOD THING being a Torres Strait Islander but it's a bit confusing when white people talk to us and we can't understand. Like my father said you have to get to know white people, and then white people can get to know you. We can't let our culture flow away. We just have to keep on with our culture. You have to get to know weaving and Island dance. When I was little I saw my parents do dancing, so I would just go and dance with them until I got used to it, and then I just danced. Some other Aboriginal, Torres Strait Islander boys dance too but they don't dance like us. Different Aboriginal people and the Torres Strait Islander tribes have different dances and different languages to us. We talk Creole English. Creole is half English and half Torres Strait Islander's language. And my second language is Miria, that's another Torres Strait language we use, and the third one is English.

JIM 13

We can't let our culture flow away. We just have to keep on with our culture.

Sexual labels: to be or not, or both or neither

As the previous boys have shown, there is so much diversity and difference out there. Sometimes the label 'different' is used to define someone as not being a 'normal' person. But who decides what's 'normal' and what's 'different'? How can the word 'different' be used to make someone feel they are inferior or unequal? Let's read what these boys, who do not label themselves as heterosexual, have to say about sexual diversity.

I THINK IT'S HARD for gay people to be out in society, because they're different, different to the majority of people. I think you're only different if you're not with the majority of people. So I'm only different if I wear my collar up and everyone wears it down. Another guy's different because he likes men and all the other boys like females. Because he's different, that's why he's thought to be an outcast. That's why he's seen not to be a normal person.
NIGEL 17

IF SOMEONE IS GAY some people cannot handle that and resort to bullying. God made everyone different for a reason!
FRANCO 13

BEING CALLED 'GAY' or 'fag' is a general insult. It's part of the vocabulary, and they don't really intend it to mean exactly what it means, they just yell it out because it's an insult. It's quite peculiar because I'm perfectly fine with people if they're gay or bisexual. I've even got a couple of friends who are. I don't see how that could be an insult. I think guys generally use it as an insult because it's like that social rule that you have to be straight and you can't be gay or bisexual.
JOHNNY 17

GROWING UP DIFFERENT

It's hard going through life,
day by day, hour by hour, heart beat to heart beat.
The world's perceptions differ internally,
externally they are but merely mirrored images.

Conflict,
like a bombardment of mirrors
each focussing on another image,
another point of view.
Fear of the unknown
Fear of unjust reasoning

My life.
Me . . .
JOEL BAKER 16

IN MY LIFE THERE is one thing that I have been told by my mum. Difference is okay! Homosexuality can be hard to accept and hard to grasp. I'm not fully gay, I'm bisexual and it's worse. Knowing that you find your friends who cat-whistle and catcall at girls handsome. Not only is it hard but very awkward. If you are different to your friends and wondering if only they knew, it's terrifying. The kind of emotional damage it could do to a young boy has the potential to be devastating. What if they knew about me? How would it affect our friendship?

Homophobia is a prejudice just like racism and ageism. It requires people to be very close minded and also highly ignorant. So are people scared of homosexuals? Are homophobes afraid that it may be a contagious disease? Well let me burst your bubble—it's not.

Are homosexuals not allowed to love or be loved? Is that what society is imposing on this group of people? You can love but only a person of the opposite sex. Well, may I be frank when I say this, 'Screw that!'.

Homosexuality is not something that just happens to you. Homosexuality is a feeling that many people experience.

No doubt my views will cop a lot of flack. But as our teacher said, the writer has the power of the pen, well computer actually.

May your life be peaceful; follow your heart.

JOEL BAKER 16

BEING BISEXUAL, PEOPLE generally assume that you're heterosexual. My best friend who's gay has now got to the stage where he thinks that if you're bisexual you should choose to be homosexual. I don't even think that the word 'bisexual' was ever used while I was at school except just to say these are the types of sexualities that there are, but otherwise it was always just an issue of you're either gay or you're straight and even homosexuality had so little visibility. It was much more accepted for girls to be bisexual. I remember I would go to parties and people would play spin the bottle or something and girls were always expected to kiss other girls but guys never ever would. Bisexuality has come to be more accepted among girls probably because it's a straight male fantasy.

Another interesting thing I found at school in my later years was guys apologising to me for teasing me about my sexuality. In both cases those guys were gay and they had been dealing with their own issues of sexuality.

ROWAN 19

Homophobia is a prejudice just like racism and ageism.

IS THIS FOR REAL?

The times are changin' and we are
complaining:
The world isn't just what it used to be,
We are evolving; the world is still
revolving,
And day by day our problems grow.

Chorus
School problems and family problems too,
Homelessness and alcohol: what are we to
do?
Break ups and fights, rape and abuse:
What is going on, has the world run loose?
Drugs and violence: is this for real?
Homosexuality: what's the big deal?

Schools across the world I urge you to
think, we go to school to learn but come
away with twelve years of stress and six
suicide attempts.

Chorus (repeat)

Now from schools to families, families:
what is going on there?
I thought that families were people who,
people who love and care.
Obviously I'm wrong, but why am I wrong,
I shouldn't be wrong.
Can we fix this problem before too long?

Chorus (repeat)

⊛ MICK CURRAN 2000

I WROTE THIS SONG 'Is this for real?' to
spread the word of how teenagers cope
with life these days. I tried to include all
the aspects that trouble a teenager. At first I
didn't include homosexuality, even though
I am gay myself and I know that this is one
of the biggest problems. I don't really care
how people take the song as long as it gets
the main message across. I hope some
others will take my example and write
about their real feelings for the world to
hear. All you teenagers out there, don't be
scared to talk about gay issues in schools.
The only way we can change people's
opinions is by showing them that we are
proud of who we are.
MICK CURRAN 17

IF I WAS GAY my mum would be kind of
strange but I reckon she would respect me
as a person. Some gay people are really
strong, they see some really hard times and
they just get on with life.
WAYNE 16

Let's go into the diary of a guy telling his family that he's gay. Johnathon below sent us excerpts from the diary he kept which explored how those around him dealt with his coming out, how they shifted and grew and learned to keep loving the guy behind the label.

EXCERPTS FROM A DIARY

24 OCTOBER 1999

'**WHY DO YOU THINK** you are?'

'MUM, I don't think I am, I KNOW!'

'Yes, but why . . . '

I ran down the beach, not caring where I went or who was looking at me. I needed to be alone for a while. It was a miserable wet day. I stood there just standing in the cold rain. It seemed to me that nobody cared and when they did they cared too much. As the tears ran down my already wet face, they were washed away, so that anyone that saw me, just thought me to be cold and wet. I walked further along the beach looking out at the menacing surf as it took its anger out on the soft, unrelenting sand. I picked up a large shell and threw it at the churning water, channelling all my anger and frustration into the throw. I sat down shivering in my cold clothes and watched a lonesome seagull, which sat riding a wave. I thought to myself, as another warm tear trickled down my face, 'Well, at least I'm not the only one leading a lonely life! Why is it that people don't want to even try to understand! Why can't they just accept me for who I am rather than if I'm gay or straight! All that's different from other guys to me is that I'm attracted to guys not girls.'

> ## I sat down shivering in my cold clothes and watched a lonesome seagull, which sat riding a wave.

I stood back up and started the tiresome half-hour walk home, dreading the fact that I had to return at all. Earlier that day, I had come out to my parents and they had seemed totally oblivious to the fact that I had just told them that I'm gay! Apart from Mum holding back tears in front of me until I had left the room and Dad saying in the most casual of voices, 'It's only a phase son, you'll get over it.' It really hurt me that they didn't even hug me once! All the stories I had read about people coming out had included them being hugged or kicked out and I felt like I was half way between both.

24 MARCH 2000

Five months down the track, I look back and realise that at times the only thing stopping me from killing myself is the support and friendship that my closest friends have shown me during these troubled times. The fact that my brother had killed himself fourteen months ago has made me realise that I don't want to be the reason for everybody to go through that much pain again, no matter how much I'm going through. At the moment I'm taking it one step at a time, trying my best at everything I attempt, to prove to people that I'm no different to anyone else.

As time goes by things change. I sit down and I look at the calendar, five months since I last wrote something. So much time, so little written, yet so much has happened. By now I have had two serious relationships and gained many friends. I have come out to fifteen friends at school (three of those being teachers), and not one of them have denied me their support or friendship because of my sexuality.

Of late there have been two guys at school who have taken to not using my name but the word 'fag' to address me. The fact of the matter is they don't actually know that I'm gay and there have been a few times that I have come close to saying 'YES I AM A FAG . . . YOU SEEM TO ALREADY KNOW ABOUT THAT SO WHAT'S YOUR PROBLEM!?' The only thing stopping me from a public outburst like that is I'm likely to receive a fist in the face and lose a few friends who wouldn't be able to accept the fact, because of their narrow-mindedness.

Being gay isn't JUST about sex as most straight people assume . . . It's about being attracted mentally and physically to the same gender and in the world we live in it's also about continuously being hurt by the people who don't understand the truth.

My parents and I have been attending PFLAG [Parents and Friends of Lesbians and Gays]. I think that going to PFLAG was one of the best things that my parents have done for me. PFLAG has brought Mum and Dad's train of thought to a more positive attitude about my sexuality. Mum and Dad both joke with me about my sexuality. For instance, I once said 'Dad . . . shhhhh! I'm trying to concentrate and can't think straight!'. He then replied, 'I didn't think you could think straight, you being gay and all!', followed by both of us laughing.

I think they find it easier to talk about after having been to a few PFLAGs.

28 MARCH 2000

I had maths and was dreading having to go, not because of the subject, but because those two guys that give me a hard time are in that particular class. For the past few weeks I've been struggling with work and not getting much done because of the two guys continually harassing me. I only accomplished half a page of work in the one and a half hour class, with all the 'FAG . . . FAG . . . FAG . . . POOF . . . PILLOW-BITER' and a few I won't mention being aimed at me continuously for the whole session until I finally got up and asked the teacher if I could go to see the student welfare coordinator. By this time I was well passed the laughing stage, I had put up with it for over three weeks and at that moment was at the brink of crying. I had previously mentioned what was happening in the class to the coordinator and she had spoken to the class teacher about it. So when I told her that it was still happening and was getting worse, she went straight to the classroom and had a chat with the two guys in question.

Half an hour later I was asked to accompany her to the middle school manager's office where I received an apology from both of the guys and their assurances that it wouldn't happen again . . . later I was told by the manager that if they harassed me again . . . even if it was in subtle ways, to tell him and they would automatically be suspended and the police would become involved because harassment of any kind is not on.

Mum and Dad both joke with me about my sexuality.

I just happened to turn it onto Ricki Lake and the topic was 'My Family Hates Me Cause I'm Gay'

12 APRIL 2000 EASTER HOLIDAYS

The Minus18 disco run by PFLAG, Melbourne, I went intending not to pick up but I did, and also GOT picked up, an amazing ego booster. And I made two really good friends out of it.

The next day, I came out to my brother while we were driving up to some traffic lights. He kept nagging me about where the disco was in Melbourne and I ended up just saying, 'Will you still love me no matter what?'. He said yes and I told him that it was on Commercial Road. He asked me what the big deal was and I had to explain that Commercial Road was known as the gay community of Melbourne. Two minutes later he looked at me and said, 'You're gay are you?', and I said simply, 'Yes I am', and to that I got a full-faced stare, and I had to remind him to look at the road.

Later I asked if he was okay with it and he asked if he had a choice to which I told him that he didn't. When we got back to his place he didn't want to talk about it so I didn't mention it again and turned on the TV. I swear I had no idea what was on but I just happened to turn it onto Ricki Lake and the topic was 'My Family Hates Me Cause I'm Gay', so I decided I'd leave it on there and watch it . . . I noticed my brother's eyes flicker from the newspaper to the screen a few times.

Later that night I came out to his fiancee, she took it great!! She told me that 'He accepts you and won't disown you or anything like that, you're still his brother'.

29 APRIL 2000

'Hi Johnathon, it's Jodie. I'm just ringing cause I think this is a special day for youuu!! And I just wanna let you know that I think you're FAAANNNTASTIC!' That was the message awaiting me on the answering machine when I got home. The reason for the phone call was that it was one year exactly since I had first 'come out'.

18 JUNE 2000

'Trav . . . there's something I have to tell you but . . . I don't really want to. Firstly . . . you remember how you said you'd love me as a brother no matter what and I could tell you anything?'

'Yeah . . . what have you done?'

'Nothing . . . '

'Well what are you gonna do?'

'NOTHING . . . Look . . . '

'Well you better tell me on the way home.'

'Why? So you don't leave me in town . . . to walk home?'

'Yup', he answered with an ear splitting grin.

On the way home after he bought me lunch, Trav began to ask me what I had to tell him. I'd start to say it and then I couldn't bring myself to . . . finally I blurted out, 'Okay, I'm gay.'

'Now if it was something like that I'd have to hit you', he said, 'so what'd you have to tell me?'.

'I told you I'm gay.'

He looked out the side window of the car taking a deep breath and said, 'Well if you're happy then I am . . . There's nothing I can do if this is how you are and I'm still your brother!'.

Later in the afternoon when we got home and he was leaving he HUGGED me! He has been the first person to hug me who I have come out to and it made me feel really good to know that he still loves me.

Being a teenager and coming out to family would have to be the scariest thing I have ever done, but I only did it because I felt comfortable with it . . . coming out is one thing that should only be done when the person coming out is ready to or things can go horribly wrong.

I admit that I am one of very few people who has had the luck to have my family's full support. I have friends who have been kicked out and whose parents have even come close to violence after their child has told them that they're gay . . . But what those friends need is to be listened to and to be loved and most importantly to know that they're loved.

■ ■ ■ ■ ■ ■ ■

Being a teenager and coming out to family would have to be the scariest thing I have ever done, but I only did it because I felt comfortable with it

■ ■ ■ ■ ■ ■ ■

7 JULY 2000

Mum told me she really hadn't accepted my sexuality and is unsure whether she ever will.

11 JULY 2000

The start of my relationship with Liam . . .

17 DECEMBER 2000

Liam and I have been together for over five months now: I love him so much!! And my parents are really accepting of him and he is even allowed to sleep in my room. I s'pose that is really showing how much they trust me. Mum has come to accept my sexuality and I'm glad.

My story is as yet incomplete and always will be as I will continue it for the rest of my life.

JOHNATHON SILVARHAVEN 15—16

MY DAD RECKONS that gay people are against religion because God didn't create humans to be like that. He would probably kill me if I was gay. My mum would be pretty angry for a bit but then I think she might calm down.
CHRIS 16

IN RE [RELIGIOUS EDUCATION] the teacher was saying how the Church teaches equality and I said, 'If it's so equal then how come women and gay people can't be priests?'. She was a bit stuck and said, 'Well, the bible says that only men can teach the word of God because God was a man, and the bible also says that men and women should be together'.

I said, 'Well, isn't that a bit dated because the bible was written so long ago?' and she couldn't really give me a straight answer which is pretty sad. The Catholic Church is supposed to be equal to everyone but they don't include homosexuals or women. If you only dig deeper into the equality thing, you find that the Church isn't really equal.
MAX 16

I FEEL VERY MUCH hindered from expressing my sexuality by the words of my mother. When she found out about me she said she would easily cut me off from the family and disown me if I was certainly gay. It seemed that all the effort I had put into coming out was burned to the ground with the words of my mother. I guess her reaction was one typical of most European and devout Catholic women of her generation. I was very much in a battle between my culture, my religion and faith, which I still hold central to my life. I was also in a battle with society and 'normality'. What felt 'normal' to me was not 'normal' to society at large. What hurt the most was that she recognised that her love was conditional and had no qualms in making them perfectly clear to me. She didn't talk to me for two months and my father and the rest of my family had no idea why and still don't.

I sought the advice of a Catholic gay priest who was able to counsel me on the place of my faith in this struggle, which was extremely comforting. When my mother found out there was a gay priest in the clergy who was filling my head with ideas that God made me gay and that it was okay to be gay, she flipped out and was prepared to challenge his position in the archdiocese by going to see the archbishop! My mother the right-wing Catholic was ready to become Pope! Anyway after a very messy fight where Mum hit me a few times in anger and threw things at me (my mother is really a lovely woman and this is not her usual style) I figured that there was only one thing to do—something that I

didn't believe in or agree with—that was to lie to her. So in a sense I went back into the closet. I was making excuses as to where I was going, that I was studying late at the library for upcoming exams or working on a group project and staying at my friend's house that night closer to the city so I didn't have to drive home just so that I could spend the night at my boyfriend's house.

I haven't always found the gay community welcoming either. I am not blond-haired and blue-eyed, I don't have a body like Ricky Martin. I discovered a superficial quality to the gay scene which was based on how many guys you picked up the other week, how thin you are, what drugs you are on and who you know. For someone who didn't care for any of that it put me in a position of disadvantage as far as chances of finding someone to have a relationship with.

VITTORIO 19

'RELIGION AND HOMOPHOBIA', BEN GERRARD 17

Handling homophobia

I WAS JUST STANDING outside a shop and there were some guys from the year above me there, and one of them came up and said, 'Oh, I see you're a faggot'. I turned the conversation around and was just talking to him and by the end of the conversation he said, 'Well have a really good day, I'll see you later'. If I'm put in that situation I just kind of slip into autopilot and talk to them. If they're being really big and macho, acknowledge that and don't try and break their little illusion straight away. If you talk really aggressively to them, they're going to talk aggressively back and then you're not going to get anywhere. Most of the time they'll say something like, 'Oh, I hear you're a faggot'. It's like, 'Oh, yes, well who did you hear that from?'. You take hold of the conversation and turn it back around. If they ask a question, turn it back and ask them what they think about it before you just rattle off your answer.
XANDER 19

MATTHEW GOUGH 17

GROWING UP AS A gay adolescent in an all male school was never going to be easy, and at times wasn't, with all the taunts and associated bullying. But because of a kind-natured teacher, life became tolerable so I'd just like to say thank you to all of the teachers out there that show compassion and understanding to the misunderstood and oppressed. You are all angels from above. Thank you!
MATTHEW GOUGH 17

I'd just like to say thank you to all of the teachers out there that show compassion and understanding

CHAPTER NINE
LIFE, PLACE & HEADSPACE

Come on in,
look around.

I'll apologise now for the mess,
haven't had time to clean things up for a while,
and you might want to avoid the dark corners,
I'm still not sure what might be lurking there . . .

I suppose you want the grand tour,
although that doesn't amount to much.

The snarling things,
the ones hiding away out of sight,
are my neuroses,
they only come out in the dark.

And the big rusting engine,
the one that's coated in dust,
is what remains of the old sex drive.
I think it might be broken,
but I keep it around.

I might need it one day,
after I clear away all the hang ups.

The little bruised and battered thing is the ego.
I don't use it much these days,
but it still grows uncontrollably
if it's massaged the right way.

'HEAD SPACE', BEN GERRARD 17

HEADSPACE

Not that I recommend trying it,
it can be a little pretentious when it's aroused.

The giant gold statue,
is my own little monument to self-pity,
It doesn't really do much,
but looking at it makes me feel better
sometimes.

Course,
other times it just weighs me down.

The big pile of dirt,
that's hiding most of my buried feelings.
I keep trying to dig them back up,
but I think I hid them all too far down.

It's amazing how hard it is to recover things
when you're not really sure where you put
them.

So that's it,
my own private little headspace.
Look around at your leisure,
and let me know if you trip over my lost
innocence.
PETER BALL 22

MY PLACE, MY SPACE, MY BEDROOM

MY ROOM IS YELLOW with blue trimming. It has posters scattered randomly on the walls like the bumps and bruises of a preschooler. The posters are pictures of my favourite bands and just other pictures that have personal meaning and suit my character. Some of the pictures and printouts include my anti-stress kit, my vampire bat sketch and photograph of lightning filling the skies during an electrical storm.

Then there is my mirror. I cut letters out of magazines then arranged them on the mirror so it defined the meaning of reflection. There is also my shelf which contains amounts of trophies, motion objects, crystals, candles and any other object that contains any sentimental value.

There is also my desk that is for ever-growing homework which haunts me at every glance, yet I still manage to feel at peace in a somewhat distorted environment.

And last of all my bed. This bed is of sacred value to me. I have slept in it the past ten years and it shows signs of age but has managed to comfort me in times of bad and good.

The scent of my room smells of eleven summers, winters, autumns and springs. It smells of the body odour released after a restless night's sleep and the deodorant which is in a constant battle to fight it. Last of all, it smells of the sage incense used during the night till each wisp of smoke has risen to a height where it no longer exists.

The sounds of music blaring from my stereo fill my room as to block out the sound from elsewhere in this forsaken world. It hums of Triple J, various CDs and tapes and sometimes, when I'm in the mood, even simply static. Also the sound of moaning, whining and talking while I sleep, and when unoccupied, my room is filled with the sound of silence.

My room tastes of cups of hot tea and Milo that I smuggle in from the kitchen as to offer warmth on a cold winter night. Also of icecreams and chilled lemonade as the summer devastates us with its heat.

The surface of my room feels as if it were an alien planet at the stroke of midnight, as I run my fingers across the walls in search of a door that may grant me freedom to relieve myself.

When I'm in my room, I feel more secure so to speak. Unfortunately while I'm outside, I must cast a mask over my face and personality and be . . . well . . . normal.

> THE SCENT OF MY ROOM SMELLS OF ELEVEN SUMMERS, WINTERS, AUTUMNS AND SPRINGS.

I'm in limbo. Outside of my room I'm emotionally happy yet when I'm inside my room I take on somewhat of a manic depressive status. The only advantage is that I know I'm smart enough to be stupid (thus meaning if I were to display my full intellect I would be tormented somewhat and be an outcast). Most people don't understand that when I say it although I believe it's true and is what's best for me. It's a kill or be killed kind of world out there, sometimes your only hope is survival, although it's harder when you have no will to live.

Why is my bedroom special? I don't know really. It's probably a replica of many teenagers' bedrooms. The only thing that separates it from others is that it makes me feel safe. Whenever I feel the need to escape from it all, all I do is retire to my quarters in the same way a sick dog goes to its little hole to die. And in there I wait.

My room is utterly private. Although there are exceptions like when my brother comes in then screams as he's pushed outside in the hope that he'll know better next time. Then there's my father who only comes in to wake me up by yelling, 'Wake up sloth!', which I believe is a near-accurate description. It's pretty much solitude, except for when I invite my friends over and we just tune out and chat for a couple of hours with the stereo blasting away.

I love my room. It's my favourite place.

What takes me to the place? My head, my heart and my legs.

BRYAN FROUD 16

WHY IS MY BEDROOM SPECIAL? I DON'T KNOW REALLY. IT'S PROBABLY A REPLICA OF MANY TEENAGERS' BEDROOMS. THE ONLY THING THAT SEPARATES IT FROM OTHERS IS THAT IT MAKES ME FEEL SAFE.

'HEAD SPACE', BEN GERRARD 17

CHRYSALIS

He stood every morning
In front of the mirror
And tried to see
Within himself
He cursed the deception
Of his lying reflection
But where else
Could he turn to find help?

He saw nothing, inevitably
But glassy triviality
The mirror made a mockery
Of his searching for identity.

Soon, the imperfection
Of his body will depress him
He puts on his clothes
He goes downstairs
And makes himself some breakfast.

His mother mistakes obsession
For selfish narcissism
She doesn't know him either
Like she didn't know his father
He divides light like a prism.

The stage inside is empty
He reeks of dusty air
So he projects a role
To plug the hole
He perceives deep within him.

Shallowness is good enough
It will have to do for now
Thoughts skip along the surface
Like a stone questing
The bottom of the flow.

He thought he could
Mould the outside
Leave the inside void
He was wrong
He wasn't that strong
Too often reality
Tore through his soft protection.

His mind asked too many
Questions to be
Submerged in some ad
Executive fantasy.

He wants to know who he is
Not what they
Perceive him to be
He knows their perception
It was his invention
He wants to go through
The looking glass.

He needs to go through chrysalis
Become the butterfly
He feels inside him
Brush his wings in the pollen
See the petals in primary colours
Looking for the perfect flower
Waiting for his finest hour
He wants to escape
Much too soon
Push himself from his cocoon
He doesn't understand
That the process doesn't last forever.

JOHN BELL 19

We've been into a lot of headspaces and heartspaces in this book. As the previous three guys show us, each life, each guy has this different space of feelings, thoughts, experiences, adventures, disasters. What's your headspace like? What's your heartspace like? What kind of space do you want in your life? How do you go ahead and be who you want to be, have the life you want, create the identity you want, live your dreams? As you've read in the first three pieces by Peter, Bryan and John, the reality is that your space can sometimes get messy, and life can be like a roller-coaster ride. But you can do some tidying, you can rebuild an even better version of your life, and you can learn to ride that roller-coaster with your heart pumping full of life.

Here are three guys telling us about their messy feelings. The first poem was actually passed on to us by the close friend of someone who wants to stay anonymous but wanted you to read his poem. Just having a close friend who you can trust with these feelings and who'll send a poem of yours to others without breaking your trust, says something fantastic about the space being created there!

I HAVEN'T GOT A NAME FOR IT YET

The suffering that you have,
is strong enough for death.
But for you to go there,
it would be too easy.
You need courage and strength,
to stay here alone. But you
don't know you're alone until there's
nobody here.

Reality is not quite what it seems
because the pain is more than
what we can feel.
Pain from the heart and
pain from the head
can drive you to pure madness.
'INCOGNITO' SENT TO US BY JOEL BAKER

PRISONER OF GENESIS

Tonight I am alone,
while the melancholic firmament
burns me with its icy stars and drowns
me with its seas of nothing.
I am nowhere—somewhere, between
yesterday and tomorrow . . . lost and
blinded in this timeless, glittering void.
And as I float past the weeping moon
I am consumed by unconsciousness
where I will dream of light and daytime.
BEN GERRARD 17

BUT THE ROAD IS UNEVEN
LIKE A CHINESE WHISPER

The school bus was always packed
and everyday we slid our tickets
in with a beep. I would sit and wish
the to and fro of that translucent cage,
its bars of shade were like a lullaby;
the crib that floated over bitumen . . .

But that dream broke, the quadrangle
awoke us, cuddling our little rebellions . . .
There I sat, dared not even cross my legs
because one girl said it wasn't manly.

On a flight of stairs to French, Tanya
told me I reeked of mull, but I took
little grief, partly because I was unable
to muster a suitably smug reply. Besides,
she couldn't see the world past her nose
and we all looked up to sewers anyway.

Outside Bindi died like a cat in a storm
    drain.
Early next morning she became
another front page face and was awash
with friends for weeks in class thereafter.
Melanie went more quietly, slipping
through the headlines. Twenty odd years
of will stuck in her arm, she faded with
    plastic
stars in her hair and a crotch full of
    ex-rumours.

Paul assures me it was suicide,
but these days it's sometimes hard to say;
Friday not so long ago, Kylie filled in
for a full-timer at the supermarket
off to farewell a first-timer who'd
OD'd with her fella at the cricket.

I saw Melanie, alone once, waiting
for a late night bus to Belconnen, brown
    hair
to the level of her breasts and make-up
    enough
for her to fit like the moon in a dark suit.
She was always beautiful but, it's said,
often broke down when alcohol
gave her the excuse . . . And Paul and I,
left behind like spare change, readily
pretend we could've been her saviours
if only we'd known her in time.
JAMES STUART 22

Shifting spaces, changing places, creating the space you want

In the following two pieces, you'll get to know what it's like dealing with homophobia and what that can lead to: depression, self-scarring, feeling sick and suicidal. Keith takes us into his space right now as he's feeling it and wondering if he can ever pull himself out. Mason looks back from a new place, a new space, a new confident self going forward to a future that's going to be so different. Even though he knows that homophobes are still out there, he has survived and is living life. Think about the space you may be stuck in right now and wondering if there's a way out, another place. And think about where tomorrow may take you as you get older, stronger and more independent.

OF PEACE. OF SOLACE. (WHAT I WANT)

THE BED HADN'T changed, but sitting on it suddenly felt different; I was there, but watching from somewhere else at the same time. The room was freezing, but I couldn't feel the cold. There were people in the house, family, ready to listen I suppose, but I couldn't talk to them. They were the reason I was like this, drinking my life away.

Detachment. That's what I was aiming for; distance from myself. As much distance as I could find in the already half empty bottle of vodka. Escape. I didn't want to be gay, I wanted to be 'normal'. So I kept up my reluctant swigging, trying to get completely out of my head, or at least numb enough to not feel anything anymore. That's why I felt different; the alcohol was severing the ties that bound me unbearably to myself, setting my mind loose to roam free, unburdened by shame and confusion. A strange sensation, one I rarely feel these days. One of peace. Of solace.

It was in a mood like this that I first took my stress out on myself. My forearms are a document that traces the more depressed times of my life, emotions inscribed in flesh as scars. I can remember nearly all of them. The first two are puncture marks, made by a stabbing compass that was aimed at veins, a short, fat mark on the back of my hand from a stanley knife, quite a few pale, faded lines and a dark purple cigarette burn. Currently I have a fresh pair of ugly red lines, about 10 centimetres long, glaring out from my left forearm.

I've never really attempted suicide. I merely went through the motions, seeing what the pain would be like, without committing myself to death. Too scared? Or unwilling to give up so soon? A good friend of mine explained to me the psychology behind 'cutting'; the theory says that we cause short-term physical pain to override long-term emotional pain. A pretty bleak assessment, but true enough in the case of my friend and I. She and I are more than a little fucked up. By anyone's standards.

Back then, I had no one to talk to. Or rather more accurately, I had lots of people to talk to, but the thought of being so open with anyone terrified me. I know what it feels like to have your intestines knot up in anxiety at the thought of who you are and what your life could be like. Count yourself lucky. My family was, and still is, unapproachable; I'm not in a position, mentally or financially, where I could deal with their rejection. The friends I have now are the same ones as before I came out, but they were unapproachable too. Insecurity made me think that they were friends who belonged to the straight version of me I had created to hide behind. Whom I still hide behind, when confronted with certain people. I have to. Fear, self-preservation and all that.

My familiar, comforting cage of self-pity was all I knew for a good ten, twelve months. I just couldn't cope. The thought of everyone I loved or even knew leaving, coupled with the other, more normal stresses and dramas in a teenager's life were too much for me. Everything stacked up, problem on problem, and got too huge. Misery loves company, and boy was mine popular. At school I retreated from people,

terrified of the rejection that I was sure would accompany any honesty on my part. Aren't they supposed to be the best years of my life?

The stigma that society has attached to homosexuality was far too great for me to deal with. In these supposedly tolerant times, television, schoolmates and the global community that I was a part of was making me feel defective; there was something wrong with me that I needed to be punished for. I was one of nature's mistakes. People who would vehemently deny being racist or sexist or homophobic still make derogatory comments, they just do it subconsciously. That was what scared me most. People who I called friends expressed these anti-gay sentiments—they didn't really mean anything by it, but at my school, a worthless little faggot can't take any chances.

There is a mighty power in words. To harm or to heal.

Sticks and stones
will break my bones,
but names have emotionally scarred me.

I've heard about a guy who ran away from his Townsville home when he was fourteen. Abusive father. He went to Sydney and lived on the streets; got involved with drugs. Sold himself to get money for food. At fourteen. Should fourteen-year-old children be made to feel that way, to take up prostitution, just because of their sexuality? After six months his mother came and took him home, only to be kicked out by his father when he came out to them.

Later on in his life he started working at his local AIDS council, providing assistance and information to anyone who needed it. Volunteer basis. In the carpark of his work he was severely beaten by three young men, ' . . . just 'cause he was a fag'. On a separate occasion, a colleague was attacked in the same car park. He retreated to the offices with the needle he was stabbed with hanging out of his neck.

Is that fair? Is there any possible justification for the trauma that the queer community has been subjected to? For the hatred that has been directed at us on a highly personal level? Can you blame me for wanting to die? That was the best way I could think of to deal with the shitty hand I've been dealt.

It was about eleven months ago that I told my closest, most trustworthy friends that I was gay, and even then it was only because I was drunk. Only eleven months. But I still haven't told my parents. I've been raised in what I would regard as a fairly tolerant family environment; my mum thinks Bob Downe (a.k.a. Mark Trevorrow) is one of the funniest men alive, and my dad is relatively sparing with the homophobic comments. It took years for me to get up the courage to tell my friends, so who can guess how long it is before I tell my parents?

I don't want to even have to think about the possibility of them rejecting me.

I don't want to have to deal with all the shit that is going to get thrown my way.

I want the legal age of consent for heterosexuals and homosexuals to be the same.

I want to be able to walk along Swanston Street, holding hands with a boyfriend.

I want to be able to be open at school, without the threat of being bashed.

Hell, I even want the right to a legally acknowledged marriage, should I ever find a nice enough guy some time down the track.

World peace, a cure for AIDS and Kurt Cobain re-animated would all be nice too, but I'm not going to hold my breath.

KEITH STEWART 17

'GUY'S FACE', BEN GERRARD 17

BOYS DO CRY

WHEN I WAS NINETEEN, I had a nervous breakdown. When other boys were exploring love and life, I was wallowing in a cesspool of self-abuse and confusion. Depressed, misguided and in a moral disarray, I posed a question to myself that would change my life forever. I asked myself if I wanted to go on living.

Yes and no. This paradox that I revealed to myself started a quest that drove me across continents and half way around the world. It forced me to explore a universe within my own psyche, a search for my own truths in life. Ten years on, I revere myself as a god, humbled by the pain, wiser for the lessons that I have learnt. Stronger for facing the darkest, most fearsome and violent terror that lurks within me. As much a part of me as the joy of life, in the light that I now choose to live in.

It was a moment, perhaps one of the most intense in my life. A moment to question all that I have ever known, all that I have ever been told and believed. A time to sort my reality from that of those who had been so much a part of my life. And although I would have never believed it at the time, it was the best thing that could have ever happened to me.

This is my story of coming out, the hard way.

I was always a strong, healthy lad. Good, honest parents. Supportive childhood, plenty of friends, no real hang-ups. Kinda spoilt really. So it was a bit of a shock when I left school, to venture forth into the 'real' world, where I began to discover the stigma, the taboo that surrounds the enigma of the homosexual. The dirty, filthy, fucking queer, faggot scum. Who me?

Starting work as an apprentice chef, I was inducted into an industry that was famous for the talents of gay men and women. After all, no one can give you a service like a gay man can. Fabulous! Unfortunately, my narrow eyes had not yet been open to the travesty of role playing, for I was fooled by the image that people project, either for reasons of protection, conformity or just plain old shock value. Ah, the naivety of youth, the paradox of thinking oneself so smart, and yet so gullible. I believed all that I could see. I had not yet learnt to read between the lines, to see through the lies, to read the silences, that say as much by not being said as by what is said. To look for the motivations that drive people, to do and say what they do, irrelevant of the hurt they cause themselves and others. Ah, the naivety of youth.

It was a time for work. So much so that I concentrated on my new career, and denied myself the nurture and self-love that is required to explore one's own sexuality, however orientated. The denial grew, with long periods of celibacy, a refusal to engage with the subject which soon grew into terror to even consider the subject. A seed of doubt had been planted by those who I considered allies, workmates and friends. The ones who called me 'mate'.

'Thanks . . . mate!'

Conformity is a funny thing. What we choose to call normal. What we choose to consider right. Morals. Truth. Lies. I soon found myself adhering to an unseen code, that of the Australian male. The Aussie Bloke. That last bastion of straight society. The myths of the heterosexual orthodoxy. Forging an image that was credible in the eyes of my new 'mates'. Hey, I could hate! I could lie! I was filled with anger at the world! I'm a Man! Respecting those time honoured traits, I became one of those most abhorrent creatures.

A homophobe.

Growing a thick skin that would protect my tender underbelly from the misguided insecure inflictions of those that posed to believe all that they self-righteously stood for. Moral enforcers. People that believed their own bullshit after being fed dogmatic lies for so long. I don't blame them,

I only have pity for their ignorance. For their refusal to discover their own light, to deny their own truths for so long.

The lie grew. For years I denied my desires. Except for those stolen moments when I thought that no one was watching, or alone at night. I could lift the curtains on my performance and relish in the fantasy world of my imagination. I could have anyone that I wanted. There was no hurt, no hate. They always did what I wanted, and more. They were always perfect. Satisfaction guaranteed. What a perfect set-up! Eh?

Then came the wonderful world of drugs. What better way to fulfil a fantasy than by getting off your face. Escapism at its best. Alcohol and dope were my choice of intoxicants. I suppose it could have been worse, smack, speed, acid. No, the first two didn't do it for me, and acid, well, it brought up too many issues, hinted at too many truths. I certainly wasn't ready for truth. I had a lot more lying to do to myself. A lot more pain to experience, before I was ready to face myself. No, it would be several years before that was to happen.

Well the years did pass, and I was able to hold down the facade. At times I think I actually started to believe it too. Then one day, I was discovered by a girl. Shock, someone actually found me attractive? I certainly didn't. She helped me see the damage that I was doing to myself. She loved me for being me, bullshit and all. I opened up to another being, and it was a long time since I had done something so noble. I began to allow the thick hide to reveal the tender emotions that had so long been suppressed. I learned to love again. She showed me to me. Showed me what I was doing to myself, the great injustice that I had committed, and all for a concept that I truly did not understand. She helped me learn to love myself again, and in the process earned my eternal love and gratitude. A friend for life.

We lived and we loved. Had fun like the best of mates do. But, in order to complete the healing process, one day a realisation came to me, a need to tackle issues that had so long been suppressed. I had to explore my sexual desires with another man. I chose to leave my home town, to travel and see the world, to get an education in life. Unfortunately, in doing so I hurt the person who had come to represent love, in its purity. For this I will always carry that burden, but through pain comes healing, so I did what I had to do, and left.

Away from home, from those that thought that they knew me, I could explore those avenues in life that I had so long denied myself. I did all the things that I wanted to. Some were great. Some were terrible. I experienced emotions that I never knew before. I laughed, I cried. I felt pure ecstasy, I experienced disgust and despair. I did it all. And in the process I discovered my truths, my loves, my dislikes. I discovered me.

I will never forget the day when I finally came to terms with it all. I woke up, ecstatic and proceeded to cry. Tears of joy. Regained emotion and self-respect. Love for myself and all that I stood for, all that I believed in. Not because someone had told me that that was the way it is, but because I had experienced it for myself. I had done it for me, and for no one else. It has become my new birthday, a re-birth-day. A day to celebrate my acceptance of my own self, my desires, my faults, my being.

My special place in the world, amongst the rich colour of the tapestry of life itself.

MASON CHIDGEY 29

So we can learn a lot from these guys. It's about loving and respecting yourself, and that can be really hard sometimes when people around you don't accept who you are. But as Nigel shows us, it is possible to create that space of self-love and respect, and to be proud of who you are.

I'M PROUD TO BE AN ABORIGINAL BOY

I'M REALLY PROUD to be an Aboriginal boy. We went on a camp and there was this Aboriginal tribe singing the song 'I'm Proud to be an Aborigine'. I was sitting down with all my friends and they were going, 'I'm Proud to be Aboriginal', and for some reason my hand just went up all by itself, and I was like shame. I was looking around and everyone was looking at me but then I noticed right deep down inside I'm really proud, I'm so proud to be an Aboriginal and I believe stuff that my family believes in.

When I went to primary school I used to believe in God and Jesus, and it's just been about a year that I've stopped believing in them. And the only reason why I've stopped is because I heard from heaps of people that if you believe in God and Jesus you're going to heaven, if you don't you're going to hell. My family don't believe in God and Jesus and I'm thinking, 'They're going to hell?'. That's not heaven to me if my family is not there. If my family is going to a burning river when they die or if they're going to be in this cage all their life, I want to be in that river to burn with my family, I want to be in that cage to be with my family. That's why I've stopped believing in God and Jesus. I just want to be wherever they are. If I'm in this golden castle with everything, all the food you can eat and never make mistakes, that's still not heaven to me. Where my family is that's my heaven, I don't care where it is or what I'm doing, that's my heaven as long as I can be with my family.

I said to Mum, 'Where are you going to go when you die?'. She said, 'I don't know son, I just want to go with Uncle Dougie who passed away and with Mum'. I said, 'Mum, I'll come with you, I don't care where it is, I'm coming'. I just want to go with my ancestors. Wherever they are I want to be there.

I'm really proud, I'm so proud to be an Aboriginal and I believe stuff that my family believes in.

a lot of people say that my friend and I are stuck up

I'm really proud, I'm so proud to be who I am and what I'm doing and I really think that I've got something going for me, and everyone says it to me. That makes me feel real good, and they say, 'Oh don't get a big head', and I get really embarrassed because I can't help it that I'm just so proud of myself. I don't mean to be stuck up—a lot of people say that my friend and I are stuck up. We only think that they're saying that because they're jealous—they're jealous that we're really close.

I believe in myself and my mates. I learnt in Aboriginal and Torres Strait Islander studies that Aboriginal people are the longest living race on this earth. And my friend and I looked at each other and said, 'I'm really proud to be one of the longest living people on this earth'. That's just what we believe when we look at each other, and I'm really proud.

NIGEL 17

NIGEL AND SABS

SKILLS FOR EVERYDAY SURVIVAL AND INDEPENDENCE

So you want to be independent? Planning to have your own place? Then you can't be dependent on women for the domestic skills of ordinary, everyday survival. You'll not only need to know how a car and lawnmower work but also washing machines, irons, stoves, vacuum cleaners and sewing machines.

Handling stress and depression

I WATCH WHAT I EAT and I try not to overeat. I make sure that I look after myself. I should do more exercise but I'm happy at the moment. I decided a couple of years ago not to get stressed out and that's really helped me. I just made that decision because the year before I'd been too stressed . . . I thought about my work too much and it just got me really stressed and that wasn't helping me at all. I just felt my head was clogged up, I had too much stress on my brain and everything wasn't feeling right. I think I was putting too much pressure on myself, being too uptight, and so everything was just getting more and more tense.

ANDREW A. 16

I'VE SET MYSELF smaller goals. My first goal is to finish school and then we'll worry about other things later.

JASON 17

I'VE HAD A MENTAL illness and it's taken a lot of time to cope with and get over my battle with it. But I am now getting on with my life. But during the battle, it made me pretty scared, frightened. It's taken me three years and help from a lot of people, too many to thank. But I know it's a thing quite a lot of people suffer from, so I am not alone.

ROB PRYKE 25

'FRIGHT NIGHT', NATHAN SMITH-FEATON 20, YPPI PROGRAM

TO RELEASE STRESS I like listening to music. I just put the radio on and listen to a bit of music. I find that if you're stressed, the radio sort of calms you down.
MARIO 16

WHEN I USED TO race, I was in the state cycling team. When I got kicked out of that, it was pretty hard on me. Some people called me a no-hoper and said, 'You won't get anywhere in life'. I've met a few guys who say, 'Look at your subjects, you're going nowhere'. I just pick myself up, I'm just here for me. When my nanna died I just got sick and tired of everyone giving me crap, so I thought, 'I don't care what they say', and I've just made myself strong for who I am. I've had enough of them and I just get on with my work and I'm going to get a good report. When they call me a nerd, I'm not that fussed. I'm not a straight A student, but I'm just a person who gets on with my life inside and outside of school.
GLENN 16

I JUST GOT SICK AND TIRED OF EVERYONE GIVING ME CRAP

I THOUGHT ABOUT MY WORK TOO MUCH AND IT JUST GOT ME REALLY STRESSED AND THAT WASN'T HELPING ME AT ALL.

WHEN I'M BEING picked on by other guys I just keep on walking. I just take it on the chin and just keep on walking.
CHRIS 16

IF YOU'RE BEING bullied, ignore it and keep going. Be proud of yourself whereas the others are not proud of themselves. You've just got to keep at it. Sometimes it's hard but people get through especially if you've got good friends and you can talk to them.
MARIO 16

The following guys, Jeff and Stephen, wrote these poems as part of the Young People Prevention and Early Intervention Program for young men experiencing mental illness and depression. They give us strong insights into their courageous efforts to 'shake the mood', quit drugs and not 'lose it'.

SOMETIMES THIS HAPPENS TO ME . . .

Sometimes this happens to me . . .
I wake up in the morning
on the wrong side of the bed.
This makes me feel depressed.
Some things I do to shake the mood
are walking to the beach,
going for a surf, going
for a pushbike ride or I just sit
down and talk to someone for a
while. At the moment I'm on
antidepressants, they help a
little, but I think it's what you
feel inside yourself that helps
conquer it. I smoke a lot of pot
so that it helps relax me.
Quitting pot for me is like
quitting your best friend. I've
done it once, I suppose I can do
it again if I really tried.
JEFF SEARLE 21

'PSYCHOSIS', CAMERON SULLINGS 18. YPPI PROGRAM

Sometimes this happens to me . . .
When I am walking down a road
and trip on a stick, I get angry
with myself and I don't know
why. When I am sitting in my
peaceful home and the power
strikes out, I feel like letting go.
But I hang in by a thread. When
the darkness of the night is
bearing and kicking at your
door, you realise that you need a
little hope that hugs and hold
you tight. When life is going
nowhere and you have many
things to do, I get angry with
what's been done and try to fight
it. I still lose it. When you finally
get the answers that you have
been dying to know, that's when
life picks you up and never lets
you go . . .
STEPHEN REYNOLDS 21

'FREEDOM OF RELEASE', BRETT COWELL 20, YPPI PROGRAM

FEELING AND DEALING WITH YOUR EMOTIONS

1 When was the last time you were worried about something? How did you feel in your head, your heart, your stomach, other parts of your body? What did you do? Would you do something differently next time?

2 What about the last time you were:

- Scared?
- Sad?
- Happy?
- Angry?
- Confused?
- Panicky?
- Frustrated?
- Lonely?

3 Do you ever feel like you're wearing a mask to hide how you're feeling or what's really going on? What kind of mask do you wear? How does it make you feel inside?

4 Do you ever hear people say boys don't express emotions? Anger is usually seen as okay for boys to express, but you know it can be pretty dangerous, it can hide other emotions, and it can lead to horrible situations. Anger that gets you thinking and acting responsibly and assertively about a situation is good. But ask yourself:

- **Do you ever feel like smashing something or someone? What do you do? When do you feel these kinds of feelings?**

- **Do you ever feel like picking a fight? When?**

- **Do people call you hot-headed or bad-tempered? Who does that? Is it praise or criticism?**

- **Do you feel sorry after you've been really angry and done something you didn't want to do?**

- **Do you feel like you can't understand why you get so angry and don't know what to do about it?**

- **How many times have you got so angry that you've hurt yourself and others physically and/or emotionally?**

If you act on your anger frequently, if you often feel guilt afterwards and confused about why it happened or how to control it, if you have a reputation among friends and family as having a hot or violent temper (even if they may praise it), if you have hurt others in anger, then perhaps there are other emotions and other stuff happening you may need to talk to someone about.

It is your responsibility to learn how to control and use your anger, and to learn to recognise what's really behind that anger. Boys are made to feel like they have to hold back a lot of feelings such as sadness, hurt and confusion, and in order to stay in power turn them into anger against another person. Instead of crying, they yell. Instead of being assertive, they become aggressive.

 Life is going to have its ups and downs, twists and turns. So many things can happen unexpectedly and at times it's going to seem all too hard. But there are things you can do to help you get through the tough times. Whatever you do, try not to bottle up your feelings. Here are some pointers:

1 Cry: It's okay to cry but many guys feel embarrassed because they're not encouraged to express what they are feeling in this way. It's important to remember that it can be a powerful way of releasing the pressure and tension that has built up inside you. It's about letting your feelings out and dealing with them.

2 Exercise: Maybe for a while staying in your room or being alone may help. But getting out into the fresh air and doing some exercise can make you feel a whole lot better.

3 Talk: Share the problem with someone you trust! It might help you to think stuff through by putting words to your feelings.

4 See a doctor or counsellor: If things seem too much to handle, it's sometimes a good idea to see a doctor or a counsellor. We all need support at times and you shouldn't feel inadequate about asking for this kind of help.

5 Plan and set goals: Sometimes when you're feeling depressed or down, the last thing you want to do is start setting goals! But it can help you to think realistically about what you want out of life and to continue to keep those goals in mind. They can kind of give your life that sense of purpose that you need to keep going especially when times get rough.

Seventeen-year-old Jordan sent us his own survival guide. It must work as he told us he is no longer suicidal and is feeling better and more in control of his life (see Chapter 7 for Jordan's story).

MY TEENAGE YEARS' SURVIVAL GUIDE

1 'BUFFY THE VAMPIRE SLAYER'

This TV show has saved my life. I absolutely love it. I am her number one fan hands down!!! I like the show so much because it's very empowering. When I'm down I watch Buffy kick some demon butt and I feel a lot better. IT ROCKS!!

2 MUSIC

I think that music is very important. Positive music (not music with 'mother fuckin'' as every second word) helps me chill out and it also helps me calm myself down when I'm stressed.

3 BOOKS, MAGAZINES ETC.

Reading helps me escape from all the trouble that sometimes surrounds me. I can separate myself from reality. That then helps me make rational decisions.

4 FRIENDS AND FAMILY

They help to keep me grounded and give me another perspective on my thoughts and feelings.

5 PETS

My pets are great because they can pick up really easily on my emotions and always give me undying love, always.

JORDAN 17

When you're feeling down, it can help to realise that there are other guys (and girls) who are going through similar stuff. They're confused or suffering from depression and feel lonely and desperate too. The only difference is that some of them won't probably admit it and just pretend that everything is going fine. Maybe they're just too scared to share what they are feeling. Every adult too has been through stuff, even if they feel better pretending to you that they haven't! Talking to people, reading and connecting with others can help you feel so much better. It might not solve the problem, but it can help you to realise that others have experienced similar pain and survived.

In the following, Tanya Lavin interviewed one of her closest friends, Steve Malcman, who is living with cancer. Steve's philosophies and attitudes tell us so much about what life can be when lived with real courage and dignity. Guys have said so much about the real meaning of strength, courage and being alive in this book, while other guys struggle living up to what Steve would call 'shallow' definitions of strength and fitting in. We think Steve is an incredible role model and that he has such an important lesson to teach all of us about putting life into perspective.

LIVING WITH CANCER

WHEN I FOUND out I had cancer, it did not hit me at first. I closeted my feelings and didn't want to deal with it. But gradually I went through stages of realisation, after all the tests, the CAT scans and the hair loss.

Because I am unwell I have had a lot of time off work, and all I can do is think of the cancer. I keep trying to look positive and look forward. I don't feel the necessity to talk about the cancer. I want to focus on getting better, not on death. Most of the treatments have been good, I've only been really sick from the treatments a small amount. I don't want the cancer to get me down.

I feel that I'm not as self-conscious anymore about having cancer as I was. Since the diagnosis I've become more easygoing about life. Life's too short, I keep focussed on the future, ignoring fights and arguments, petty things. I've bottled up talking or thinking of death. If I die I die, there is no point worrying.

I had been afraid before chemotherapy and radiotherapy of what it was going do to me, my looks, how I'd feel afterward. Now I don't care about those shallow things as much. Having cancer has also made me question and think more about how people answer the simple greeting, 'How are you?'.

To other guys in similar situations, don't lose hope. If you do you will fall down deep into depression. Keep looking forward. Keep in touch with your dreams and reality and what you want in life.

If you are a friend of someone living

with cancer, never look back, look forward with them. Enjoy life with them and don't treat them any differently. It's an illness, it's something that happens. Don't look at them any differently. Cancer patients want to feel comfortable so you have to be there for them. You don't have to always talk about their problems, and you can still talk to them about your problems. That makes them feel great, not different, and it has gotten me through hard times.

I've noticed some of my friends are calling less to go out. Others have been really good and it feels good catching up, talking. Some have been very supportive, visiting me in hospital. When I'm feeling down, receiving a phone call makes me feel better. I remember I didn't notice my first treatment because of all the friends that came to visit. I enjoy talking freely on the net with friends and with other young people with cancer, and that's helped get a clearer picture of my situation.

Having cancer has brought life into perspective. Being gay has made it even harder to deal with the cancer sometimes. It can be hard meeting people who can deal with your cancer and you being gay. But I won't settle for just anybody. They have to accept all of me.

STEVE MALCMAN 20 WITH TANYA LAVIN 18

> **when I'm feeling down, receiving a phone call makes me feel better. I remember I didn't notice my first treatment because of all the friends that came to visit.**

ON RELIGION

Repression breeds contempt
Of the ones that keep him down
No longer content with his leash
He hates being led around
Where does personal belief end
And Indoctrination start?
When Individuality appears
Dogmas fall apart
MAXO 17

I LIKE ME!

I'VE LEARNT SO MUCH and am able to see
how far I've come. I now have wisdom and
maturity to go with my passion and can
confidently say I am growing up. I'm not
saying I don't get depressed—everybody
does—but I'm now able to take
responsibility for what is wrong in my life
in a way that is productive and not self-
destructive. I look back on my life and
have now learnt that everything has
happened for a reason and has shaped me
into the person I am proud to be today.
You can lose battles but if you don't lose
the lessons it's all been worthwhile. I LIKE
ME! That is my victory and I know I'm
becoming a man. I hope we can now send
a message of hope to all young men—
whatever their race, socioeconomic status,
sexuality or religion—that they are here for
a reason, and encourage them not to let
anything prevent them from realising their
full potential. To be proud of who they are
and what they have to offer the world.
BEN GERRARD 18

NO REGRETS

In times of trouble,
through thoughts of doubt,
do you ever wonder what it's all about?
Could have been this, why done that?
But in the end,
it's where you're at.

Through turns of luck,
and shades of green.
All the chances that could have been.
When you look at it,
at the end of the day,
here: now.
You did it your own way.

No regrets! Be proud to say.
Living my life.
Loving it!
My way.
MASON CHIDGEY 29

> I look back on my life and have now learnt that everything has happened for a reason and has shaped me into the person I am proud to be today.

ACKNOWLEDGMENTS & ATTRIBUTIONS

Attributions

Page 39 'Inner Beauty' excerpted from 'Sexuality and Physical Disability' by George Taleporos in Carl Woods (ed.) *Sexual Positions: An Australian View,* Hill of Content, Melbourne, 2001, with kind permission from the publisher Michelle Anderson.

Page 132 Photo of Steven Hodge (Prince Charming) and Jacqui Blaney (Snow White) in Ballet Theatre of Queensland's performance of *Snow White*, 2000, with kind permission from Ballet Theatre of Queensland, Steven's family and Jacqui's family.

Pages 175–6 Duy 18 and Siva 18 pieces excerpted/edited from research interviews conducted by Ms Jane Grant for MEd thesis, Students With Refugee-Related Experiences: Deconstructing the Categories, University of Melbourne, 1998.

Photos of Frankie Fantasia: thank you to The Look Studios, Adelaide.

Notes on the contributors

Due to the need for confidentiality, many of the contributors chose not to provide details about themselves. Some used pseudonyms or first names only. Others may appear more than once with different ages because they contributed several pieces over the course of the project. However, some contributors wanted you to know a little bit more about themselves and we've provided space for them here. If you wish to contact any of the contributors, please write via Wayne and Maria at **boysstuff01@hotmail.com**.

Joel Baker 'I am currently attending high school. During my growing up I always knew that I was in fact different to the rest of the boys. Whilst they loved looking at cars that drove by and loved getting dirty, I was a homebody helping my mum cook and playing games indoors. A loser you might say. As I grew up I tried to make my own personality not going along with conventional society. Though bullies have tried to mar my existence I knew that I was me and I was proud. I am a bisexual youngster and in life I hope to be a role model to others and my goal is to break homophobic boundaries that I know are present in society.'

Peter Ball is a poet and Gold Coast dweller with an Arts degree; he has had poems published in *Voiceworks*, the *Rave Young Writers* page and *Verso*.

John Bell is a young writer. He had an on-again, off-again relationship with God at a Church of England school in Sydney, and is now at university. He dreams of a life in music, but rock journalism may have to do.

Mason Chidgey is a first-generation Australian born to an American mother and English father. Mason's childhood was spent in the Javan highlands and then later in the suburbs of Perth. Mason's journey into adulthood was at times traumatic, but has certainly given him an ability to turn any perceived failure or mistake into a lesson, making his experiences of life, both for him and those he shares his life with, all the more richer.

Having spent many years travelling, Mason has now returned to Perth, living close to the city with Anthony, a pillar of propriety and sound critic. He is currently pursuing studies in culture and in creative writing.

Brett Cowell 'The painting *Freedom of Release* is one of the ways I would express psychosis. My mental illness sprang out of a deep depression, then drugs kicked in hard. It gave me a different perspective on life and how the mind can be affected if not looked after. I got thrown into a pit, then was gradually released. God, time, friends and family, and will power have let me live a tad easier.'

Mick Curran 'Other than being gay, I am also totally blind and have had a few other visits to hospital over the last seventeen years. And I really regard my sexuality as a very small part of the problems over my life. There are much more important things such as keeping healthy, getting through my studies and the rest of my life with a visual impairment etc. Also I would like to thank my parents, my brother, my grandparents and all my friends for being so accepting and supportive through my life.'

Damien 'I am in Year 10. I am easy-going, like to have fun and I live with foster parents.'

Frankie Fantasia 'I am a hairdressing apprentice and I'm living on my own. My ambition is to work hard and be successful at what I do, and have a house and family of my own one day.'

Michael Flood runs workshops on violence, relationships and sexuality for young men and women, and teaches gender studies at the Australian National University, Canberra.

David Freir enjoys cricket, basketball, music, outsmarting his sitter and parents, cooking, sleeping and eating.

Bryan Froud 'A brilliant light can either illuminate or blind. How do we know which is which till we open our eyes?'

Ben Gerrard has begun a professional writing course at Deakin University in Melbourne and is working toward getting into acting.

Kevin Hunt 'I've lived in South Hedland all my life. I live at home with my parents and younger brother, Cody. I'd like to end up a teacher, preferably an English or high school language teacher. The main point of my story was to show what extremes kids can be pushed to if they're brought up with certain values and attitudes pushed upon them by society. The issue of youth suicide is growing each year and a lot of the deaths are a result of kids feeling that they don't fit into society or the picture society has of who they should be.'

Matthew Gough 'Embrace what you have, you only have a lifetime.'

Tim Harrison 'I try to be friendly to others even if they aren't really friendly to me.'

Steven Hodge has been studying ballet and other forms of dance since he was five and is now a member of the prestigious Ballet Theatre of Queensland.

Jacob 'Be yourself, be different, and live life to the fullest.'

Johnny was born in Australia and lives in Melbourne.

Tanya Lavin is a Deakin University nursing student and vice-president of QWomyn.

Mark 'I am in Grade 6. I have lots of pets. I live with my brother Damien, and Ian and Brett my foster parents.'

Simon Moss went on to great success in his schooling career, achieving a result of 99.6 and winning several academic prizes. His most cherished memories, though, come not from study but from his school's historic first soccer premiership in which he played a part, and the experiences he gained in the Outdoor Program leading younger students walking in Kosciusko National Park. In his pursuit of being a modern-day 'renaissance man', Simon has now deferred his studies to travel around Europe, improving his language skills and experiencing different cultures.

Gavin Nicklette 'I love my friends and it took a terrible tragedy for me to realise this. Don't take your friends for granted, and never forget to tell them how much you appreciate them.'

Nigel is from Mt Isa. He loves basketball and his greatest asset is his family.

Podge 'When I look down in the shower I notice I'm male. Apart from that, in the battle of the sexes, I'm on a grassy hill listening to the faint roar of artillery and looking in the opposite direction.'

Rob Pryke lives on the Central Coast of New South Wales. He works at a local store and believes we need to take life as it comes. 'I had a breakdown three years ago and Young People Prevention and Early Intervention Program (YPPI) has helped me get back on my feet. I am working again and enjoy being the editor of the YPPI fanzine *The Rave*.'

Daniel Scarparolo 'I have finished Year 12 at Corpus Christi College in Perth, Western Australia. My interests are more in the lines of the arts with such things as drama, music, singing and writing. I am hoping to complete a journalism course at Curtin University but that is not my main ambition. Along with journalism I hope to complete a creative writing major and hopefully get some well-rounded writing skills instead of a lot of the slap-dash writing I am doing at the moment.

My story is semi-autobiographical and relates to an ongoing saga that has filled up most of my last year of high school. I am aiming to show that there is a hidden meaning behind every action and our true motives are very rarely revealed, especially in today's emotionally repressed society.'

Jeffrey Searle 'I wrote about an experience that totally changed my life. It gave me a different perspective on people's feelings and outlooks on life, in the way that personal experience can change the way of the individual's thinking.'

Nathan Smith-Featon 'I write down my thoughts in the form of songwriting, poetry and art. Sometimes if I have to express my emotions, I create art or write them down because it helps get it all off my chest. I enjoy sport, feeling fresh and looking good.'

Keith Stewart 'Well, I've lived in Melbourne all my life and have achieved my VCE [Victorian Certificate of Education]—no small emotional, mental and physical effort, believe me. During school, acting in the annual productions proved to be an enjoyable and effective way of staying sane. Imagery in writing and art has always been of interest to me. My writing usually takes the form of fiction. I received a Highly Commended award in the Rotary Club of Richmond's Slade Literary Award (1997).'

James Stuart studied at Newcastle University and moved to Sydney to work. He was editor of the university's student paper *Opus*.

George Taleporos is a consultant and research student with a physical disability. He is currently undertaking a PhD in psychology at Deakin University. His research focusses on sexuality and body image in people with physical disabilities.

Jonard Ubalde is an undergraduate student at the University of Western Sydney. He is an active member of Amnesty, the Australian Conservation Foundation and SchoolWatch, which promotes anti-homophobia in New South Wales schools.

David Van Pelt is an undergraduate student at Deakin University aspiring to become a secondary teacher in the areas of health/human development and physical education. He has a love of both sport and music and plays keyboard for local rock band Rainmaker. As a secondary health and PE teacher, David hopes to inspire his students to enjoy physical activity, be aware of health risks and above all, make the most of and enjoy life.

James Wall is from Townsville, currently residing in Melbourne. He is looking for more exposure for his writing and can be contacted on jp_wall@hotmail.com.

Jesse Whinnen lives in Adelaide and his mum, Maria, is the author Maria's best friend! He writes: 'It's not fair the way people don't think about others and tease and bully them.'

Daniel Witthaus currently works for Moonee Valley Youth Services as a youth outreach and support worker. He has over four years' experience working in programs and projects that support same-sex attracted young people. For two years Daniel has worked in a number of secondary school settings, addressing and exploring sexual diversity and homophobia.

Wayne and Maria wish to thank . . .

Over 600 boys and girls, young men and women have participated in the larger research and writing project we have been conducting, through interviews, questionnaires, discussion groups and the development of writing, art and photography. We wish to thank every single young person for their time, insights, honesty, questions, good humour, inspiration and strength even while discussing very difficult and traumatic experiences. We have really appreciated and been strengthened by your encouragement of us and the work we are doing. You are inspirational and have much to teach the older generations about love, respect, courage, and the celebration of diversity.

We wish to thank the following people particularly for their support, patience and participation in this project at various steps on the way. Due to the need for confidentiality, not all the people we would like to thank can be mentioned below. You know who you are: please be aware that your support will be ultimately appreciated by the many readers of this book and is certainly gratefully acknowledged by us.

■ Maria would particularly like to thank those enthusiastic mothers who approached her in the supermarket or rang her from their workplaces or homes around Australia and introduced their sons who 'had something to say'. Also, those students who met her at various school and writers' events and asked to be part of this book or encouraged their friends to contribute.

Thanks to parents who supported their sons, introduced their sons, chased their sons to meet deadlines: Violet Bokody; Kate Carr; Elena and Maurice Castrechini; Robyn Collis; the Curran family from PFLAG Victoria; Paula Dennan; Moira Deslandes MP (SA); Maude Frances, Australian Centre for Lesbian and Gay Research, Sydney University; Kerry Harrison; Moira Henderson; Diane Hodge; Gail James; Marion Lovejoy; Mara and Carmine Maresca; Sharon Moss; Cherylyn Murray; Cathy and Ian Norris; Tony and Eva Pallotta; Julie and Ralph Olivieri; Teresa Savage; Ian Seal and Brett Widlich.

■ Wayne would like to extend a very special thanks to Maria Baira for her incredible support, friendship and help in connecting him with some wonderful and inspiring Aboriginal boys such as Nigel and Beade, who are incredible role models for all young men. Maria Baira's support, vision, commitment to social justice and determination in her own life have been a powerful source of inspiration.

■ Wayne would also like to thank the following Aboriginal educational workers in Queensland and Western Australia, who assisted him with setting up interviews with Aboriginal/Torres Strait Islander boys and who liaised with their parents. Their support for our work is very much appreciated: Valerie Lenoy; Retz Oddy; Raba Solomon.

■ Thanks to teachers and principals who allowed students to be interviewed and surveyed, who encouraged students to contact us or who encouraged us with the project:

Wendy Boggs, Perth, WA

Wendy Buck, Oodnadatta Aboriginal College, SA

Antonio Castello and Matthew Henry, Traralgon Secondary College, Vic.

Brother Brian Clery, Aquinas College, Perth, WA

Amanda Collins, English teacher, Port Hedland, WA

Bill Deegan and Peter Shanahan, principal, St Paul's College, Adelaide, SA

Ian Elder, principal, Sacred Heart College, Sorento, WA

Judith Field, Mount Scopus, Melbourne, Vic.

Mary Frier and Graham Bastion, principal, Golden Square Secondary College, Bendigo, Vic.

Pat Gay, St Kilda Park Primary School, Vic.

Jane Grant, Maribyrnong Secondary College, Vic.

Peter Henderson, Vermont Secondary College, Vic.

Dominic Herne, Waverley College, Sydney, NSW

Laura Higgins, Canberra College, ACT

Kristie Lewis, Hawthorn Secondary College, Vic.

Jeremy Ludowycke, principal, and staff, Princes Hill Secondary College, Melbourne, Vic., and students who provided valuable comments on the manuscript

Marie Lyall, principal, and David Beeton, Corrimal High School, Wollongong, NSW

Shelia Masters, Perth, WA

Jacqui Nell, Perth, WA

Angeline Salpietro, Caroline Chisholm Catholic College, Braybrook, Vic.

Linda Santolin and Year 10 boys at Christian Brothers' College, St Kilda, Vic., for valuable comments on the manuscript

Glenn Sargent, Plumpton High School, Sydney, NSW

Lyn Scott, principal, and Michael Crowhurst, Sydney Road Community School, Melbourne, Vic.

Andrew Syme, principal, Scotch College, Perth, WA

Sue Tucker, head of English, La Salle College, Perth, WA

Michael Waters, principal, and Harriet Houghton, Forest Hill College, Vic.

Karen Wells, Mullauna Secondary College, Vic.

■ Thanks to other persons and organisations who made contacts, chased leads, sent material and put us in touch with contributors:

Christine Bakopanos, Foundation House, Vic.

Kaye Boulden, Equity Programs Unit, Education Queensland

John Brown and the Men's Focus Group participants, Department of Health, ACT

Eric Kwok Ching Chu

Shirley Dally, Department for Education and Children's Services, SA

Fiona Delisle and Sally Marsden, Connexions/Jesuit Social Services, Collingwood, Vic.

Dan Disney, outreach youth worker, Richmond Federation, Vic.

Education Queensland

Dr Murray Drummond, lecturer, School of Physical Education, Exercise and Sport Studies, University of South Australia (Dr Drummond lectures in the sociocultural aspects of health and human movement. His primary research interests are men, sport and masculinities. He is specifically interested in men's and boy's body image and male eating disorders, particularly in relation to sporting subcultures. He is currently involved in a number of funded research projects including a project investigating men, body image and eating disorders in 'at risk' sports. Dr Drummond is a recipient of a University of South Australia supported researcher award reflecting his past research achievements)

Carmel Fleming, Eating Disorders Resource Centre, Brisbane, Qld

Robert Gaetano

Craig Garrett, editor, *Voiceworks*, Express Media, Vic.

Lisa Gibbs, Arthritis Victoria

Wayne Glenn, youth worker, Young Fathers and Lifeskills project worker, Eaglehawk, Vic.

Melinda Hartwell, Splash Art Studio, NEAMI Psychiatric Disability Support Service, Vic.

Dr Sue Headley, Australian Clearinghouse for Youth Studies, University of Tasmania

Alix Hunter, Splash Art Studio, NEAMI Psychiatric Disability Support Service, Vic.

Ian Hunter, Canberra Education Department, ACT

Thomas Jia, Murri community worker, and the Indigenous Young Fathers Support Group, Centacare, Qld

Andy Jones, Australian Conservation Foundation Education program, Youth Action Council, Vic.

Yorgo Kaporis, artistic director and choreographer, 'Ilinden' Macedonian Cultural Association, Rockdale, NSW

Tim Kerslake, Canberra, ACT

Bernadette McCartney, social worker, Crossroads Reconnect, Salvation Army, Vic.

Kieran MacGregor and Nan MacGregor, PFLAG

Dr Khairy Majheed, men's relationships worker, North Eastern Regional Migrant Resource Centre, Vic.

Leonie Mills, Spaghetti Circus, Mullumbeena, NSW

Jai Milner, Youth Action Council, SA

Margaret Mitchell-Hill, Western Sydney Area Health Service, NSW

Darryl Murray, resource coordinator, Family Planning, Qld (for sending writing and photography from two projects: Rite-Up: Personal Experiences About Growing Up with boys from various Brisbane schools; and Through My Eyes: Snapshots of Relationships with students from special education units and disability schools in Qld)

Kelvin Nather, regional disability and welfare coordinator, Vic.

Jenny Nolan, regional disability and welfare coordinator, Vic.

Jeanne Norling, Student Welfare and Support Branch, Department of Education, Vic.

Dr Barrie O'Connor, director, Institute of Disability, Deakin University, Vic.

Lyn O'Grady, Crossroads and Galaxy Program, Salvation Army, Vic.

Michelle Sabto, Melbourne, Vic.

Zoe Scrogings, Young People Prevention and Early Intervention Program, Central Coast Area Health Service, NSW (YPPI is a community-based early intervention program with a focus on recovery, in which young people can choose to participate in the Creative Arts Project to enhance self-expression and creativity)

Luke Simington, The Warehouse, Sydney

Mark Trudinger, Qld

Jonard Ubalde, Sydney, NSW

Teresa Valentine, Education and Services, Arthritis Victoria

Adrian Walter, Brisbane, Qld

Kayleen White, Transgender Victoria

Daniel Witthaus, youth outreach and support worker, Moonee Valley Youth Services

■ Thanks also to friends and significant others who supported us and the project, found contributors, contacted organisations, put up with our regular updates, took photos, loved us through it all:

At the School of Health Sciences, Deakin University: Dr Shona Bass, Rachel Carlisle, Associate Professor Caroline Finch, Professor Sandy Gifford, Professor Mark Hargreaves (Head of School), Alana Hulme, Maria Karvelas, Suzy Kelly, Shelley Maher, Bernie Marshall, Catherine Martinson, Sharon Melder, Dr Daniel Reidpath, Dr Damien Ridge, Margaret Sheehan and Professor Laurie St Leger (Dean of the Faculty of Health and Behavioural Sciences) for their inspiration, support and friendship

Dr Lori Beckett, Faculty of Education, University of Technology, Sydney

Christian Capurso

Rob Chiarolli (particularly for photos, food, a nurturing masculinity and love) and Steph Chiarolli (for love, and for being a fabulous daughter, and in the hope that the guys in her life will be special)

Greg Curran

Luciano Di Gregorio

Matt Dury (Freedom Centre, Perth WA)

Jon Eliot (deceased 1989, but who's still there. Jon's love made Maria grow, and writing his life story was the beginning of Maria's writing and social activism journey; and it was through that book *Someone You Know* that Wayne and Maria met, became friends, and decided they would write together one day!)

Maria Fantasia and other girlfriends in Adelaide (for love and still hanging in there with Maria!)

Rebecca Galvez (for her constant support and friendship to Wayne)

Jacqui Griffin, SchoolWatch (committee monitoring homophobia in schools)

Madelaine Imber

Carmela Luscri

Michael and Daniel Maresca for allowing Maria access to lots of personal photos and to their friends for allowing their photos to be published: Paul Berlangieri, Stephen Berton, Mark and Matthew Bombardieri, Mark Coppola, Nicole Donnelly, Matthew Fazzari, Giovanni Licari, Anthony Parisi, Michael Re, Aaron Rosada, Tony Sacca, Steven Stefanopoulos, Adam Tropeano

Michael Pendrey and the Pendrey and Phillips families

Bill Phillips (deceased 2000, a dear friend who encouraged Maria to do this book 'for the boy I wish I could've been')

Annie Ruddy (who now lives in the United States but whose support and email contact with Wayne through this journey has been so amazing and significant—absent in body but always connected in spirit)

Ian Seal

Alan Stafford (for love, for his own disruptive masculinity and for a Sydney home for Maria)

Mateusz Szelag and Chris Rillo (for ongoing love and support of Maria)

■ A special acknowledgment to Rex Finch from Finch Publishing for first approaching Maria with the idea of compiling a book for girls by girls, which became *Girls' Talk: Young Women Speak Their Hearts and Minds* (1998), and who has supported the publication of this book.

■ Also our special appreciation of Elizabeth Weiss, publisher, and Simone Ford, editor, at Allen & Unwin whose vision, passion, good humour and fun lunches will always be remembered. We would also like to thank copy editor Mary Rennie, who worked on the manuscript, and designers, Antart, for an awesome design that has brought the book to life.

■ For transcribing over 200 interviews: Pat Bentley and Geraldine Stack. For technical support with taping and recording equipment: John Cooper, Alan Cosstick, Cameron, Janice and others at Audiovisual Learning Resources Services, Deakin University. Also thanks to Tania Corbett, secretary, Curriculum Section, Murdoch University (Wayne's life support while on leave at Sydney University producing this book) and Susan Vukovic, Information Technology Services, Deakin University (Maria's computer whiz!).

■ Wayne and Maria would also like to acknowledge the funding and support offered for this project by the School of Education, Murdoch University, and the Faculty of Health and Behavioural Sciences, Deakin University.